Bruce L. Gates

Atkinson Graduate School of Administration
Willamette University

social program administration: the implementation of social policy

PRENTICE-HALL, INC., Englewood Cliffs, New Jersey 07632

Library of Congress Cataloging in Publication Data

Gates, Bruce L
  Social program administration.

  Includes bibliographical references and index.
  1. Social work administration—United States.
  2. United States—Social policy—1960-   I. Title.
  HV91.G36   361'.973   79-24495
  ISBN 0-13-817767-8

PRENTICE-HALL SERIES IN SOCIAL WORK PRACTICE
Neil Gilbert and Harry Specht, editors

Editorial/production supervision and design by Judy Brown
Cover design by Phyllis Erwin
Manufacturing buyer: Ray Keating

Printed in the United States of America

10 9 8 7 6 5 4 3 2 1

Prentice-Hall International, Inc., *London*
Prentice-Hall of Australia Pty. Limited, *Sydney*
Prentice-Hall of Canada, Ltd., *Toronto*
Prentice-Hall of India Private Limited, *New Delhi*
Prentice-Hall of Japan, Inc., *Tokyo*
Prentice-Hall of Southeast Asia Pte. Ltd., *Singapore*
Whitehall Books Limited, *Wellington, New Zealand*

to Ruth and Kil

contents

3

social program implementation: the demand for accountability 61

4

assessing need 100

5

assessing barriers to utilization: the problem of access 141

6

management control 173

7

8

9

conclusion:
sources and directions
of program change 280

bibliography of cases 295

preface

The preoccupation with matters of policy in recent years has caused many students of social welfare to overlook the importance—and policy significance—of administrative behavior in social welfare organizations. To restore needed perspective, I have endeavored to link the theoretical and political dimensions of social policy and its formulation with the norms, decisions, decision support structures, and actions underlying contemporary administrative practice into what I have called the *social welfare enterprise*—the large-scale, organized response to problems of individual and societal well-being. To achieve this linkage, I have focused upon the social program, which is seen here as both an instrument of policy and a central element in the multifaceted organizational and political milieu through which policies are implemented, controlled, and administered.

The social program is an instrument of policy because it manifests, in theory at least, a planned and coordinated set of activities—centering upon specific issues of who gets what and how—which are undertaken in pursuit of broad policy objectives. In practice, however, the pluralistic political processes through which they are formulated generate policies inherently vague, consequently leaving many specific questions surrounding social program implementation unanswered. It is now that the program as an organizational entity becomes important. In the uncertainty of desirable action under prevailing policy, the social program becomes the object of control by the numerous organizations and interests upon which it is dependent for essential resources. Hence, the social program must be seen not only as an instrument of stated social policy, but also as an instrument of the various groups and organizations desiring to use the program as a vehicle for promoting their own interests.

The role of the social program administrator is seen as one of altering, responding to, or otherwise reconciling the many diverse and often conflicting sources of authority that would seek to influence program operations. More important, the administrator by tradition brings to this role a commitment to the norms of efficiency, effectiveness, and accountability. The text illustrates—and through the exercises outlined in the Bibliography of Cases allows students to experience—the ways in which these traditional administrative norms are understood and pursued. It also shows how and why apparently mundane administrative decisions may have far-reaching policy implications.

In reading what follows, the student will probably experience many of the same frustrations I encountered while compiling and organizing the material. The recurring problem was achieving the conceptual simplicity necessary to the analysis of why and how without whitewashing the complexity and frequent intractibility of social program implementation and administration. There are, as the reader will see, few simple solutions to administrative problems in the social welfare enterprise; rather the implementation of social policy is replete with paradox and contradiction. It involves numerous interdependent decisions and actions—each rational by itself but when combined with others created a whole that is apparently irrational. In this regard, the reader will doubtless encounter some observations and contentions with which he or she will take vehement offense, for I have tried to confine what follows to a description and analysis of what apparently *is* rather than what *ought* to be.

There are many individuals who made substantial contributions during the preparation of this book. I would especially like to thank Harry Specht, George Brager, David Garson, Cecil Hinsey, Phyllis J. Day, Theodore Walden, and Dale F. Pearson, each of whom read the entire manuscript and provided numerous valuable suggestions regarding its general thrust and content, and Michael White and Earl Littrell, who provided insightful comments on specific sections of the text. I am especially indebted as well to William G. Scott for his always timely encouragement, support, and indirect though significant substantive contributions. These individuals should not be held accountable for errors of fact or interpretations of value which are, of course, solely my responsibility.

I am also indebted to the students in numerous seminars at the Atkinson Graduate School of Administration and Lewis and Clark College and members of the Salem Area Social Services Commission who were subjected to endless conceptual false starts and dead ends during the years this book was in preparation; two in particular, Richard Mockler and Cathy Webber, have been especially helpful.

During the project I have been blessed with assistance that transcended all realistic expectations for secretarial support. Barbara Dixon, who not only typed the many manuscript drafts but on countless occasions soothed the fevered brow and smoothed the ruffled feathers, deserves my undying gratitude.

And finally, I am indebted to my wife, Vickie, who provided the most valuable and persistent of criticisms, who carried the burden of maintaining some semblance of family life during this effort, and who, together with our mutual friend Frank, provided the emotional support without which this book would have been impossible.

Salem, Oregon
November, 1979

The social welfare enterprise and its administration are the principal concern of this book. The enterprise is defined as that set of formal organizations charged with the responsibility for implementing social policies—those policies designed to promote specific aspects of individual and societal well-being through the planned distribution of valued goods and services.

The focus of social policy implementation is the administrative program, seen here as an open system that often cuts across the boundaries defined by more traditional organizations. This, plus the fact that social policy goals and program objectives are vague and imprecise, compels the view that, as well as an instrument for policy, the program is also a complex political arena in which various groups try to promote their interests.

The perspective adopted in this book is primarily external—from the inside of the program looking out. The nature of the program's external environments, how those forces shape the program's general objective of matching services to needs, and the role of the administrator in responding to and shaping those forces define the primary concerns of the chapters that follow.

social welfare and social program administration

1

Not long after the first man stepped on the moon in 1969, the National Aeronautics and Space Administration (NASA), the organization responsible for that feat, initiated a nationwide poll among schoolchildren. Students were asked to answer the question, "If we can go to the moon, why can't we . . . ?" Significantly, many of the responses expressed concern with finding solutions to this nation's social ills, problems with cities, crime, poverty, health, housing, and so forth. More important perhaps, is the fact that the ability to administer large-scale enterprises was seen as one key to the solution of these problems.

The short period during which the "space age" was prominent in the national consciousness did indeed signal a time of great administrative promise. Thousands of people, hundreds of public and private organizations, scores of professions, and billions of dollars were mobilized and coordinated by NASA in the achievement of a major national and technological triumph. In many ways it was the pinnacle of a long history of organizational and managerial techniques that had harnessed the vast technological potential of the Industrial Revolution. In many ways, and for reasons of varying complexity, that development has failed to address the problems raised in, "If we can go to the moon, why can't we . . . ?"

This book deals not with NASA but with the evolving administrative technology of a much larger organizational milieu with a far more complex set of objectives, here called the *social welfare enterprise*. Certainly not a common term, it is used purposefully for three reasons: first, to convey the idea that social welfare, in addition to being an issue of major public concern, is also big business, since the mid-seventies consistently accounting for about 60 percent of total governmental expenditures in the United States;[1] second, to stimulate thought about conceptual alternatives to the "welfare state," a concept that has achieved symbolic status on a par with socialism or capitalism, thereby rendering dispassionate analysis a virtual impossibility; and third, and probably most important, to emphasize the fact that the enhancement of well-being is, increasingly, the responsibility of large-scale, formal organizations.

As defined here, the social welfare enterprise is that set of formal organizations, both public *and* private as well as those in the not-for-profit or voluntary "third sector;" upon which individuals are directly or indirectly dependent for certain aspects of their well-being. These organizations either provide direct "in-kind" social or human services, distribute a variety of cash or cash subsidies to individuals meeting defined standards of need or eligibility, or provide funding and other resources to organizations engaged in those activities.

the
social welfare enterprise
as an "organization"

Because large-scale, formal organizations permit collectives to transcend the limited knowledge and skills possessed by a single individual, they have become contemporary society's primary instruments for solving complex problems. In the ideal at least, societal problem solving using formal organizations entails four logical and straightforward steps. First, the rather abstract idea of "problem" is defined, redefined, and eventually translated into a general goal to be achieved by the organization. Second, the general goal is factored into a variety of sub-goals, functions, and tasks, which when performed according to plan will lead to the achievement of the major goal. Third, each of the sub-goals, functions, and tasks is made the responsibility of a single organizational unit. And fourth, the process of goal factoring and organizational matching continues until each organizational member is confronted, not by the vagaries of an unmanageable, complex problem, but by a manageable and often routine task. "*If this factoring is accurate,*" notes Victor Thompson, "rationality in terms of each unit will be rationality in terms of the organization as a whole."[2]

Once factored, however, problem solving via the method of formal organizations still requires that some set of controls be imposed to ensure that each of the specialized organizational units contributes in harmony to the achievement of the desired end. The creation of a coherent whole from its separate parts is the general purpose of an organizational structure, which embraces two interdependent objectives: first, to facilitate the flow of information between the organization and its larger environment and among its specialized operating units; and second, to ensure effective coordination and integration among those units. The social welfare enterprise is characterized, however, by the most complex of organizational interdependencies, what James Thompson has called reciprocal interdependence,[3] in which the output of organizational unit A becomes the input to organizational unit B, whose output in turn is fed back as input to organizational unit A. An example is found in a juvenile court referral to a state child welfare agency, which, in turn, places the child in one of a variety of child welfare programs. After a certain period—during which the child may progress through a random series of programs—he or she may return to the courts.

Because the appropriate interdependencies are often shrouded in uncertainty, organizational entities characterized by reciprocal interdependence require the most complex and flexible of information flows and structural mechanisms if they are to be effective; this is true even under the most ideal of conditions. But the organizational and administrative problems faced by the social welfare enterprise are compounded by another difficulty: it is charged with the implementation of policy within a pluralistic society, which is generally characterized by the existence of multiple sources of authority. The effect is that different organizational units within the enterprise (even different activities within the same unit) will often be influenced by and held accountable to different authorities and different means of control, which threaten the workability of the necessary reciprocal relationships and ultimately the effectiveness of organizational solutions to complex problems.

The remainder of this chapter is concerned with the various means by which the enterprise is and might be factored into specialized organizational units; our principal focus will be the social program. In chapter 2, we shall consider the principal defining characteristics of the social program, seen herein as the primary focus of administration efforts in the enterprise. In chapter 3, we shall investigate the reasons behind and the effects of multiple sources of accountability upon the implementation of social policy and programs. Chapters 4 through 9 are concerned primarily with information, what is required, how it is generated, and how it is used by program administraters and the program's major constituents in evaluating and improving program accountability, efficiency, and effectiveness.

from norms to programs:
a hierarchy of social decision

Analysis is the examination of cause and effect relationships, whether action and reaction in physics, stimulus and response in psychology, price and demand in economics, or intervention and cure in health care. Any goal statement or statement of intent can be subjected to further analysis by asking the questions of *why* and *how*. Answers to the question of *why* will provide a higher order rational for the existence of a goal, or often more correctly a series of alternative values that serve to rationalize the existence of the goal. Answers to the question of *how* ultimately force the analyst to confront the more technical, detailed issues regarding the means by which that goal is to be achieved. Oftentimes, it is difficult to know how this chain of means and ends should be defined, how far in either direction it should extend, or even where one should start. The answers depend upon the purpose of the analysis, and for our purposes it is sufficient to focus upon four elements in the social hierarchy of decision: norms, policies, plans, and—at the bottom but perhaps the most important—programs.

SOCIAL NORMS AND THE CONCEPT OF WELFARE

It is often difficult to distinguish the substance of social welfare from the symbolism, the reality from the myth. To identify something called the social welfare enterprise in a way that can facilitate a useful analysis of cause and effect and that can contribute to our understanding of this most complex phenomenon is to invoke assumptions regarding not only the "proper" nature of society but also the individuals who comprise it. In the end the norms that are socially and politically accepted will determine the nature of the social and individual "problems" to be addressed by the social policies and programs.

Most Western thought is characterized by a very sharp conceptual distinction between the individual and the larger collective of which he is a part. The concept of social welfare, with its direct focus upon the nature of interdependencies between the individual and the society, directly confronts this separation. Social welfare is a response to apparent disparities between the behavioral assumptions and expectations comprising societal institutions and the actual behaviors of societal members. For this reason, social welfare efforts can alternatively be viewed as repressive or liberating political instruments; they can be directed at changing repressing institutions or at altering individual behavior to comply with those institutions.

According to Harold Wilensky and Charles Lebeaux,[4] two alternative conceptions of welfare, reflective of this dichotomy, are predominant. In the first, the *residual* view, it is the individualistic ethos that wins out. Social welfare is seen as an organized response to temporary failures in the two "natural" American institutions that provide for individual needs; the family and the free market economy. The residual conceptualization of welfare is most closely associated with what we know as "public dependency" and is centered upon the satisfaction of income and consumption needs that arise from ill health, family disintegration, and economic crisis. It thus emphasizes temporary relief through the redistribution of income and the provision of various rehabilitative services. The residual conception of welfare is most closely associated with the philosophy and programs of the New Deal, in which it is expected that formalized welfare efforts will diminish once the disruptive crisis has passed.

In the past half century since the passage of the New Deal programs, the political recognition that economic dependency is a collective responsibility has expanded to include an ever-widening variety of new, legitimate dependency relationships. According to Richard Titmuss, the pre-eminent British scholar on social welfare:

> With the gradual break-up of the old poor law, more "states of dependency" have been defined and recognized as collective responsibilities and more differential provision has been made in respect to them. These "states of dependency" arise for the vast majority of the population whenever they are not in a position to "earn life" for themselves and their families; they are then dependent people. In industrialized societies there are many causes of dependency; they may be "natural dependencies" as in childhood, extreme old age and child-bearing. They may be caused by physical and psychological ill-health and incapacity; in part these are culturally determined dependencies. Or they may be wholly or predominantly determined by social and cultural factors. These, it may be said are the "man-made" dependencies. They include unemployment and underemployment, protective and preventative legislation, compulsory retirement from work, the delayed entry of young people into the labour market, and an infinite variety of subtle cultural factors ranging from the "right" trade union ticket to the possession of an assortment of status symbols.[5]

The expansion in both the number and scope of legitimate dependency relationships leads to a second conception of welfare, the *institutional* view. In contrast to the residual view, which is concerned primarily with "public welfare" efforts, the institutional conception of welfare focuses upon the *total* range of physical, psychological, and social needs and problems possessed by *all* members of modern industrialized society. Within the institutional view there is no abnormalcy, no stigma, attached to the consumption of welfare services; rather the need for services and benefits is seen as a natural outgrowth of the increasing complexity of modern society. The institutional and residual conceptions of welfare are obviously polar extremes, reflecting respectively the humanitarian and instrumental motives that—in dialectic opposition—underlie any social welfare effort. Most welfare theorists and practitioners will conclude that, while the social welfare enterprise currently manifests elements of both conceptions, social policy and program developments since the Depression indicate a slow but persistent move in the direction of the institutional conception. Many of the services now provided under Title XX of the Social Security Act, the Older Americans Act, and under the auspices of myriad child welfare programs, to name but a few—services available to poor and non-poor alike—support this contention. These services, note Alfred Kahn and Sheila Kamerman, are

> Social inventions to fit our era and not, as once thought, temporary, second-best substitutes until the old "basic" institutions of family and church are restored. The latter type of thinking would be akin to the view that public education could be foregone once the family updated its capacity to teach.[6]

While the continued industrialization of American society is seen by most welfare scholars as a primary force in creating these new dependency relationships, it is equally the source of resources required to support the institutional conception. An economy that does not generate sufficient capital to maintain industrial growth cannot afford to divert resources to institutions formally charged with the responsibility for individual well-being, a fact known only too well in many of the less developed countries of the world. The pressures to establish universal education and adequate systems of health care and to provide for the poor or otherwise deprived inevitably yield to the more basic necessity of reinvesting capital simply to maintain the economic machinery. Thus, the institutional conception of welfare depends upon both the continued generation of economic surpluses and the organizational infrastructure created by industrialization.

Yet, especially in this time of tax revolt, the likelihood of a prolonged energy and natural resource crisis occupying public and political attention, and a general mistrust of government, it is not at all clear that—the opinions of the experts notwithstanding—American political *attitudes* demonstrate a willingness to support an increasingly pervasive and more costly social welfare enterprise. Indeed, as we shall see repeatedly in the chapters that follow, the inability of policy makers to reconcile the ideological and practical disparities between the institutional and residual poles is a major factor contributing to the complexity—particularly their respective costs and benefits—of social program administration.

SOCIAL POLICY

Somewhat lower down in our chain of means and ends is social policy, which is seen here as a subset of the larger domain of public policy. A policy, in the classic formulation of Harold Laswell and Abraham Kaplan, "is a projected program of goals and practices,"[7] and the distinction between policy in general and public policy specifically, likewise in classical formulation, depends upon who makes policy decisions. In David Easton's formulation, public policies are authoritative decisions formulated, adopted, and implemented by individuals—acting in their legitimate appointed or elected roles as legislators, executives, administrators, judges, and the like—"who engage in the daily affairs of the political system," and who are "recognized by most members of the system as having responsibility for these matters."[8]

The substance of any public policy is manifest in some statement of more or less coherent goals arranged in order of priority. The goals reflected in any public policy statement—for example "to become energy independent," "to eliminate crime," or "to provide adequate health care for all individuals"—represent but one of many possible causal linkages between a set of alternative norms and a set of action alternatives adopted to achieve them. A policy goal, in the words of Pressman and Wildavsky, "points to a chain of causation between initial conditions and future consequences."[9] Central to the analysis of any policy, then, is a theory or a set of competing theories used to explain and justify action, and central to social policy are theories of benefits and their distribution.[10] Clearly, any policy will have distributive and redistributive implications; any policy will raise the questions that comprise the classic question of politics: who is to get what and how. Social policy is unique, however, in that its goals, technologies, and intended consequences are consciously redistributive.[11] As it will be used here, a social policy is manifest in any authoritative decision or set of decisions that *explicitly* addresses some specific aspect of individual and societal well-being by *explicitly* addressing the redistribution of benefits among various classes of individuals.

SOCIAL PLANS AND PROGRAMS

Plans reflect the fundamental strategies for achieving policy goals and, following the formulation of Herbert Simon, may be classified as two principal types: substantive plans and procedural plans.[12] The *substantive plan* is the conceptual instrument by which broad, often vague and open-ended policy goals are factored into successively more concrete and more manageable (ideally measurable) objectives and activities. At some point where a relatively well-defined objective—one that can be treated as relatively independent of other objectives embodied in the plan—is combined with a general means for its attainment, the substantive plan will have generated a *program*: an organized set of activities undertaken in pursuit of a more or less specific objective. That is, a program represents a conceptual synthesis of both an objective and a set of concrete actions directed toward its attainment. To illustrate, suppose that a municipal government has adopted a policy that has the broad goal of increasing the quality of housing stock within the community. It thus falls upon a local government department, say the Department of Community Development, to formulate a plan for achieving the policy goal. Such a plan might specify, among others, the following objectives: to stimulate an improvement in new housing through a revision in existing zoning laws; to stimulate home renovation by making low-cost home improvement loans available; and to foster pride in home ownership through the promotion of various "self-help" activities undertaken at the neighborhood level. Each of these objectives, together with its strategy, provides the basis for identifying a specific program.

But programs are not self-implementing; left unaddressed in either the statement of policy or the substantive plan are those decisions and actions that will affect the day-to-day operations of the program and likely its ultimate success as well. Thus, a second type of plan—what Simon has called the *procedural plan*—must attend the definition of alternative programs. Within the procedural plan are embodied the various administrative mechanisms—rules, guidelines, standard operating procedures, reporting requirements, and the like—that create, in Simon's terms, the "psychological environment of decision."[13] These "givens" direct the attention and delimit the behavior of program staff to ensure that day-to-day decisions and actions conform to the intended substance of the plan. Thus, the procedural plan adopted by the Department of Community Development may require that loan program staff adhere to specific eligibility criteria for low-interest loan applicants; may limit the amount of the loan and the nature of the improvements financed by it; may specify certain neighborhoods as having higher priorities than others in case available resources exceed demand; and may require a monthly report of loan applications and disbursements by neighborhood—all in the interests of ensuring that specific aspects of program behavior are in compliance with policy intent.

In effect, it is through the provisions of the procedural plan that an appropriate organizational structure is superimposed upon the conceptual hierarchy of decision. As such, rational organizational functioning obviously demands that the two elements of planning be compatible and the controls exerted through the provisions embodied in the procedural plan do, in fact, further the achievement of substantive objectives. For well-structured problems, clearly formulated policy goals, objectives and strategies, and well-defined patterns of organizational control, the achievement of compatibility between the two planning components may be feasible. Where problems, goals, objectives, strategies, and patterns of control are unknown, unclear, or unagreed upon, the two plans may be in substantial conflict. That is, adherence to the proscriptions in one may render adherence to those in the other an impossibility. Since they are often the more tangible and the more easily monitored, and since they are the principal mechanisms for ensuring program accountability, it is often the case that procedural provisions exert the stronger influence over the conduct of program activities (at the expense of achieving program and social objectives). Regarding this pervasive conflict, Victor Fuchs has remarked with respect to medical care and health:

> I am impressed by the widespread confusion between process and product, the tendency to identify medical care with health even though the connection is a fairly limited one. I wonder if that same confusion does not exist in other aspects of society, for example, schooling vis-a-vis learning, litigation vis-a-vis justice, or police work vis-a-vis public safety?[14]

A major reason for this confusion is that the social program is *both* an instrument of policy *and* an organizational entity that consequently spans the two most important functions in any organizational setting—planning and control. The inherent conflicts between these two functions will be a major issue explored in the chapters that follow.

programming
the social welfare enterprise

Because of resource, political, time and other constraints, not all plans and objectives will generate operational programs. Hence a major element in the hierarchy of social decision is *programming*—deciding upon the nature, size, and optimal mix of programs to be implemented. The conceptual map that results from the programming process is often called the *program structure,* which outlines the logical (and organizational) relationships among programs, the functions they perform, and the broad goals that each is designed to pursue. In such a conceptual map, decision makers have a powerful tool for: (1) identifying the need for new programs, (2) assessing sources of program duplication and overlap, and thus possible inefficiencies, and (3) identifying clusters of programs whose activities require coordination. While social programs have in most cases simply evolved in fragmented and unplanned response to political and social pressures of the time, there is substantial interest in creating an idealized program structure for the social welfare enterprise, because it would apparently provide a basis for more rational system-wide decision making. Perhaps the best known, most widely used, and most comprehensive of many such attempts has been developed by the United Way of America.

The United Way of America Service Identification System (UWASIS) hierarchically arranges, as Figure 1.1 shows, programs and various service aggregates in relation to eight interdependent human and social goals: Optimal Income Security and Economic Opportunity; Optimal Health; Optimal Provision of Basic Material Needs; Optimal Opportunity for the Acquisition of Knowledge and Skills; Optimal Environmental Quality; Optimal Individual and Collective Safety; Optimal Social Functioning; and Optimal Assurance of the Support and Effectiveness of Services through Organized Action.[15]

The second level in the hierarchically organized taxonomy identifies thirty-three different categories of services systems, each of which is aligned with a major human and social goal. For example, the goal of achieving optimal income security and economic opportunity is assumed to be dependent upon the functioning of four primary service systems: the Employment Services System, the Income Security System, the Economic Development and Opportunity Services System, and the Income Security and Economic Opportunity Support Services System.[16]

The third level in the taxonomy currently identifies some 231 specific

FIGURE 1.1:
the UWASIS typology of human and social services

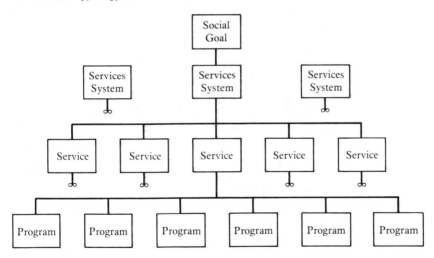

Source: United Way of America, UWASIS II: A Taxonomy of Social Goals and Human Services Programs *(Alexandria, Virginia: United Way of America, 1976), p. 13.*

11

services, each aligned within its appropriate parent service system. For example, within the Employment Services System are identified three specific services: "Employment Procurement Services, Employment Training Services, and Special Employment Assistance Services for Exceptional Individuals and Groups (Aged, Handicapped, and Other Disadvantaged).[17]

Finally the service level is currently subcategorized into some 587 specific programs, each directed toward the achievement of a more or less specific objective. The Employment Procurement Services Category, for example, contains three separate programs: "Employment Assessment and Guidance, Pre-Job Guidance, and Job Search Assistance and Placement."[18] Furthermore, each program element contains a general description of the activities normally performed in the conduct of the program and a general description of program output or "product." To illustrate, the following description is provided for Pre-Job Guidance Program.

> Pre-Job Guidance is a program designed to help individuals who need to learn the basic tools of obtaining employment to suit their particular skills and talents. Program elements include advice pertaining to some or all of the following: vita or resume preparation; dress and personal appearance; filling out applications and writing letters applying for a job or responding to a job ad; interview techniques; taking employment tests; and providing general orientation to occupational choices. The program may operate on a one-to-one basis or on a group basis.
> *Program Product*
> Number of persons guided in the techniques of obtaining employment.[19]

THE NATURE OF THE PROGRAM STRUCTURE

While an extremely valuable taxonomy (and this is indeed all the United Way intended it to be), the UWASIS framework does *not* reflect the actual organizational structure of the enterprise; it is but a useful conceptualization. Although the *taxonomy* is factored and arrayed hierarchically with discrete programs seen as ultimately contributing to the achievement of a single goal, the actual method of factoring and structuring is far more diffuse and complex. There is, to be sure, no singular organizational "system"—no singular basis of information flows and integration—that parallels the conceptual Employment Services System, promotes its goals, and coordinates its allied services and programs. Rather the actual structure of the enterprise is multidimensional, cutting across and thus influenced by a multitude of organizational "systems," each defined by a different method of factoring and different structural relationships. Some possibilities are shown, together with examples, in Table 1.1.

TABLE 1.1:

bases of specialization in social welfare

Basis of Specialization	Exemplified by:
Purpose (or program)	Public assistance, corrections, recreation, vocational rehabilitation
Skill (or process or service)	Social casework, group work, vocational counseling, health care services
Clientele	Children, adults, veterans, the unemployed, the elderly, the poor
Auspices (or sponsorship)	Government (federal, state, local, state-local), Voluntary not-for-profit (sectarian, non-sectarian), Private for and not-for-profit, and Joint partnerships
Geographical (or location)	Geographical jurisdictions, catchment areas, and boundaries of service

Source: Harold Wilensky and Charles Lebeaux, Industrial Society and Social Welfare *(New York: Free Press, 1965), p. 248.*

While social program objectives, in a general sense, are related to the achievement of broad human and social goals, the *specific* nature of those objectives will be greatly influenced by the organizational and political milieu in which they are implemented. That is, the actual program objective cannot be separated from the means adopted to attain it. Consider, for example, a youth care program that has the objective of promoting independent living skills of children from troubled homes; within the UWASIS framework, this objective is instrumental in achieving a broad social goal labeled, "optimal social functioning." But the objective also explicitly embraces a specific clientele—children and, depending upon the service modality employed, perhaps their families—and implicitly will focus upon a particular geographical area; its implementation will thus require the cooperation of other geographically specialized organizations, like the courts, having jurisdiction within that area. The program will probably be funded primarily under governmental auspices, which may involve all levels of government, but a private foundation may provide supplemental funding and a private, not-for-profit provider may actually deliver the service. And the "service" itself may actually be a combination of different service modalities—some casework, group and individual counseling, perhaps some educational or vocational services, and possibly drug abuse rehabilitation services. While not always apparent in the program's espoused purpose, the actual implementation of program objectives will doubtless be influenced by all of the other bases of specialization. Rather than ordered hierarchically, these influences might look as shown in Figure 1.2.

13

FIGURE 1.2:

sources of influence over actual program implementation

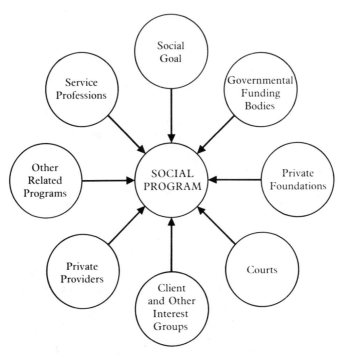

Figure 1.2 considers only a single program. When one considers a whole series of programs that might be in operation at the same time and in the same jurisdiction, it is not difficult to see why the social welfare enterprise is often considered to be, not a coherent "system," but rather a fragmented agglomeration of organizations, services, programs and frequently contradictory purposes. To better understand the organizational complexity of the enterprise, it is important to identify the principal reasons underlying its various and overlapping patterns of structural specialization or factoring. To be sure, many of the reasons are attributed to a history of unplanned, crisis-provoked evolution. But there are persistent patterns in this evolution that help to explain its organizational complexity, which are referred to here as the four "isms": professionalism, federalism, pluralism, and political and organizational symbolism.

Professionalism is the primary force that creates skill or service factoring of the enterprise, and the significant consequences of professionalism for our purposes are two. First, professionals have a particular way of looking at problems, not surprisingly in a way that will take maximum advantage of available professional knowledge and skills (or simply the

14

treatment modalities that are currently in vogue within the profession). Second, the professions have historically been resistant to intrusion by external sources of authority. Thus, a physician will view a person as a set of medical problems; the counselor will concentrate upon, say, family or employment problems, and so on. Moreover, few of the uninitiated are able to penetrate the formidable barriers that surround increasingly specialized professional knowledge.

The antithesis of this view is *holism*—the idea that the individual is not the possessor of a set of discrete maladies, but is rather a "whole" person possessing a total range of highly interrelated needs. The response of the specialized professions to the challenge of holism has been interesting because it has taken two contradictory tacks. The first consistent with what Gilbert and Specht have called the "service perspective"[20] of professional behavior, posits the idea that the professions themselves should adopt a more holistic view of their clients; in essence, the professions would become more generalized. The recent reemphasis upon the family practitioner in health care is an example of this perspective.

The second response, consistent with the "status enhancement"[21] view of professionals, in which high degrees of professional specialization are maintained, relies to a far greater extent upon organizational solutions to the problem of creating a holistic social welfare enterprise. Networks for coordinating access to service, designed to channel persons in need to the right service at the right time, would overcome the pockets of specialized, professional expertise. This solution is what most call *service integration.*

In contrast to the skill orientation provided by professionalism, federalism promotes, at least in theory, organizational factoring along distinctly geographical lines. Within this view, authority and responsibility are defined with reference to geographical subunits; the subunits may parallel the classic three-tiered model of government, or they may involve special jurisdictions, like specially identified neighborhoods, or substate regional jurisdictions responsible for coordinating, say, health care or aging services within a given geographical area. Yet the jurisdictions that often provide services must frequently rely upon higher level jurisdictions for funds, and many of these higher levels are organized around functional departments, which provide funds through often restrictive categorical grants-in-aid. The effect is to balkanize the structure of social welfare organizations and programs within a given region, because the dominant and important relationships with other agencies are often vertical—those that define the all-important flow of dollars.

The Federal-State human service "system" is organized vertically around categorical programs based upon different pieces of Federal legislation. The strongest relationships in the system are the vertical ties between a Federal categorical agency; a State bureau which administers the Federal-State program; local offices of the State agencies; and client groups, professional organizations and congressional subcommittees or individual Congressmen who have a particular interest in the program.[22]

The essence of the third ism, pluralism, is *purposeful* fragmentation, the deliberate avoidance of concentrated sources of power and authority. The new administrative watchword of pluralism, "multiple sources of accountability," cuts across functional, client-oriented, and geographic bases of factoring to embrace all three. The classic argument on behalf of pluralism, and in defense of fragmentation as a strategy for adhering to its principles, is that of ensuring representativeness. That is, a diffuse system of overlapping agencies—each, perhaps, differing only slightly—provides the public with many points of access for influencing agency decision making. With a single hierarchical organization, decisions and actions can be rationalized and made internally, away from public scrutiny. In a system comprised of many highly interdependent entities, many more decisions must be worked out in interagency process and are subject to a greater degree of public exposure and public control.[23] In short, purposeful fragmentation has a positive value because it provides the political and organizational milieu with a set of safety factors against adopting the wrong "one best way" of defining and achieving objectives.

Central to the working of pluralist democracy is the availability of the knowledge, incentives, and the resources for groups with similar interests to organize in response to public issues; the group bias of pluralism is thus consistent with a clientele orientation. One of the key strategies used in the War on Poverty during the sixties and today in Title XX is to foster the self-organization and hence the participation of disadvantaged groups that had been consistently denied access to benefits of the political process. With respect to some groups, particularly children, the elderly, and the handicapped, this trend has continued into the seventies through the creation of specialized social service programs and agencies designed to be responsive to their particular needs.

The final "ism"—symbolism—is an often overlooked, but especially important explanation for organizational complexity in the social welfare enterprise. Recall that, at some point in the planning process, the responsibility for the various goals and programs that comprise the substantive plan must be assigned to a concrete organizational entity. This raises an extremely important question in social policy and program implementation: Who *does* what? It is a question that frequently involves issues of jurisdictional turf, precedence, tradition, and legality, as well as the more instrumental question of which organization is best qualified. But often superseding these more traditional issues, as Murray Edelman has suggested, is the symbolic value attached to the assignment of functional responsibility to organizational units.

> The administrative system is . . . a rather sensitive instrument for highlighting those political functions that are widely, if ambivalently, supported. It has time and again been necessary to change the hierarchical locus of a function precisely to facilitate such highlighting, even though there was no reason to suppose that the locational change meant a shift in policy direction or in the relative influence of interested groups.
> What we have here is a fascinating application of a well-known psychological phenomenon: that we screen precepts and interpret them in relation to a preconceived organization of reality. In administrative activity the organizing conception is very plainly presented and reiterated. It is given first in the very name of the agency.[24]

There are a number of recent examples to support Edelman's contention that the symbolic value of where responsibility is located in the larger organizational setting is a crucial element of policy making and implementation. For example, it is argued that President Kennedy's attempt to highlight urban problems in the sixties by establishing a Department of Urban Affairs was unsuccessful because it seemed to oppose rural interests. President Johnson, on the other hand, succeeded in establishing a Department of *Housing* and Urban Development, in large part because the powerful construction lobby saw in the name that housing was to be a major strategy for dealing with the urban problem. While ambivalent on Kennedy's earlier proposal, the support of the housing industry for HUD was a prime factor in its eventual establishment.[25]

Apart from symbolizing the existence and particular definition of a problem of public concern, administrative restructuring may possess tangible benefits as well, for as President Johnson (a clear advocate of the method) once remarked: "The best way to kill a new idea is to put it in an old-line agency."[26] There are, however, costs associated with highlighting new or redefined problems with new or reorganized administrative structures. While the strategy may help to overcome the vested interests, relationships, and procedural inertia that exist in all large organizations, it also takes time to establish new internal and external working relationships that contribute to effective administration. It is, says Anthony Downs, inevitable that there will be a learning process in dealing with new problems in new ways.[27] In commenting upon many of the welfare programs that proliferated during the sixties, Downs further notes that while the problems they addressed were multifaceted and highly complex, the governmental structures and processes were narrow and fragmented. Problem solving required a degree of cooperation and coordination among governmental institutions that they were ill-prepared to achieve.[28]

social program
administration

While some social welfare programs may be completely embedded within the structure of a single "organization"—the federal retirement insurance program operated by the Social Security Administration is one such example—more often that not the nature of social welfare program objectives and strategies will require program implementation to cut across a variety of organizations, whose objectives and bases of specialization may be quite different than those of the program in question. That is, the benefits of most social programs are seldom rationalized, financed, produced, distributed, and the results evaluated—in short, social programs are seldom implemented—by a single coherent organizational entity. Rather, even for the simplest of programs, implementation may be influenced by a multitude of organizations. In this regard, as Pressman and Wildavsky have pointed out, it is "useful to conceive of 'organization' in an extended sense, so that it encompasses those whose cooperation is necessary for the program to be carried out."[29]

The extended view of organization can be effected if one conceives of the social program, not solely as an instrument for the achievement of a singular, stated goal, but as an *open system* that is dependent in different ways upon various groups and organizations in its environment. Within this view, social program implementation is seen to require the support of a fluid coalition of often contending interests, each of which is engaged in the promotion of its goals.[30] Social program success thus requires that the interdependencies among these interests—and between them and the program—be effectively managed.

In the open system view, organizational interdependencies center upon the control of resources; groups and organizations in possession of crucial resources are in a position to levy control over program operations. Perlman and Gurin have identified five major types of resources upon which any social welfare program will be dependent.[31] First, it will require a continuous supply of service users, whether utilization is the result of personal desires or initiatives, the result of a referral from another agency or program, or compelled by a political, administrative, or professional authority.

Second, the program requires financial resources. With a fee-for-service or sliding fee scale mode of delivery, financial resources are dependent upon the number of service users, which in turn is dependent upon the program's methods of providing service access. In addition to those controlled by program users, financial resources will be controlled by a variety of institutional sources of funds—legislatures, agencies within all levels of government, charitable organizations, and third party providers like insurance companies. Significantly, each of these organizations may be engaged in the promotion of goals that differ from those officially attributed to the program. The net effect is that seldom will funds be provided with no strings attached, but will usually be accompanied by various restrictions designed to further the objectives of the organizations having control over funds.

Third, the organization generally requires some form of mandate or license from legislative or administrative body to perform a given service.

Fourth, the program obviously requires human resources, be they paid staff or volunteers, professional or nonprofessional personnel. It is clear that required knowledge and skills are closely linked to the nature of the service provided and to the various restrictions embodied in the legal mandate to provide those services. Many social welfare programs are locally governed by volunteer boards of directors; the ability to acquire and maintain this valuable resource helps ensure that a bridge is maintained between program and community interests. Finally, the program requires administrative personnel which, as we shall see throughout this book, must possess an increasingly sophisticated set of analytical, political, and coping skills.

Fifth and finally, required is information about the environment in which the program operates and the interdependencies that will often determine program success. Also required is information about internal program operations, which is essential for maintaining accountability to external groups, controlling what must be controlled, and furthering effective program operations.

In the chapters that follow, the program is seen as an open system, enmeshed within the constellation of other programs and organizations that comprise the social welfare enterprise. Our focus will be primarily external—from the inside of the program looking out—emphasizing the ways in which environmental forces influence program operations and administrative behavior.

Despite its attractiveness as a means of understanding organizations, the open systems model presumes a noninstrumental role for the program; its purpose is merely to survive. And yet the social welfare enterprise has been previously defined in purposeful terms—as that set of formal organizations engaged in the promotion of various aspects of individual and societal well-being. Thus, while we shall see that the specific goals and purposes attributable to a given program are often vague and imprecise,

I will argue that the general purpose of all social welfare programs is one of achieving the *correct match of services to needs*. How that general purpose may be understood, supported, retarded, diverted, and generally influenced by the external forces to which the program will be held accountable, and the role of the program administrator in understanding, accommodating, and shaping those forces are the subjects of the chapters that follow.

This chapter began with a brief reference to NASA and the administrative potential manifest in that organization's accomplishments. Compared with the role of the social program administrator, the scientists, engineers, and administrators at NASA were indeed fortunate. They had a known goal for which there was widespread, virtually unwavering popular support; social programs do not. They possessed for a time an almost bottomless well of financial and human resources; social programs do not. They possessed a sound theoretical basis if an unproven technology for achieving their goals; social programs do not. The organization itself was relatively isolated from the nontechnical community and "messy" social problems; social programs most definitely are not. Perhaps most important, participants in the space program were engaged in what was believed to be one of the most prestigious activities ever undertaken by the federal government; social program participants are not. Despite these differences, the social welfare enterprise is consistent with NASA in one extremely important respect: both are founded on the belief that well-administered formal organizations are contemporary society's most effective instruments for solving complex problems.

notes

1. U.S. Department of Health, Education, and Welfare, "Social Security Bulletin," 42, no. 6 (June 1977), 12.

2. Victor Thompson, *Modern Organization* (New York: Alfred Knopf, 1961), p. 15.

3. James D. Thompson, *Organizations in Action* (New York: McGraw-Hill, 1967), pp. 54–82.

4. Harold Wilensky and Charles Lebeaux, *Industrial Society and Social Welfare* (New York: Free Press, 1965), pp. 138–40.

5. Richard Titmuss, *Essays on the Welfare State* (New Haven: Yale University Press, 1959), pp. 42–43.

6. Alfred J. Kahn and Sheila B. Kamerman, *Social Services in International Perspective* (Washington, D.C.: U.S. Department of Health Education and Welfare, undated), p. 7.

7. Harold D. Lasswell and Abraham Kaplan, *Power and Society* (New Haven: Yale University Press, 1950), p. 71.

8. David Easton, *A System Analysis of Political Life* (New York: Wiley, 1965), p. 212.

social welfare and social program administration 21

9. Jeffrey L. Pressman and Aaron B. Wildavsky, *Implementation* (Berkeley and Los Angeles: University of California Press, 1974), p. xv.

10. Martin Rein, *Social Policy* (New York: Random House, 1970), p. 5.

11. See Theodore Lowi, "American Business, Public Policy, Case-Studies, and Political Theory," *World Politics*, no. 6 (July 1964), pp. 677–715.

12. Herbert A. Simon, *Administrative Behavior*, 2nd ed. (New York: Free Press, 1957), p. 96.

13. *Ibid.*, Ch. 5.

14. Victor R. Fuchs, "The Economics of Health in Post-Industrial Society," *The Public Interest*, no. 56 (summer 1979), p. 18.

15. United Way of America, *UWASIS II: A Taxonomy of Social Goals and Human Services Programs* (Alexandria, Virginia: United Way of America, 1976), p. 8.

16. Ibid., p. 15.

17. Ibid., p. 15.

18. Ibid.

19. Ibid., pp. 51–2.

20. Neil Gilbert and Harry Specht, *Dimensions of Social Welfare Policy* (Englewood Cliffs, N.J.: Prentice-Hall, 1974), p. 129.

21. Ibid.

22. DeWitt John, *Managing the Human Service "System": What Have We Learned from Service Integration?* (Denver: Center for Social Research and Development, University of Denver, 1977), p. 4.

23. Herman L. Boschken, "Interorganizational Consideration in Coastal Management," *Coastal Zone Management*, 4, nos. 1/2 (1978), 52.

24. Murray Edelman, *The Symbolic Uses of Politics* (Urbana: University of Illinois Press, 1964), pp. 3–4.

25. James E. Anderson, *Public Policy-Making* (New York: Praeger, 1975), p. 106.

26. Cited in Ibid.

27. Cited in Francine Rabinovitz, Jeffrey Pressman, and Martin Rein, "Guidelines: A Plethora of Forms, Authors, and Functions," *Policy Sciences*, 7, no. 4 (December 1976), 401.

28. Cited in Ibid.

29. Pressman and Wildavsky, *Implementation*, p. xviiin.

30. See, for example, Daniel Katz and Robert L. Kahn, *The Social Psychology of Organizations* (New York: John Wiley, 1966), and Jeffrey Pfeffer and Gerald Salancik, *The External Control of Organizations* (New York: Harper Row, Pub., 1978).

31. Robert Perlman and Arnold Gurin, *Community Organization and Social Planning* (New York: John Wiley, 1972), p. 172.

The program is the strategic and organizational element that links social policies with their eventual outcomes. Fundamental to this linking function are the parameters of social programming—the major categories of policy decisions that provide the essential "givens" within which the programs will operate.

Social policies are consciously redistributive, and thus the major parameters of social programming address the classical political questions of "who is to get what and how." The legislative history of social policy suggests that the answers to this question were largely determined by political conditions of the day, rather than by a master social policy plan.

Nonetheless, every social program possesses an eligibility parameter which determines "who gets" and an allocation parameter which addresses the issue of "what." The issue of "how" is largely dependent upon two additional classes of decision: the financial and service delivery parameters. The range of possible choices within each parameter, the manner in which each is understood and rationalized, and how they are combined to create the current spate of social welfare programs are the major focuses of this chapter.

parameters of social programming: who gets what and how

2

Social policies as we have seen in the previous chapter are redistributive; they represent a conscious effort by political decision makers to alter the prevailing distribution of benefits and well-being among various groups or classes of individuals. In a political economy such as our own this ultimately means modifying, through programmatic intervention, distributive patterns that would prevail were existing economic and political forces left unaltered. As previously formulated, the key social policy issue is: who is to get what. But how is such a momentous issue broken down and restructured into a set of more or less concrete decisions that can provide the basis for program design and implementation?

Oftentimes—as anyone who has been asked to draft a policy statement already knows—it is difficult to know where to start in its attendant chain of means and ends; it is difficult to know what norms and values should be treated as given. Does one start with abstract but almost universally shared social purposes—for example, to "promote happiness," to "eliminate crime," or to "reduce human suffering"—and work slowly downward until a coherent set of logically appropriate objectives and activities is identified; or does one initiate the process more humbly with, say, organizational or program objectives assumed as given? Because social programs are the embodiment of means as well as ends, we shall focus in this chapter on the middle levels in the hierarchy of social decision, upon a variety of givens—what Alfred Kahn has called parameters of programming[1]—that provide the individual program with a more or less unique identity as but one of many instruments for implementing social policy. We shall see that the parameters span both normative and more technical concerns and thus serve as essential linkages between policy and program. And while the specific parameters selected are a matter of analytical level and perspective, two of the parameters to be discussed—the eligibility and allocation parameters—pertain to the issue of who gets what. The two remaining parameters—the financial and service delivery parameters—address the remaining issue of how.

the eligibility parameter

The existence of a "need" or an "unmet need" has become an increasingly important political-economic justification for redistributing benefits in

American society; to meet particular needs is the social program's primary mission. Yet as we shall see in a later chapter, the concept of need is extremely difficult to make operational. As a consequence, it is initially useful to view social programs as targeting their benefits on the basis of various eligibility criteria, which operationally define the intended recipients of social program allocations. It is important to note at this point however, that those in need may not be the same as those who are eligible, and vice versa. It is entirely possible—for example in the case of a retired millionaire who receives his monthly Social Security check—for an individual to be eligible but not to need program benefits. Conversely, some individuals will need but are not eligible for program benefits, such as is often the case with underemployed single persons.

But what groups of individuals are eligible to receive social welfare allocations and how are they identified? Should essential goods and services or cash assistance be made available as a matter of right to all citizens, or should their distribution be somehow limited? Obviously, it depends upon one's point of view. But as it has evolved, the social welfare enterprise has developed four principal eligibility criteria that both rationalize and operationally define the recipients of allocations. These are the means-tested, the status, the compensatory, and the diagnostic criteria of eligibility.

FOUR MAJOR CRITERIA OF ELIGIBILITY

Were one to expand the distributive causal chain of social policy upward in pursuit of successively higher order ends, it would likely culminate in a fundamental question of social philosophy: what is the nature of mutual responsibilities to be assumed by the individual and the larger society of which he or she is a part? Put another way, to what extent and in what ways are the individual and the elements of the larger society to be dependent upon one another for their well-being and ultimately their survival?

Any dependency relationship is comprised of two actors; as we have seen, social policies and programs can be and are rationalized in two different ways. First, they may be justified in purely humanistic terms, wherein the collective is seen to recognize and accept a moral obligation to support various types of dependencies. The goal is simply the promotion of individual well-being with little or nothing expected in return; this justification is consistent with welfare's institutional conception. The second treats the promotion of individual well-being as an intermediate goal of social policy, with social programs the instruments for resolving, through intervention at the level of the individual, a variety of broad, complex social problems; this is the residual conception of welfare.

The residual conception of welfare suggests that social allocations be distributed only to those individuals meeting some financial "inability to pay" or *means-tested* criterion of eligibility. Social welfare programs that limit eligibility to individuals meeting a means test—normally an asset and income criterion defined as some proportion of average or median income —are often labeled *selective* programs. The public assistance programs, state general assistance programs, and many social service programs adopt the means test as a major (but not the only) eligibility criterion. In contrast, the non-means-tested programs—primary and secondary education, the social insurance programs, protective services for children, and many special services for the elderly, to name a few—while possibly invoking other criteria of eligibility are not premised on one's ability or inability to pay. Social welfare programs not invoking a means test as a criterion of eligibility are often called *universal* programs.

Proponents of the selective strategy argue that the means-tested programs reflect the most cost-effective use of scarce societal resources, since publicly controlled resources are expended only on those persons unable to afford essential goods and services in the marketplace. Moreover, they contend, one's willingness to pay is the ultimate test of the value one places upon any good or service; in the absence of this test (known by economists as the "law of demand") it is likely that goods and services will be overconsumed. In short, eligibility to redistributive programs should be limited to those unable to pay.

The universal position, in contrast, holds that if certain goods and services—health care, for example—are deemed essential to all individuals at one time or another, then they should be made available to all citizens as formal rights, regardless of one's income. Moreover, in concert with those favoring an institutional conception of welfare, universalists argue that were benefits made universally available to all citizens, there would be no need to support a separate welfare system for the poor. The stigma attached to the use of a separate system—stigma that is not only demeaning but that may be the most important factor in retarding service utilization by those in genuine need—would thereby be eliminated. In this vein, Irwin Garfinkel remarks,

Americans do not like welfare programs. This is true of beneficiaries and nonbeneficiaries alike. One of the things that beneficiaries find objectionable is that in order to receive benefits, they must declare themselves to be poor. In a country in which stress is put on economic success and in which the dominant ideology is that "with hard work anyone can make it," to declare oneself poor is almost synonymous with declaring oneself to be a failure.[2]

However necessary or unnecessary it might be, in application the means test is administratively burdensome, prone to error, and often defies either humanitarian or administrative precepts of rationality. For most means-tested programs—including the Supplemental Security Income Program (SSI), food stamps, Aid to Families with Dependent Children (AFDC), and state and local general assistance programs—an applicant's means must be separated into current income and assets, like a bank account, a car or a house. Even if income is within eligibility limits, assets may prove disqualifying. On the surface this seems reasonable, for why should the public support persons with no income, but in possession of assets that could easily be turned into cash to meet necessary expenses? Of course there is the story of the elderly woman who applied for Supplemental Security Income benefits and was told that the $1,500 she had saved to cover the expenses of her own funeral exceeded eligibility limits. If she would go out and blow $500 on a new color TV, she was told by the person processing her application, she would then be eligible.[3] This illustrates the principal dilemma that is confronted in formulating formal eligibility criteria. While individual situations may fall within a legal or moral "grey area," the criteria must dichotomize: one is either eligible or one is not. Actually, SSI is among the least complex and least perverse of the means-tested programs.

The Aid to Families with Dependent Children program is probably the most complex and most perverse. While some states have adopted an approach that simply provides a flat cash grant to all eligible recipients depending upon family size, others apply an individualized approach that bases the size of the grant upon a case-by-case determination of family needs.

> There are detailed, specific allowances for specific needs per family member. Detailed budgeting is designed not only to control overall program costs but also to check what is thought to be extravagant living. Thus there are usually no allowances for television sets, or, in many areas of the country, telephones. This means, of course, that if a caseworker sees forbidden (not budgeted for) items in the house, the recipient is forced to come up with a satisfactory explanation or face possible fraud charges.[4]

In this highly individualized and highly discretionary process, an applicant's means (including allocations from other programs like food stamps, medical assistance, and public housing) are compared against a state-defined "need standard," which both determines eligibility and the amount of cash allotment to which the applicant is entitled. The family budget is often separated into a number of parts, such as a basic living allowance, an allowance for shelter (home ownership may be allowed provided that the character of the dwelling is considered "reasonable"), and for special need items, like transportation or educational expenses.[5] Each of these needs must be reviewed, most investigated and verified, and weighed against the need standard, a process that may take several weeks and require substantial time and effort on the part of program personnel and applicant alike. The standards are frequently complex and subject to continuous alteration, and because individual needs and resources change with changing personal circumstances, both eligibility and the size of the allotment are—in principle at least—subject to constant review. In practice, however, budgetary and manpower limitations generally dictate that detailed reviews cannot be performed for all programs beneficiaries but must be performed selectively, at the discretion of often poorly trained intake and eligibility workers. As in the initial intake process, this leads to the distinct possibility that judgments about applicant eligibility will be governed *not* by formally established criteria, but by welfare workers' "personal perceptions of 'proper' standards of morality or behavior."[6]

Perhaps the most serious indictment of the means test as it works in application, however, is that while it serves as a barrier to getting *on* welfare, paradoxically it creates *dis*incentives for individuals to get off. While receiving AFDC benefits, an individual's earnings are subject to the "thirty and one-third disregard," meaning that the first $30 and an additional one-third of a recipient's earnings are disregarded in computing benefit levels; this rule was originally implemented both to improve the adequacy of benefits and to provide some incentive for welfare recipients to work. Nonetheless, the effective "tax" of getting off welfare creates a substantial loss in income—a person earning $120 would "lose" $60 in cash benefits ($30 plus one-third of the remaining $90)—as well as a loss in numerous basic services.

A second set of eligibility criteria pertains to an individual's *status* as the member of an age group, a resident of a particular community, and so on. Family allowance programs as adopted in some European countries invoke status criteria, as do programs for children, the elderly, and the residents of low-income neighborhoods in this country. Probably the purest expression of welfare's institutional ideals, the rationale underlying the distribution of allocations on the basis of status criteria is explained by Gilbert and Specht as follows.

> Eligibility is conditioned upon belonging to a category or group of people having common needs that are not met by existing institutional arrangements. . . . Need may be attributed to as large a category of people as an entire population, such as in the case of health care in

England, or to a delimited group such as working mothers, children, and residents of low-income neighborhoods.[7]

Operationally, status criteria are implemented by limiting program eligibility to persons possessing certain definable sociodemographic characteristics which, while requiring documentation and verification, involve administrative procedures that are less complex than those of means-tested programs. While they may invoke additional criteria as well, examples of programs premised upon status criteria include many child welfare programs, a variety of programs under the Older Americans Act, and many programs fully or partially supported by the provisions of Title XX to the Social Security Act.

A third criterion, here called the *compensatory* criterion, is used to direct program allocations to persons "who have made social and economic contributions . . . or who have suffered unmerited disservice at the 'hands of society.' "[8] Examples include special programs for Native Americans, blacks and other racial minorities, the handicapped, as well as various programs for women. Significantly, while compensatory in nature, eligibility to such programs—like the status-oriented—is made operational through the use of definable sociodemographic characteristics.

By far the largest of the compensatory programs are those for veterans and the social insurance programs, the latter targeted to individuals with a sufficient history of work: retirement insurance, disability insurance, Medicare, workers' compensation, and unemployment compensation programs. Social insurance benefits were made available to workers upon retirement as part of the original Social Security Act; in 1939, these benefits were made available to their survivors and dependents. In 1960, identical benefits were extended to individuals who, for any reason, became permanently and totally disabled after having worked the required number of quarters; the level of benefits was the same as if the individual had worked until the age of 65. Workers' compensation program benefits are available to workers who have suffered a work-related injury or illness, and unemployment compensation is available to workers during short-term periods of unemployment. In every case, the principal criterion governing eligibility to the social insurance programs is a sufficient work history.

The final set of criteria, called *diagnostic* criteria, is the most troubling to administer because the standards that separate the eligible from the ineligible are the least susceptible to objective definition. While intake workers may have difficulty verifying a welfare applicant's true income and assets, at least it is theoretically possible to construct clear means-tested standards. The same is true for specific status and compensatory eligibility criteria. In contrast, the diagnostic determination of eligibility—in the form of a court adjudication, a psychiatric or medical review, an administrative or a caseworker determination—may involve a substantial amount of "built-in" discretion on the part of the individual making the diagnosis. Programs invoking diagnostic criteria rely to a great extent upon professionalization to guard against arbitrary and unwarranted eligibility judgments.

MULTIPLE ELIGIBILITY CRITERIA

To summarize thus far, the eligibility parameter has been seen to include four principal criteria: eligibility on the basis of means-tested, status, compensatory, and diagnostic criteria. But were one to attempt at this point classifying all social welfare programs according to these criteria taken singly, many wouldn't fit. For the most part American programs incorporate multiple elegibility criteria.

For example, the disability insurance program invokes both the compensatory criterion of sufficient work and a diagnostic determination of disability; a similar determination occurs with respect to workers' compensation programs. Some social service programs invoke both means-tested and diagnostic criteria, in the sense that a diagnostic process may identify a need and, after acceptance into the program, an income review may be performed to determine how much, if anything, the individual will pay.

But by far the largest set of programs adopting multiple eligibility criteria are the so-called categorical public assistance programs, which incorporate a combination of means-tested, status, and in some cases diagnostic criteria as well. The categorical public assistance programs include those under the original public assistance titles of the Social Security Act of 1935: Old Age Assistance (OAA), Aid to the Blind (AB), and Aid to Dependent Children (ADC). In 1950 a fourth category, Aid to the Permanently and Totally Disabled (APTD) was established for those with insufficient work to qualify under the disability provisions of social insurance. Originally administered at the discretion of the states, in 1973 Old Age Assistance, Aid to the Blind, and Aid to the Permanently and Totally Disabled were combined into a single, federally administered program, the Supplemental Security Income Program.

In 1950 support for a parent or legal guardian was included in the ADC program (prior to that time support was intended for the children only) and the name changed to Aid to Families with Dependent Children (AFDC); further in 1961 in part to stem the tide of criticism that the welfare system was responsible for family breakup and also to ameliorate the effects of an especially severe recession at the time, AFDC benefits were extended, at the discretion of the states, to include families with an unemployed father, creating the AFDC-U program. The alternative for those poor who did not *also* satisfy the various status criteria imposed by the federal categorical, public assistance programs—impoverished couples with no children, single males and females—there remained the bottom rung of the welfare ladder, the highly discretionary and parsimonious state and local general assistance programs.

By confining eligibility to various subsets of the poor—poor and blind, poor and elderly, and so on—American categorical assistance programs attempt to confine benefits to the "deserving poor," those unable or legitimately excused from the obligation to work. As Martin Rein has noted:

> Common sense and public policy have always insisted upon the distinction between those who could work and those who could not. Social programs were designed to reflect those policies. But the dichotomy between the unemployed and the unemployable, . . . is inherently vague.[9]

A dominant characteristic of American social policy and program since the Depression has been the expanded use of administrative mechanisms for resolving the vague distinction between the unemployed and the unemployable. Because this approach requires the establishment of schema for separating the population into definable employment-related subgroups, the development of methods for assigning each individual to the appropriate category, and the maintenance of different programs and organizations for each, it is natural that the implementation of the categorical approach to welfare will be administratively intensive and complex. Such is the case even when the categories of individuals to which allocations are to be distributed are well defined; when vague, however, the importance of provider discretion in policy and program implementation increases dramatically. As we shall see shortly, such vague distinctions pervade the allocation parameter as well.

the allocation parameter

Closely related to decisions regarding eligibility—indeed, it is difficult to treat them separately—are those concerning the allocations to which specific groups and individuals in need will be entitled. Debate regarding the appropriate decision within the allocation parameter of social programming generally focuses upon two primary issues: (1) the quantitative amount of allocations to be distributed, and (2) the qualitative characteristics of those allocations. The latter is the primary focus of this section and as is the case with the need parameter, different programs manifest different conclusions to this issue.

Social welfare allocations are of three major types: (1) intangible "opportunities," like access to jobs; (2) cash transfers; and (3) noncash, tangible allotments—usually called *in-kind services*—like food, shelter, and social services. A major question embraced by this parameter concerns the relative merits of distributing cash as opposed to in-kind services, and like the selective-universal debate regarding program eligibility, the issue involves both philosophical and practical concerns.

The United States is characterized by a "mixed economy," in which the distribution of benefits occurs through a mixture of government-controlled and market institutions. Supporters of cash allocations tend to favor greater reliance upon the marketplace as the most efficient means of distributing benefits. Usually "liberal" economist (liberal is defined with respect to economic thought, not necessarily contemporary political persuasion), they base their position on the two fundamental assumptions of neoclassical economic theory: the existence and supremacy of the "sovereign consumer" and a marketplace characterized by "perfect competition."

In brief, the theoretical underpinnings of the economists' view and the cash allocations position is as follows. Each individual is a sovereign consumer, assumed in possession of a unique set of wants and preferences which, when revealed and satisfied through the act of consumption, increase his happiness or "utility." In addition, the sovereign consumer is assumed to be in possession of perfect information regarding two central prerequisites of rational individual choice: (1) the total range of available consumption alternatives (present *and* future) and (2) the degree to which each will contribute to his overall utility. Behaviorally, the sovereign consumer is a utility maximizer, in dogged pursuit of his well-being. But he is also assumed to experience a phenomenon known as marginally decreasing utility: the more that is consumed of a particular good or service, the less the contribution to one's overall utility.

The role of the marketplace under the assumption of perfect competition is elegant in its simplicity, with suppliers assumed to respond quickly and effortlessly to the revealed preferences of consumers as expressed in the act of consumption. When new preferences arise, suppliers move to meet the demand; when demand declines, suppliers shift to more lucrative markets. When the assumption of perfect competition is combined with the theory of the sovereign consumer, the conclusion of neoclassical economic theory is this: the cost of government in-kind services (the basic cost, excluding administration, delivery, etc.) will *always* exceed the total utility derived by the individual service user. Hence, one can reap the same gains in consumer happiness for less money (or more gains for the same expense) by distributing cash rather than services.[10]

The in-kind service argument questions both the normative and factual assumptions of neoclassical economics, and for a variety of reasons promotes the idea that it may be desirable to control the distribution of *benefits* by controlling individual *patterns of consumption.* First, it may be argued, the notion of consumer sovereignty is largely a myth. In contrast to the idea that consumers possess innate wants and preferences to which producers automatically respond in the marketplace, the myth of consumer sovereignty is built upon the very plausible observation that wants are, in fact, *created* by producers specifically and society in general.

> In fact, not only do producers determine the range of market goods from which consumers must take their choice, they also seek continuously to persuade consumers to choose that which is being produced today and to "unchoose" that which was being produced yesterday. Therefore to regard the market, in an affluent and growing economy, as primarily a "want-satisfying" mechanism is to close one's eyes to the more important fact, that it has become a want-*creating* mechanism.[11]

In effect, the myth of consumer sovereignty questions the perfect information assumption that is a crucial characteristic of the sovereign consumer. Not only is it possible that the "real" consumer may have inadequate information about the range of consumption alternatives (for example, the relative "quality" of various service options), but also that want-creating forces in the market may distort the individual calculus that links consumption decisions to ultimate individual happiness. Of course, one way of dealing with this distortion is to provide all individuals with a sufficient amount of cash to ensure that, amidst the nonessentials, a sufficient balance of essentials would be consumed. But the monetary costs would doubtless be prohibitive. Moreover, policy makers may wish to compel some individuals to consume certain essentials—mental health and drug rehabilitation services, for example—that individuals would not want, regardless of their incomes. In short, one way to promote the desired distribution of benefits—to ensure that milk is consumed rather than beer—is for government to provide the essentials, or otherwise stimulate individuals to consume them.

A second reason for distributing services rather than cash arises because policy makers may desire that benefits accrue not only to the recipient of the allocation but to other persons as well. Economic theory is highly individualistic, assuming that the utility of the consumer is the one that counts, period. In contrast, many social welfare programs may reflect a desire to distribute benefits to persons other than the recipient alone. This is true, for example, in the AFDC program, in which the largest proportion of the cash allocation is intended to benefit not the recipient, but rather her children.

Many programs, moreover, are intended to benefit the community or society at large. Policy makers may rationalize the provision of health care services on the grounds that they will help prevent the spread of contagious disease, thereby protecting the larger community as well as providing benefits to the user. Similarly, adequate housing may prevent crime and disease. Education may prevent an unmotivated, untrained, and unsocialized future generation. Child care may benefit taxpayers by helping a mother get off welfare or prevent her from going on by enabling her to work or obtain job training. In each of these cases, the rationale for providing services rather than cash is one of promoting consumption patterns that help to reduce *negative externalities,* essentially the costs borne by the larger community were the services not consumed.

Third, there may be insufficient reason for the market to provide certain services, even were cash made available to potential users. This is the case, for example, when benefits are indivisible, accruing to the community at large, and when a user fee is either infeasible or deemed inappropriate; national defense, parks, libraries, and roads are examples. Or there may be insufficient financial incentives, as is the case with many services for children, for private organizations to provide services deemed desirable by policy makers.

Finally, as the growth of in-kind service programs during the sixties demonstrates, because it is cheaper financially, distributing in-kind services is cheaper *politically* than distributing cash.

At the philosophical level, the cash-versus-services debate is symbolically embedded in images of the "competent" sovereign individual versus the coercive, paternalistic state. As economist Lester Thurow has remarked:

> At the heart of the economist's love affair with cash transfers is the doctrine of absolute consumer sovereignty. Everyone is his own best judge of what should be done to maximize his own utility. Real public policies must face up to a modification of this simplistic view—some individuals are not competent to make their own decisions.
>
> Obviously, it is a difficult problem to establish any individual's degree of incompetence, but the existence of incompetence is a problem that neither governments nor economists can ignore.
>
> Governments have a whole range of public policies that can be pursued to supplant consumer sovereignty, but one of the mildest and least coercive of these is the public provision of goods and services in kind. Such in-kind aid can be used to influence individuals to make those decisions that society thinks they would make if they were "competent."[12]

Like most symbols, the dichotomy reflected in the cash versus in-kind services debate is in reality too simple. In fact, the social welfare enterprise invokes a continuum of allocation strategies—of which cash and the direct provision of services are merely the two poles—for controlling consumption and the distribution of benefits. Those to be discussed here include opportunities, cash transfers, credits and vouchers, social services, social utilities, and social interventions.

As used here, *opportunities* involve no allocation of any tangible good or service, but rather create access to benefits previously denied certain groups.[13] Perhaps the most important is the opportunity for political mobilization of groups previously denied access to full participation in the political process; the Equal Opportunity Act, through the establishment of the Community Action Programs, created such opportunities for poor residents of urban neighborhoods; the Older Americans Act has created similar opportunities for seniors. The Rehabilitation Act of 1973 is designed to improve opportunities for persons with physical and mental handicaps. The Civil Rights Act of 1964, and the various affirmative action efforts that followed, have created numerous job and educational opportunities previously denied women and racial minorities. Almost by definition, opportunities incorporate compensatory criteria of eligibility.

A *cash transfer* is the allocation of a sum of money from one individual or institution to another; it differs from a wage or fee in that payment is made in lieu of any service rendered or a transfer of property ownership. Social welfare cash transfers redistribute benefits in one or a combination of two general ways. First, as is the case with the categorical AFDC and SSI programs, as well as the general assistance programs, benefits are redistributed from taxpaying citizens to eligible program recipients; revenues are generated from current tax revenues. Or, as is the case with private pension and insurance programs, as well as workers' compensation and unemployment insurance programs, cash transfers effect a distribution of benefits from present to future; revenues for these programs are generated from a payroll tax on employers and employees, with the administrative agency serving as a steward for these funds until disbursed.

Retirement insurance (OASDI), also financed from a payroll tax, redistributes cash in both ways. It redistributes benefits from present to future and—since, in proportion to contributions, ultimate benefits received are less for high-income contributors than those with lower incomes—it also redistributes benefits from rich to poor. And finally within the disability provisions of OASDI, benefits are distributed from workers to those no longer able to work. As is the case with opportunities, once the cash transfer has been effected, government has little direct control over individual consumption patterns.

If policy makers desire to exert a greater degree of control over program beneficiaries by limiting or promoting the consumption of specific goods and services, they may elect to distribute not cash, but a variety of *credits*. A major mechanism for doing so is the American tax system. A method for generating the revenues that permit governments to spend, the particular tax system selected together with its various sanctions and provisions can (and does) have a profound impact upon the distribution of benefits within society. Alternative taxing systems are generally labeled as either progressive or regressive, depending upon whether members of the higher or the lower income strata respectively bear a proportionately greater share of the tax burden. As applied in America, the federal income tax system is, at least in theory, progressive: the higher one's personal income, the higher the tax rate and hence the proportion of income that will be paid in taxes. The property tax, state and local sales tax, and the taxes paid by employees in support of the social security system are regressive, since the tax *rate* does not increase in proportion to income.

Although progressive in theory, the provisions governing the implementation of the American federal income tax tend to provide the wealthy with certain advantages not available to the poor. Whatever the reasons used to justify them—interest group pressures or tradition—the federal government allows, through the tax system, advantages for certain classes of expenditures; in effect, government is subsidizing and promoting the consumption of certain goods and services. The two primary devices for subsidization via the income tax system are the tax *deduction* and the tax *credit;* a deduction reduces the level of taxable income and the tax credit reduces the individual tax burden by an amount, within limits, equal to the amount expended on a qualifying good or service.

A subsidy provided in the form of a tax deduction, as is currently allowed for such essentials as medical care expenditures and the taxes and interest paid toward the purchase of housing, is inequitably biased in favor of those with higher incomes in a progressive tax system. Suppose, for example, that two families with different incomes each spend $3,000 for property taxes and mortgage interest during the year; each may reduce its taxable income by $3,000 by claiming a deduction for taxes and interest. The higher income family in, say, the 50 percent tax bracket reduces its tax burden by 50 percent of $3,000 or $1,500 because it is engaged in the purchase of a house. The lower income family, say in the 25 percent tax bracket, reduces its tax burden by only 25 percent of the cost for taxes and interest, or $750. Those too poor to pay income taxes or those who use the standard deduction receive no subsidy for housing through the tax system.

These inequities can be reduced substantially (although those too poor to pay income taxes still receive nothing) if the expenditures for certain essential goods and services are deducted, not from before-tax income, but the tax itself. Government can allow a tax credit rather than a tax deduction as is now the case within limits with respect to child care expenditures.

Through the provision of such exemptions and the various other special provisions in the complex system of federal, state, and local taxes —such as special provisions for the blind, the handicapped, the elderly, and for children—agencies of government are able not only to provide a measure of relief, but to exert substantial, though relatively indirect and unobtrusive, control over such diverse behaviors as work and leisure patterns, consumption and savings habits, the willingness to incur personal debt, the propensity to marry, and family size and structure.

An additional credit, a *voucher*, is a form of scrip designed to limit current consumption to certain goods and services. Food stamps are vouchers. The Medicare and Medicaid programs use a similar strategy of promoting restricted comsumption, with the federal government reimbursing medical care providers for services rendered to eligible individuals; educational benefits to qualifying veterans are distributed in a similar way. While the use of various credits reflects an attempt by policy makers to control what is consumed, beneficiaries are still free to choose their own source of supply and, if necessary or desired, to supplement the value of the credit with personal income. Food stamps may be redeemed in any supermarket; any qualified medical care provider may be selected by a Medicaid or Medicare beneficiary; and veterans may enroll in any approved educational program.

Finally, policy makers may believe or taxpayers may demand that it is necessary to control not only *what* is consumed by program beneficiaries, but also the *qualitative characteristics* of the good or service. For example, food stamps obviously encourage the consumption of food, presumably yielding nutritional and health value to the recipient; personal tastes, however, dictate the specific food items that are consumed. Suppose it is determined, however, that Chinese food provides the greatest nutritional value per dollar, and that—variations in personal tastes and wants notwithstanding—the consumption of Chinese food is to be encouraged. Government may choose the market as the distribution medium, by subsidizing or contracting only with providers agreeing to comply with government specifications pertaining to the quality of Chinese food; this is the approach adopted in health care services. Or government may opt to provide the in-kind service itself.

In recent years it has become common to distinguish between two broad categories of in-kind services. The first of these, and the largest in dollar expenditures, is the *general social services*—health care, education, housing, and employment training services.[14] In the United States, these are provided by a mixture of public and private institutions, with those provided privately the object of numerous government-defined and - imposed standards of quality. Primary and secondary education is, of course, the only general social service made universally available by agencies of government.

A second category of in-kind services, the smallest but among the fastest growing and most complex, is the *personal social services;* a partial listing of services within this category is given in Table 2.1. To better understand the role of the personal social services, it is useful to further subdivide this class of social allocations into two categories that reflect the general purpose of each: the social utilities and the social interventions or case services. The *social utilities* are personal social services that are seen to "enhance development and socialization or provide information and access"[15] to other social programs. Thus, the social utilities are strongly aligned with the institutional conception of welfare in that their use often carries little or no stigma and is, indeed, a matter of personal choice, not compulsion. In contrast are the *social interventions* or case services, designed to serve people with "maladjustments, problems, illness, difficulties."[16] Although benefits of the social intervention will doubtless accrue to the

TABLE 2.1:
a partial listing of the personal social services

---

* Child welfare, including adoption, foster home care, children's institutions for the dependent and neglected, protective programs for children
* Family services and counseling
* Community services for the aged
* Protective services for the aged
* Homemaker and home help services
* Community and senior centers
* Child care
* Vacation camps for children, the handicapped, the elderly, average families
* Information and referral services
* Congregate meals and meals-on-wheels
* Self-help activities among handicapped and disadvantaged individuals
* Youth counseling and services
* Protected residential arrangements for youth
* Specialized institutions for several categories of children and adults

---

Source: Alfred J. Kahn and Sheila B. Kameran, Social Services in International Perspectives *(Washington, D.C.: U.S. Department of Health, Education, and Welfare, 1976), p. 31.*

individual client, most will accrue to the society at large in the form of a "problem solved" and a concomitant reduction in negative externalities.

The principal distinction between the social utilities and the social interventions—that the former provide benefits only to the user and the latter a share of benefits to the larger community—may be difficult to discern in practice. One could distinguish by saying that consumption of the utilities is a matter of personal choice, and interventions the result of economic, political or administrative compulsion. Relatedly, one could say that social utilities can be provided either publicly or through the market-place, while interventions are most often provided under governmental auspices. But these distinctions often break down in practice, and, indeed, many of the personal social services may be classified as *both* utilities and interventions, depending upon their presumed purpose. Take the example of child care. In one sense child care services may be regarded as a social utility, since it is one response to the changing role of the American family in modern society. Within this view, child care is properly seen as a means of enhancing child development and socialization. On the other hand, child care may be viewed as a social intervention, as an instrument that simply permits a welfare mother to obtain training and to work. Note as well that the specific, *qualitative* characteristics of the service may differ as the general purpose differs. One need merely provide shelter, supervision, and maintenance for the intervention, not a child development component, as would be the case were child care defined as a social utility.

who gets what: a programmatic synthesis

If one combines the various choices within the eligibility and allocation parameters into a matrix, as has been done in Figure 2.1, it is possible to classify the major programs that comprise the bulk of this nation's social policy. Additionally, the matrix gives some idea of the myriad and complex interrelationships that exist among the various programs. Programs shown as occupying more than one cell in the matrix manifest multiple eligibility and allocation components. For example, most credit programs pertain to specific services and thus occupy both the Credits and General Social Services columns. Similarly, the SSI program may invoke different sets of eligibility criteria and is shown as occupying the Status, Means-tested and Diagnostic rows. Most of the cash transfer programs shown in Figure 2.1 —AFDC, SSI, state and local general assistance, and the various social insurance programs (including Medicare)—have been previously dis-cussed, and will not receive further attention here.

FIGURE 2.1:

who gets what: selected American social welfare programs

ELIGIBILITY PARAMETER	ALLOCATION PARAMETER				Personal Social Services	
	Opportunities (Major Legislation)	Cash Transfers	Credits	General Social Services	Utilities	Interventions
Compensatory	Equal Opportunity Act Civil Rights Act Rehabilitation Act	OASDI (retirement, disability insurance) Unemployment insurance Worker's compensation	OASDHI (Medicare) Veterans' Programs			
Status	Older Americans Act	AFDC SSI general assistance	Medicaid	primary and secondary education public housing CETA	Programs under the Older Americans Act Programs under Title XX	Work Incentive Program
Means-tested		AFDC SSI general assistance	food stamps Medicaid	public housing CETA	Programs under Title XX	Work Incentive Program
Diagnostic		AFDC SSI			Programs under Title XX Programs under the Rehabilitation Act	

The food stamp program is unique in that it was the first major social program for the working poor and is the only noncategorical, means-tested assistance program in the social welfare enterprise. Medicaid and public housing services invoke both means-tested and status criteria of eligibility, the latter because eligibility and allocation particulars will vary with one's place of residence. In contrast, food stamp eligibility criteria and benefit levels are uniform nationwide.

Among the most significant service programs are those operated under the auspices of Title XX of the Social Security Act, signed into law in 1975. Title XX authorizes a specific grant to the states to support a variety of personal social services; in general, the specific purpose of services provided—whether utilities or interventions—and specific eligibility requirements are at the option of the states. However, services are limited to those earning less than 115 percent of a state's median income. Because specific services vary from state to state the importance of Title XX is less in the "who get what" parameters of social programming than in the "how" issues of delivery and finance. As a result, it will receive greater attention in a later section of this chapter.

The legislative history of these programs indicates that most were conceived and implemented in response to the needs of particular groups of people or the need for certain essential goods and services. What is not immediately apparent from Figure 2.1, but what has nonetheless occurred, is the way in which the eligibility criteria of specific programs are tied to those of other programs to create a variety of "subsistence packages" for various classes of the general population. For example, consistent with the work incentive provisions of the AFDC program, AFDC recipients are automatically eligible for WIN benefits. AFDC recipients are also automatically eligible for food stamps, a variety of personal social services, subsidized public housing, and Medicaid (in fact, Medicaid benefits continue for four months following the termination of AFDC benefits). Persons receiving cash assistance from the social security program are also automatically eligible for the Medicare program. Moreover, if an individual's retirement or disability income from social security and private insurance or pensions is sufficiently low (an increasingly frequent occurrence in periods of high inflation) he or she will also become eligible for benefits under the SSI program. Many recipients of SSI are also eligible for Medicaid and food stamps. On top of these, a number of programs at the state and local levels of government are designed either to supplement (by providing, for example, emergency payments to recipients of AFDC benefits) or to fill the gaps between the federally supported public welfare programs; some states are required, for example, to further supplement the federal portion of SSI.

Why is the set of social welfare programs so diverse and complex? The most plausible answer is that it simply "happened," with policy makers adopting the expedient path of building upon and refining existing legislation as new needs emerged and became legitimate claimants of public support. Reinforcing this piecemeal development are the ways in which social welfare funds are generated and, in an often roundabout way, the benefits distributed to those in need.

the finance parameter

In the preceding two sections we have seen that social welfare programs can be classified in two dimensions: the nature of the allocations they provide, and the various need groups to which they respond. Some programs will differ only marginally from others, providing a similar but not identical allocation on the basis of similar but not identical eligibility criteria. A large share of the complexity in these and other dimensions of the social welfare enterprise can be directly traced to the many ways programs will receive funds. In this section we will investigate the various sources of revenue and the various methods used to finance social welfare programs.

WHO PAYS: SOURCES OF SOCIAL WELFARE FUNDS

Certainly the most direct means of funding social welfare programs is through the adoption and imposition of a user fee; the user pays for the service rendered. Hence, the amount of revenue available to the program is directly dependent upon the fee and the magnitude of utilization. This is the funding strategy employed within the majority of the social services and a large number of personal social utility programs as well—education, health care, child care, housing, homemaker services, nursing care, and the like. Within this mode, services may be rendered by profit-making or "proprietary" entities, such as some hospitals, psychiatric treatment centers, and many nursing homes; they may be provided by not-for-profit organizations like private universities, or youth care and counseling centers; or the fee-for-service strategy (normally as a sliding fee scale) may be employed in some public programs as well. Few such programs, however, are self-supporting; most are subsidized in one way or another by various public funds. And most user fees, moreover, are subsidized in part through the availability of numerous credits and deductions in the income tax system. The effect: even when services are delivered and financed on a direct fee-for-service basis, seldom does the user bear their full cost.

Private charitable organizations like the United Way, the Red Cross, and a variety of foundations dealing with more specific service areas are a second source of social welfare funds. Although allocations are sometimes made to individuals, Red Cross disaster relief for example, most funds from charitable organizations are allocated to private, not-for-profit service organizations. The most common mode of funding is what is known as deficit financing, in which the charitable organization agrees to underwrite the difference between program costs and revenues obtained from other sources, which may include user fees, individual contributions, funds from government agencies, and funds provided by other charitable organizations. Although charitable organizations may receive governmental funds, those generally available for disbursement to social welfare programs come from contributions from businesses and individuals.

In the health care field, the largest portion of service costs are borne by a third source of funds, the so-called third party providers or insurance companies; premiums, of course, are paid either by individuals or by their employers as part of fringe benefit packages. In 1976, it was estimated that 76 percent of the American population had some type of insurance coverage for hospital and surgical services.[17] Increasingly smaller percentages had some type of coverage for other health care costs: three-fourths of the under-65 population had private insurance that paid part of the cost of in-hospital physicians' visits and related hospital services like X-ray and laboratory examinations, drugs, and nursing services; three-fifths of this population had coverage that paid some of the costs of physician in-home and office visits; and only about one-third had any coverage for long-term care. Less than one-fourth of the under-65 population had dental protection, although largely as a result of collective bargaining agreements, dental coverage is the fastest growing segment of health insurance.[18]

Virtually all Americans over age 65 are covered by the two Medicare programs, hospital care and the optional Supplementary Medical Insurance program. Many, however, also purchase complementary insurance from private providers to cover the cost of Medicare deductibles for physician services and nursing home care, and for services totally excluded by Medicare, such as drugs and private-duty nursing services.

The insurance principle—pay now, receive benefits later—is also used to provide funds for all of the state and federal social insurance programs—retirement and disability insurance, workers' compensation, and unemployment insurance. Funds are raised through a series of payroll taxes on employees, employers, or a combination of both. The funds are collected by the appropriate agency of government (in some states workers' compensation coverage may be in the hands of a private insurance provider, or employers may elect to be self-insured) and held in trust until payment to a qualifying individual is warranted. By law, these funds must be kept separately from other government revenues and expended only in support of that program's administration and to provide benefits to qualified recipients.

Such special purpose funds are also raised by levying taxes on property owners within special taxing districts at the local level of government; this is generally the case with primary and secondary education, water and sewer services, fire protection, and sometimes with public transportation. These special taxing districts create a complex, overlapping mosaic of revenue-generating entities, upon which must also be superimposed the general taxing powers of municipal and county governments. Unlike funds generated by special taxing districts, revenues generated by general purpose governmental entities are not necessarily earmarked for any specific purpose; rather they are general funds, to be expended in accordance with the priorities of the local citizenry and its elected officials.

The revenue-generating and expenditure patterns of both special and general purpose governmental entities are usually based upon the simple nonredistributive premise that the beneficiary will pay for governmental services, whether this be a resident, the owner of a business, or an employee within a defined jurisdiction. The "beneficiary should pay" rule is sometimes the subject of fierce debate, as is often the case with public transportation (which I see as a social service because of its significance for the general problem of service access). The costs of operating public transportation systems make total financial support through user fees infeasible. Some are subsidized by a payroll tax, others a property tax; the question of method is often one of who benefits most. A payroll tax to support public transportation is indicative of the conclusion that businesses and their employers reap the greatest gains, while a property tax levy indicates the conclusion that the greatest gains will accrue to residents of the community.

State governments generally employ one or a combination of two mechanisms for generating operating funds, the sales tax (also used by some counties) and the income tax. From a purely monetary standpoint, the sales tax distributes some of the costs of operating state government to nonresidents, who may nonetheless be consumers within the state. Despite exemptions in some states for food, medicine, and other necessities, sales taxes are highly regressive, imposing a proportionately greater burden on the poor than the well-to-do; they are also complex and expensive to administer. A large number of states generate funds through an income tax, and although this method of generating revenues has the potential to be highly progressive, most states have been reluctant to use their income tax system as a device for redistributing income and for redistributing the burden of operating state government to those most able to afford it.

Although the federal government possesses a variety of revenue-generating capabilities—including excise taxes, estate and gift taxes, and customs duties—its income tax on corporations and individuals is clearly the most important, accounting for $270 billion or 87 percent of federal non-trust-fund revenues in fiscal 1978.[19] Of this total, better than $100 billion was expended in support of noninsurance social welfare programs. Some benefits financed by these revenues—for example, cash assistance payments under the Supplemental Security Income programs—were provided directly to individuals by an agency of the federal government. But the majority of benefits were delivered to individuals by various state, local and private agencies, which were largely funded through a complex system of intergovernmental transfers known as grants-in-aid.

THE GRANT-IN-AID

The federal grant-in-aid is probably the single most important source of funds for social programs. At present, the federal government funds and administers somewhat better than 500 different grant-in-aid programs of which nearly 60 percent pertain to social welfare purposes.[20] Moreover, these numbers actually understate the true magnitude and complexity of federal grants-in-aid because they assume that grants for the same purposes, but to different jurisdictions, are the "same." With respect to Title XX, for example, the same grant-in-aid program is actually different for each of the fifty states.

The dramatic growth in federal grants-in-aid since 1950—from $2.3 billion to better than $70 billion in 1978[21]—may be traced to a variety of legal, political, and economic reasons. The most important of these is the tremendous revenue-generating capability of the federal income tax, a far more efficient and effective instrument than any of the state and local taxing methods. Coupled with the fact that in recent years "state and local revenues have lagged behind citizens' desires and demands for public services," the grant-in-aid has become an effective instrument for "bridging this gap between revenues and expenditures."[22] That the federal government's revenue-generating capabilities are needed to bridge the revenue-expenditure gap at the state and local levels is insufficient explanation for the myriad different grant-in-aid programs, however. A single program—a flat cash grant to state and local governments to cover their operating deficits—would suffice; indeed, this is the philosophy underlying the federal General Revenue Sharing program, which provides grants for unrestricted use to state and local governments. But what about the remaining 500-odd programs that are somehow restricted to the performance of certain activities? Staff at the Brookings Institution state the rationale as follows.

The case for specifying, either broadly or narrowly, the nature of the activity to be supported rests on the belief that national priorities are different from state and local priorities—that even if they had greater resources state and local governments would fail to meet some important national needs.[23]

This divergence of priorities, the Brookings analysis continues, may occur for three reasons. First, state and local governments may spend too little on services of apparent national importance because the negative externalities of *not* providing those services will be borne by other jurisdictions. An obvious example is a community experiencing a strong emigration of young people. No need, the community may argue, to bear the costs of educating and training people who will eventually benefit another community. Second, state and local spending priorities may not take into account the needs of some disadvantaged citizens, "especially those with little power and status in the community."[24] This observation provided the rationale for the first of the major social grants-in-aid—the categorical public assistance titles of the Social Security Act of 1935. Third and finally, states and localities may be unwilling to underwrite high-risk, innovative methods of delivering services. An example is the health maintenance organization (HMO), a prepaid health care plan that emphasizes prevention. Because service utilization requires no (or only a nominal) fee-for-service, a major barrier to service utilization is eliminated; health problems are thus diagnosed and treated before they become major problems. And since the HMO is committed to providing needed health care to its members but receives only a flat yearly fee, there is an obvious emphasis upon prevention, and upon the provision of low-cost but effective health care. The establishment of such organizations requires funds, and in 1973, through the Health Maintenance Organization Act, Congress promoted the establishment of HMOs by providing assistance to local groups in the form of cash grants, contracts, and loans.

To achieve various national objectives through state and local government and to satisfy a number of political constraints as well, Congress and the federal bureaucracy possess a bewildering array of different grant-in-aid instruments which defy simple classification. Indeed, grants may be classified in *at least* six different ways, and virtually all require multiple classification.[25] First, grants may be classified according to *specificity of program purpose* and the degree of grantor control; these range from the most restrictive *categorical grants* to less restrictive *block grants* to the virtually unrestricted General Revenue Sharing program. Second, grants may be arranged with respect to their *intended effects* on grantee expenditure decisions, whether the grant is intended to stimulate new activities or merely assist in supporting grantee activities already undertaken. The *level of match* is a third way of classifying grants; some may require no contribution by the grantee, other programs a low match (25 percent is common) and others a high match like 50 percent or 67 percent. Some programs, moreover, require that the grantee match be in the form of cash; others permit the substitution of in-kind services or facilities to satisfy the matching requirement. Fourth, grants may be classified according to *eligible recipient*—state or local government, a specific agency within state or local government, a special purpose or general purpose governmental entity, the type of local government (county or municipality), or a private, not-for-profit organization. Fifth, grants may be arrayed according to *restrictions on the level of funding;* some will be open-ended with limitless appropriations, while for others Congress may have imposed a funding ceiling. Sixth and finally, the *method for determining the distribution of funds* to various recipients will differ from grant to grant; some distribute funds to eligible recipients on the basis of an arithmetical formula, others on the basis of grantee competition, others on a combination of the two, and still others depend simply upon the number of program users—such as food stamp and AFDC recipients —within a state or local jurisdiction.

Clearly, a detailed analysis of the whys and hows behind each of the different grant strategies is impossible here, but one dimension—the method for determining the distribution of funds—bears further discussion because it is distinctly tied to the idea of program need. A large number of grants for social programs incorporate specific formulas, as defined in enabling legislation, agency guidelines, or unwritten agency rules, for determining the amount of funds to be allocated to eligible jurisdictions, predominantly state governments. Formulas may be used in categorical grant programs like child welfare services, block grant programs as with Title XX, and in general revenue sharing as well. The main feature of the formula approach is that, while the granting agency may maintain substantial control over *how* the funds are spent, the grantor usually has little control over the *level* of funding received by the eligible jurisdiction. Thus, while the regulations, restrictions, and requirements governing the actual performance of child welfare services, for example, may be endless, the responsible federal administrator does not specifically control a state's level of funding; that is the function of the formula.

Formula grants are primarily used in support of activities of state government and are generally intended to underwrite state programs already in existence; normally a state match is required. Especially significant are the different allocation formulas used in different programs and how each is justified. The most commonly used are formulas that incorporate a state's *population* as the basis for determining funding levels; Title XX uses such a formula. Population as an allocation factor is often invoked when federal policy makers desire to raise the general level of services provided by the states. Since it may be assumed that a state's service costs are proportionate to the size of its population, a per capita allotment is deemed appropriate.

A second commonly used allocation factor is state *per capita income,* which is generally seen as a proxy for the jurisdiction's fiscal capacity to provide basic services; hence, states with lower per capita income populations are assumed to possess a lesser fiscal capacity than those with higher income residents. If formulas based upon population are intended to raise the general level of services in all states, those based upon income are frequently used to *equalize* fiscal capacity among the states. It has been noted that grants using a per capita income formula may lower the state tax burden that would otherwise have been imposed in the absence of the grant, and thus "help to bring about a certain measure of income redistribution."[26] Major social programs incorporating per capita income as at least one of the factors in their allocation formulas include vocational education, child welfare services, medical assistance to the states (Medicaid), construction of community mental health facilities, and drug and alcohol abuse prevention and treatment.

Finally, the federal allocation formula may include factors that are indicative of program need within a jurisdiction; this is accomplished through the use of measures of the *population-at-risk,* or the group of persons most likely to possess specific problems and, thus, to be in need of certain services. Specific measures may include the number of persons below median income, or various demographic measures like the number of children ages five to seventeen or those over age sixty-five. In many cases, however, program grants that are intended to address specific needs and need populations may be made strictly on the basis of total population counts because no better problem indicator is available. It has been suggested, for example, that grants for Vocational Rehabilitation Services; Alcohol Abuse and Alcoholism Prevention, Treatment, and Rehabilitation; as well as Drug Abuse Prevention and Treatment services are among those for which no indicator better than aggregate population is known to exist.[27]

Whereas formula grants are usually directed at state government for purposes of providing continuing support of ongoing activities, a second type—the *project grant*—often bypasses state government and is used to stimulate new programs and activities primarily at the local level. Moreover, whereas the formula grant generally allows little grantor discretion regarding the levels of funds allocated to the grantee, quite the opposite may be true with respect to the project grant, or as it is sometimes called, the discretionary grant. It has been observed, however, that to decrease the administrative burden and to avoid charges of cronyism, "federal agencies tend to use their own administratively determined formulas to set aside funds for each state or region in the country."[28]

The project grant is competitive in nature, requiring potential recipients to submit specific, detailed proposals of activities to be undertaken and estimated costs. Normally these activities pertain to the conduct of various research, demonstration, and training projects; examples of programs funded in this manner include Head Start; the start-up costs for HMOs; child welfare research, demonstration, and training projects; and many model and demonstration projects for the elderly. The project grant is a relatively new and the most narrowly focused of the federal grant-in-aid strategies. Its increasing popularity from the 1960s to the present may be attributed to a number of factors:

> a heightened concern over critical urban needs; the widespread view that state governments were constitutionally and philosophically unwilling or incapable of dealing with these needs; the difficulty of using the traditional state plan approach under formula grants to target on social problems at the community level; the absence of reliable substate allocation data; a growing interest in employing nongovernmental as well as governmental agencies as grant recipients; and the desire to stimulate innovative approaches to the solution of particular problems.[29]

As stated in the above, a significant feature of the project grant is that applicant eligibility is oftentimes not restricted to governmental entities. Thus, in many program areas—but especially with respect to the general and personal social service programs—there is a sharing of eligibility (and the potential for competition) among general and special purpose local governments and private nonprofit groups. Prevention of this potential conflict, and the promotion of some degree of regional coordination in the arena of local grantsmanship, were major factors behind the recent establishment of a fourth or substate regional level of government, exemplified in the general purpose Councils of Government, and the special purpose Area Agencies on Aging and Health Systems Agencies.

The effects of and the arguments against this cacophony of federal grant-in-aid programs are numerous, complex, and not subject to simple empirical verification. Among the most mundane but most persuasive arguments is that the burden of paperwork and red tape brought about by the complex (and continuously changing) federal conditions accompanying grant funds substantially increases the costs of state and local administration. A second point pertaining especially to programs having low matching requirements is that they cause state and local policy priorities to be biased in favor of national interests. As Deil Wright has commented:

> To say that state and local officials must pay attention to actions in Washington is an understatement; what happens in D.C. is part of the daily operating realities for numerous state and local officials.[30]

This revision in priorities is, of course, the desired consequence of many grant-in-aid programs, but it raises serious philosophical issues regarding the constitutional separation of powers between federal and state government, as well as the more practical difficulties that arise from the sometimes ephemeral nature of federal grants: national priorities (and grants) may change more quickly than the grantees' abilities to respond. Readily available when problems achieve popular awareness, federal funds may quickly be reduced, withdrawn, or the restrictions attached to their use substantially altered once national preoccupations with certain problems wane. State and local jurisdictions must then face the difficult choice of either dismantling programs before they have had a chance to work (the fate of many Office of Economic Opportunity programs) or of shifting funds from other programs of equal or higher priority.

These are just some of the problems that confront virtually all agencies and programs dependent upon funds from federal grants-in-aid. But with respect to those for social welfare purposes, they are further compounded, as the Brookings analysis points out, by a further fundamental dilemma.

> The most difficult questions to be answered in designing federal grants for social programs are how narrowly to specify the services to be provided and in what detail to regulate how the money is to be spent. On the one hand, since the purpose of the grant is to change the priorities that would otherwise have prevailed at the state and local level, there is a temptation to write very detailed regulations to ensure that the national purpose is actually being carried out. On the other . . . , detailed rules may fail to reflect the realities of local situations . . . and may actually prevent them from spending the money effectively.[31]

As a result, there has been a significant shift in recent years from the more restrictive categorical grant approach to a greater use of block grants in the health care area, in law enforcement, in manpower and employment training, in community development and in the general and personal social services. This is one of most significant aspects of Title XX, which essentially consolidated a number of restrictive categorical grants to the states for social services into a single block grant.

Capping a ten-year period during which federal spending for social services had increased by better than 1,000 percent, in 1975 Title XX removed the responsibility for service planning and priority setting from Washington and vested it in state and local decision makers. Among the most important of the many objectives of the Title XX strategy are: (1) to allow each state to tailor its service programs to its unique needs and priorities with a minimum of federal intervention and with a maximum of local citizen participation, and (2) through grant consolidation and a regional planning process to reduce the service overlap and fragmentation characteristic of the previous categorical programs.

PURCHASED SERVICES

Largely stimulated by the provisions of Title XX, purchase-of-service contracts have become an additional major source of funds for service providers; indeed it may well be that purchase of services on a contractual basis has become the predominant mode of social service delivery in the United States.[32] The funding and performance guidelines under contracts are generally more restricted and precise than under most grants-in-aid; in addition, unlike many grants, the contractor is legally liable for failure to perform the required function. Contracts may exist between different levels of government. The Social Security Administration contracts with state agencies to perform specific administrative functions—primarily eligibility determination and updating of recipient files—associated with the Supplemental Security Income program; actual payments are made by the federal government. Contracts may exist between programs or between programs and agencies within the same level of government; thus a youth care program may purchase drug rehabilitation services from a community mental health agency rather than performing the service itself. But probably the most important purchase-of-service agreements are those existing between a governmental program and a private not-for-profit service provider; such would be the case were a local government to contract with the Salvation Army to provide food under the auspices of the city's emergency food program.

Purchased services offer several advantages over the direct provision of services by a government agency. First and probably foremost, many services can be provided less expensively by private providers than by governmental agencies. Wages are normally less than those required by civil service regulations and, as is sometimes the case especially with church-affiliated providers, may not even meet federally established minimum wage guidelines. Moreover, private providers often have access to community resources—funds from local charitable organizations and volunteers—not normally available to governmental agencies.

Second, contracts with private providers often offer greater flexibility and innovative potential than agencies of government. Since purchase of service contracts are of short duration (seldom longer than a year) contract specifications can be altered as needs for program change arise. If the levels of resources or unmet needs change, contracts can be initiated or terminated accordingly, whereas staffing changes under civil service regulations are virtually impossible to effect quickly. One must view the potential for flexibility with caution, however. In many cases, private agencies become quasi-governmental entities, dependent upon governmental resources for continued survival. Moreover, private agency staff develop strong personal and professional ties with governmental personnel and with influential members of the community, making radical program change or termination often no less difficult than in government.

Third, many private not-for-profit service providers are governed by boards of directors, comprised of members of the local community. They thus possess ties to the general community often lacking in more bureaucratic governmental settings. It may be far simpler, as a result, to gain community approval for a controversial program—such as a halfway house—if initiated and promoted by a private agency rather than imposed by an agency of government. Equally significant, private boards frequently display a mix of personalities and skills that is both representative of community attitudes *and* appropriate to the particular service provided. Thus, it would not be surprising to find on the board of directors of a halfway house a judge, a police officer, a former inmate and others with ties to the constituencies and institutions upon which program success depends. While this may be an extremely valuable attribute, it may also lead to conflicts in accountability, with the private provider of necessity torn between responding to the various represented community interests and the requirements imposed by providers of funds.

Fourth and finally, the purchase-of-service strategy allows program administrators to concentrate upon program planning and strategy, free of operational demands. But even if the day-to-day operational burden is reduced, the overall administrative burden may not decline significantly; emphasis may simply shift. In the purchase-of-service strategy, contract specifications must be drafted, requests for proposals must be publicized (if competitive bidding is required), proposals reviewed and evaluated, and contracts negotiated. Once in effect, continous performance monitoring and evaluation are required to ensure that contract specifications are being met and that program operations are attaining their objectives.

the delivery parameter

Of the four parameters of social programming, service delivery, which "refers to the organizational arrangements among distributors and between distributors and consumers of social welfare benefits in the context of the local community,"[33] is the least susceptible to neat description and analysis. This is due largely to our lack of understanding and a commensurate lack of useful models with which to describe and to assess the effects of all but the simplest of interorganizational processes, functions, and structures. Indeed, one finds that the most commonly analyzed of service delivery alternatives focuses upon a single structural concept—the decentralization of authority—and a single effect—responsiveness—with different studies often yielding different and even contradictory conclusions.[34] This suggests, then, that other factors are equally significant, but even in the smallest of communities the total number of possible interorganizational arrangements—formal and informal alike—can be staggering.[35] This, coupled with the fact that service delivery is probably as dependent upon such abstractions as community leadership, attitudes, and culture as it is upon identifiable organizational arrangements, makes—as a cursory examination of myriad service delivery experiments clearly reveals—valid generalizations extremely difficult to draw.

ASSESSING THE DELIVERY NETWORK

While conclusions regarding the effects of various administrative arrangements upon service delivery requires further research, there is some agreement upon the attributes of an effective delivery system, even if we may not know how best to achieve them. In particular, an effective delivery system is characterized by comprehensiveness, accessibility, continuity, a lack of fragmentation, and accountability to the service user.[36]

A service delivery network is *comprehensive* if it provides a range of benefits in sufficient amounts, of sufficient quality, and over a sufficient period to have an impact upon the human and social problems of concern to the local community. Clearly, then, the two most important factors affecting comprehensiveness are a community's financial and human resource base and the willingness of local decision makers to conceive of social and human programs as having sufficiently high priority to divert resources from other community functions and needs. In this regard, we have already seen how grant-in-aid funding may both augment the community's resource base and, through restrictions on the use of those funds, effectively alter prevailing community priorities in accordance with those of the grantee.

A service delivery network is *accessible* if there is a general absence of barriers to the use of services by those in need. Although sometimes equated solely with the geographical location of service facilities in relation to a community's residential patterns, accessibility is affected perhaps in more important ways by financial and individual motivational and cognitive barriers as well; the significance of these barriers, moreover, will likely vary among various subgroups in the community, creating the serious problem of unequal access to services. Since the elimination of such barriers is an obvious prerequisite if services are to be correctly matched to needs, most students of social welfare have come to believe that the provision of access—through outreach services, information and referral programs, and special transportation programs, to name but a few—itself be considered as a vital social service.

Continuity refers to the interorganizational accessibility relationships within the total set of programs and agencies comprising the local service network. Discontinuity implies an inability of the network to respond sequentially to an individual's needs; its assessment thus requires we understand the functioning of interorganizational relationships over time. Significantly, the elimination of discontinuity requires as well an understanding of the logical sequence of services required to resolve a single problem or a set of multiple problems and needs possessed by the service user. If that logical sequence is known, but the necessary services do not exist or there is a breakdown in referral or channeling capabilities among existing services, the network is discontinuous. If the problem is unemployment, for example, discontinuity would be characterized by the existence of a job training program that is not closely linked to an employment placement program.

Discontinuity may result from *fragmentation* of the service network, which occurs when there is uncertainty about or gaps between the programs within which services are available. For example, a person may be in legitimate need of special transportation services, services actually provided by a number of different community programs, but which are targeted to specific groups of individuals; unless the person in need also happens to be a member of one of these groups, the services will likely be denied. We have seen that social programs may provide benefits, be targeted to specific populations, or some combination of both, resulting in a large number of different programs for different combinations of people and problems, creating dilemmas of duplication and overlap among programs that differ only slightly. With respect to this dilemma—and in reference to the federal grant-in-aid system, which is largely responsible for its creation—the Advisory Commission on Intergovernmental Relations has noted:

> The problem of program numbers is not that of duplication and overlap . . . but excessive specificity with clusters of several grants . . . in the same narrow program area. Often a single social problem has been attacked from many directions, with programs distinguished by the particular activity they support, the clientele groups they serve, the manner in which services are delivered, or the places on which they focus.[37]

And finally, the service network is *accountable* if it is responsive to the user's often unique problems and needs, and if it also maintains some process or set of processes—judicial hearings, for example—through which users are able to redress their grievances.

It is probably beyond our political, organizational, and administrative capabilities to create and maintain a service delivery system that maximizes all desirable service delivery attributes, because there are fundamental tradeoffs, and hence choices, that must be made both within and among each. Consider, for example, comprehensiveness and the frequent debates surrounding its dual ideals of sufficient quantity and quality of services, two concepts that may be inversely related for a given level of resources. If policy makers must decide between quantity and quality, does comprehensiveness mean a large number of readily accessible but low quality services, or does it mean high quality services available to only a few? Or consider accountability. Can the various elements in the network be held accountable *only* to the service user and perhaps to his unique wants, which may be different than the community's definition of needs? Or must it also be accountable to groups—funding bodies, the courts, professionals, citizen advisory groups—with legitimate authority to determine needs and to control other aspects of the network's operation?

Tradeoffs between network's attributes are equally difficult to resolve. If we improve accessibility and accountability, for example by establishing a large number of store front, multiservice agencies uniquely geared to the needs of a neighborhood, we run the risk of increasing fragmentation and discontinuity; if, conversely, we reduce fragmentation and discontinuity through organizational centralization, we risk a reduction in both accessibility and accountability.[38] Although the tradeoffs among desirable service delivery attributes are numerous, the relative values of each unknown, and the appropriate mechanisms for their implementation uncertain, an often proposed solution to the multifaceted problems of service delivery is *service integration.*

SERVICE INTEGRATION

Although its purpose is generally seen as one of improving the five service delivery attributes described above, there is little agreement on a specific definition of service integration. One very general definition, however, is given by the following:

> The linking together of two or more service providers in order to treat clients' needs more comprehensively.[39]

Within this general definition it is useful to distinguish conceptually (although it is often difficult to do so in practice) between linkages that truly *integrate* and those that merely *coordinate* the delivery of services, the former denoting in the words of Morris and Lescohier, "a new unitary structure," and the latter a strengthening or a smoothing of the "relationships of continuing, independent, elements such as organizations, staffs, and resources."[40] Since service integration requires the establishment of wholly new organizational elements, it is important to note—the persistent use of the term, integration, notwithstanding—that the bulk of linkages established to date have focused upon the improved coordination of existing organizational elements.

The establishment of linkages among clients, programs, agencies, and services can be conceptualized in two different ways, conditioned as an HEW report indicates, by one's level in the organization.

> Human services personnel at different levels in the organization perceive the integration of services differently. Service delivery personnel tend to view it as a 'bottom up' process, while administrators tend to see it as an issue of organizational structure.[41]

Within the latter or "top down" view, integration is achieved through a variety of general and special purpose agencies that coordinate activities and the flow of funds within a defined geographical jurisdiction. The use of existing general purpose governmental entities upon which to build coordination capabilities is predominant, especially at the local level of government. Particularly in recent years, the general purpose capabilities of state governments have been augmented by the establishment of specialized umbrella, state departments of human resources.

Common linking functions performed by such organizational superstructures include: the colocation of a number of different services in numerous decentralized multiservice facilities; the promotion of centralized intake procedures, which includes a comprehensive evaluation of a client's needs and the development of a complete service plan; comprehensive information and referral and outreach programs; client tracking and case management support services; and the coordination of a variety of supportive services, such as day care, that permit users to take advantage of other needed services.[42]

The bottom up view, in contrast, focuses upon the integration and coordination of services at the level of delivery; it is assumed to be performed by professional service generalists and is designed to achieve

> effective meshing of the simultaneous and sequential treatment activities with complex cases, interventions which clients cannot coordinate themselves and in which meshing is the precondition of effectiveness.[43]

One way in which this has in part been achieved in the personal social services is through *staff out-stationing* or the placement of service workers directly within organizations not ordinarily providing casework services—caseworkers in hospitals, in mental institutions, in prisons, and in schools. In effect, the caseworker acts as a personal "broker" of services not normally provided within that institutional setting. This is an interesting and useful model, but professional and organizational rigidity frequently limit its effectiveness in practice, especially in attempts to integrate the supportive personal social services with the more established general social services. As Kahn and Kamerman note, "since the other systems 'give' very little, the personal social services suffer from loss of identity, disorganization, and decreased effectiveness."[44]

When the importance of integration of services at the level of delivery is recognized by administrators, solutions are generated that "do not ordinarily reorganize service delivery on the front line."[45] Thus, administrative solutions to case integration tend to accept as given professional and organizational compartmentalization, concentrating instead upon the establishment of low-cost mechanistic integrating devices, such as nonprofessional referral specialists, who "neither deliver the service nor are accountable for service integration."[46] In sum, then, the top-down and bottom-up views of service integration reveal a fundamental conflict between the two important sets of relationships in the service delivery process—those existing among providing organizations and those between the organizational milieu and the user. In the top-down approach interorganizational relationships may be centrally coordinated, planned and harmonious, but they may not result in the "correct" set of services to meet individual needs; in the bottom-up approach, integration may achieve a correct match between services and needs, but it may also result in interorganizational relationships that are unplanned, uncoordinated, and unharmonious.

What are the effects of service coordination and integration efforts to date? In 1971, the Department of Health Education and Welfare at a cost in excess of six million dollars initiated forty-five Service Integration Target of Opportunity (SITO) projects nationwide, which were designed to promote interagency coordination in the delivery of services at both the state and local levels. The principal coordinating mechanisms established as a result of the program included: fiscal linkages, such as joint agency budgeting processes and purchase of service contracting; personnel linkages, facilitated through joint use of staff, staff out-stationing, colocation, and joint training; planning and programming linkages, through joint policy making, joint planning, information sharing, and joint evaluation; administrative support linkages, achieved in part through common record keeping and information systems and common central support services like grants management; core service linkages, effected through common outreach, intake, diagnosis, referral, and transportation services; and case coordination, achieved through integrated case consultation, multiagency case conferences, and the establishment of case coordinators and multi-agency case teams.[47]

Three significant conclusions merge from evaluations of the forty-five projects.[48] First, the funding guidelines and eligibility criteria that are a central facet of federal service grants-in-aid made fiscal linkages among different organizations and programs virtually impossible to manage effectively. To remain accountable to federal, state, local, and private funding agencies (all four of which may support a program) monies flowing into service providing agencies must be held and dispensed from identifiable funds, since each of these funds is restricted as to use. Despite this fact, when joint fiscal efforts were able to overcome these constraints on the use of funds, there is some evidence to suggest that service continuity and accountability to service users improved significantly.

Second, a significant barrier to better coordination—primarily with respect to those linking strategies that might have substantially improved both accessibility and continuity—was the problem of organizational "turf." Seemingly, the maintenance of a distinct organizational identity among the total network of different providing agencies (an identity that helps enhance organizational survivability) takes precedence over the possibile benefits to the service user of a continuous and easily accessible delivery system.

Third and possibly most revealing, as evidenced by how few of the SITO projects were continued beyond the federal funding period, none of the potential benefits of improved coordination was apparently worth the burden of continued coordination efforts. A significant outcome of the projects, however, was the identification of numerous gaps in existing services, although little scrutiny was given to the effectiveness of existing services. This has led one observer to comment:

> Most reorganizations leave us with one fundamental fact about human services integration: the services themselves are unchanged and there-fore not usually integrated. There is a reluctance to examine the hard question of whether services are doing any good and a corresponding reluctance to accept the conclusion that coordinating or managing a set of services, if they are ineffective will not make the services themselves effective.[49]

Reviewing these and other integration and coordination efforts, Robert Agranoff and his colleagues have concluded that service integration techniques have been largely ineffective because the theoretical perspectives that guide them are themselves fragmented. In particular, they argue that service delivery is a mutidimensional process, comprising linkages among organizations, programs, services, and the policies that guide their implementation; effective integration, then, can only occur if all dimensions are treated as a system of highly interdependent variables. The key to their approach is a comprehensive view of social policy development and program implementation, "with an eye for the forest rather than just the trees, with the focus of inquiry encompassing more than the adoption or rejection of a particular decision, activity or program."[50] It is to the interrelated processes of policy development and program implementation that we now turn our attention.

notes

1. Alfred J. Kahn, *Theory and Practice of Social Planning* (New York; Russell Sage Foundation, 1969), p. 208.

2. Irwin Garfinkel, "What's Wrong with Welfare?" *Social Work,* 23, no. 3 (May 1978), 188.

3. Michael Nelson, "The Desk," *Newsweek,* September 11, 1978, p. 17.

4. Joel F. Handler, "Federal-State Interests in Welfare Administration in Joint Economic Committee, *Studies in Public Welfare,* Paper 5, pt. 2, *Issues in Welfare Administration: Intergovernemental Relationships,* 92nd Congress, 2nd session (1972), p. 24.

5. Joel F. Handler and Ellen Jane Hollingsworth, *The Deserving Poor* (Chicago: Markham, 1971), p. 90.

6. *Federal Register,* Vol. 44, No. 54 (March 19, 1979), p. 16,451.

7. Neil Gilbert and Harry Specht, *Dimensions of Social Welfare Policy* (Englewood Cliffs, N. J.: Prentice-Hall, 1974), p. 67.

8. Ibid.

9. Martin Rein, *Social Policy* (New York: Random House, 1970), p. 327.

10. See for example, Donald S. Watson, *Price Theory and Its Uses,* 2nd ed. (New York: Houghton Mifflin, 1968), pp. 96–97.

11. Ezra J. Mishan, *The Costs of Economic Growth* (New York: Praeger, 1967), p. 110–11.

12. Lester Thurow, "Cash Versus In-Kind Transfers," *American Economic Review,* 64, no. 2 (May 1974), 193.

13. Gilbert and Specht, *Dimensions of Social Welfare Policy,* p. 88.

14. Alfred J. Kahn and Sheila B. Kamerman, *Social Services in International Perspective* (Washington, D.C.: U.S. Department of Health, Education and Welfare, 1976), p. 31.

15. Ibid., p. 7.

16. Ibid.

17. Marjorie Smith Carroll, "Private Health Insurance Plans in 1976: An Evaluation," *Social Security Bulletin,* 41, no. 9 (September 1978), 3.

18. Ibid.

19. Office of Management and Budget, *The United States Budget in Brief, Fiscal Year 1978* (Washington, D.C.: Office of Management and Budget), p. 66.

20. Deil S. Wright, *Understanding Intergovernmental Relations* (North Scituate, Mass.: Duxbury Press, 1978), pp. 136–37.

21. Ibid., p. 135.

22. Ibid., p. 133.

23. Edward R. Fried and others, *Setting National Priorities: The 1974 Budget* (Washington, D.C.: Brookings Institution, 1973), p. 172.

24. Ibid., p. 173.

25. For an overview see Wright, *Understanding Intergovernmental Relations*, pp. 138–41; and Advisory Commission on Intergovernmental Relations, *Categorical Grants: Their Role and Design* (Washington, D.C.: Advisory Commision on Intergovernmental Relations, 1977).

26. *Advisory Commission on Intergovernmental Relations, p. 101.*

27. Ibid., p. 103.

28. Ibid., p. 100.

29. Ibid., p. 104.

30. Wright, *Understanding Intergovernmental Relations*, p. 136.

31. Fried and others, *Setting National Priorities: The 1974 Budget,* p. 174.

32. Robert Harris, "Landmark in Social Services or More of the Same," *Search. A Report from the Urban Institute,* 8, no. 2 (Winter 1978), 8.

33. Gilbert and Specht, *Dimensions of Social Welfare Policy,* p. 108.

34. James E. Hartling, *The Structure of Human Service Delivery Systems* (Austin: Center for Social Work Research, School of Social Work, University of Texas at Austin, 1977).

35. The number of possible interrelationships increases geometrically as the number of identifiable organizational entities increases. Consider, for example, a very small community in which there are four levels of government, ten service providing agencies, twelve funding sources, ten distinct client groups, twenty distinct service programs, and six different methods for achieving interorganizational linkages. This situation represents 576,000 different possible combinations of relationships that might be used to tie the network together.

36. Gilbert and Specht, *Dimensions of Social Welfare Policy,* p. 109.

37. Advisory Commission on Intergovernmental Relations, *Categorical Grants,* p. 287.

38. Gilbert and Specht, *Dimensions of Social Welfare Policy,* pp. 110–11.

39. Robert Agranoff and Alex Pattakos, *Dimensions of Services Integration* (Washington, D.C.: Project Share, Human Service Monograph Series), April 1979, p. 166.

40. R. Morris and I. H. Lescohier, "Solutions to Welfare Dilemmas," in *The Management of Human Services,* eds. Rosemary C. Sarri and Yeheskel Hasenfeld (New York: Columbia University Press, 1978), pp. 22–23.

41. Cited in Agranoff and Pattakos, *Dimensions of Services Integration,* p. 156.

42. Ibid., pp. 150–51.

43. Alfred J. Kahn and Sheila B. Kamerman, "Options for the Delivery of Social Services at the Local Level: A Cross National Report," in *Reaching People: The Structure of Neighborhood Services,* eds. Daniel Thursz and Joseph Vigilante (Beverly Hills: Sage Publications, 1978), p. 97.

44. Ibid.

45. Ibid.

46. Ibid.

47. DeWitt John, *Managing the Human Service System: What Have We Learned from Integration?* (Denver: Center for Social Research and Development, University of Denver, 1977), p. 13.

48. Ibid., pp. 14–37.

49. Agranoff and Pattakos, *Dimensions of Services Integration*, p. 154.

50. Ibid., pp. 83–84.

The American political process generates social policies that are inherently vague, with the effect that policy is essentially made during the process of program implementation. Vague policy blurs the traditional distinction and separation of powers among the legislative, administrative, and the judicial branches of government. A principal issue thus becomes: to whom or what source of legitimate authority is the program to be accountable?

Accountable behavior, whether by an organization or an organizational actor, is behavior that is somehow responsive to a legitimate source of authority. If, as is the case with social welfare programs, there are many such authorities, the issue of accountability possesses two dimensions. First is the set of all authorities to which a decision or action might be held accountable. And second is the dimension of control, the various means used by legitimate sources of authority to influence decisions and actions.

The existence of multiple sources of accountability, each exerting influence over a limited range of program decisions and activities, threatens the integrity of the program and thus its ability to achieve its purposes. The role of the social program administator is one of creatively managing and responding to these often contradictory forces in an effort to achieve program integrity, a prime prerequisite of program effectiveness.

social program implementation: the demand for accountability

3

In the preceding chapter, we saw that a social program was identified by some combination of decisions regarding who was to get what and how. While this combination of decisions generally defines what the program is supposed to do as a single element in the total realm of redistributive strategies, it often fails to specify exactly how these decisions are to be implemented. Given an eligibility criterion, for example, using what specific information and by what specific procedures shall program staff actually determine who is eligible for program allocations? In the absence of detailed procedural plans governing such day-to-day program decisions, there may be abundant opportunity for the exercise of discretion by administrators and providers responsible for the program's implementation.

Because discretionary behavior may lead to decisions and actions detrimental to the achievement of desired program outcomes, it is common for policy makers to impose a bureaucratic structure upon program activities, which is designed to limit discretion and channel behavior. To be effective, however, bureaucratic controls like specialization, routinization, and standardization require an element of certainty that, for a variety of reasons, is often lacking in the social welfare enterprise. First, social policy goals and program purposes are seldom stated clearly and are subject to wide degrees of interpretation by different groups in the policy-making community; hence, the ultimate objectives of the program may be uncertain. Second, the results of social programs are seldom amenable to precise verification; in even the simplest of programs there may be substantial disagreement regarding the nature of program results. Third, policy makers often lack the theoretical relationships linking actions with results and thus lack the basis for determining what specific set of actions and decisions is to be preferred. And fourth, even when the preferred set of responses may be known, policy makers often lack the necessary controls to ensure that actual responses are in compliance with those that are preferred.

In varying degrees, these problems will confront any program in any organizational setting; such is the nature of efforts to define and ensure purposeful organizational and individual behavior. But they are exacerbated in the social welfare enterprise because program implementation occurs by "remote control"; the substantive parameters of the social program—which define what it is supposed to do—are generally determined by central authorities in pursuit of national goals, but program implementation—the actions and decisions that determine what the program actually does—occurs in the local community. Both conceptually and organizationally, the circuitous channel from central policy to decentralized implementation is riddled with ambiguity and uncertainty. It affords those groups and individuals in positions of power, and upon whose cooperation and support successful implementation depends, substantial opportunity to influence program operations and hence the substance of social policy. What some of these principal forces are, how they may attempt to influence program operations, and the possible roles of the program administrator in the implementing process are the major questions addressed in this chapter.

vague policy: the genesis
of the accountability dilemma

In theory, American government is designed to guard against the misuse of authority by creating a separation of powers among the Congress, the administration and the judiciary. Congress is given the authority and responsibility for enacting laws, the administration the authority for enforcing and implementing those laws, and the judiciary the authority and the responsibility for their interpretation. Fundamental to the separation of powers is the maintenance of accountability, the establishent of mechanisms to ensure that each branch of government behaves in accordance with established principles or with the expectations of a defined set of actors in the political process. Hence, Congress through the legislation it adopts or fails to adopt is ultimately held accountable to maintaining the public interest; this is enforced through the power of the vote. Congressional actions must also be accountable to constitutional and other legal constraints as interpreted and enforced by the courts. The actions of the judiciary are ultimately accountable to the facts and prevailing interpretations of existing law.

In simpler times and within the realm of simpler theories, administrative accountability meant that administrative decisions and actions—in short, the implementation of public policy—were to be held accountable to the legal statutes established through the legislative process. The administrative theories of Woodrow Wilson as developed in the late nineteenth century dominated thinking about American public administration for better than half a century. Through education and the professionalization of the civil service, Wilson maintained, an apolitical cadre of administrative experts could best carry out the policies generated by political institutions.[1] And the image of an efficient and loyal bureaucracy, implementing public policy with dispassion and dispatch, was the model of American public administration throughout the first half of this century. Although the clear conceptual separatism between politics and administration is in wide disrepute today,[2] it seems less because Wilson's theories were fundamentally incorrect than because the nature of American government has changed so drastically since his time.

This country's first 150 or so years were dominated by the principle of laissez faire, a reliance upon the market economy for the creation of the social order and of limited government activity aimed primarily at maintaining the conditions within which that economy could flourish. Legislation during this period was principally concerned with allocating the spoils of an expanding economy among various private groups, such as the railroads, the utilities, and other interests seen as comprising the necessary foundation for industrialization and economic development. Public policy during this period reflected "virtually self-executing laws."[3]

Three major developments during this century have substantially and irrevocably altered this simple view of policy and program implementation. First, in an effort to deal actively with a large number of complex foreign and domestic problems, various administrations have proposed and Congress has adopted a multitude of policies that leave many substantive, procedural, and organizational issues surrounding their implementation unanswered. Second, because many public policies concern the redistribution of power and wealth from one group to another, the political relationships among contending interests have become increasingly interdependent and complex. Thirdly, and often overlooked, state and local governments are no longer the relatively sovereign political entities of earlier days, but have increasingly become the instruments through which national public policy—but particularly social policy—is implemented. Laws and policies are no longer self-executing, but rather afford a wide measure of uncertainty and discretion in administrative decision making, discretion that renders Wilson's notion of an apolitical public administration obsolete. The once sharp distinction between policy formation and policy implementation upon which Wilson's theories were predicated is now blurred because political and administrative decisions and procedures have become so highly interdependent.

Policy making in America today is generally characterized as a pluralist process of bargaining, compromise, and coalition-building among individual and institutional actors who may possess divergent and even incompatible goals and fundamentally different views on the nature of the problems that policy is to address. Particularly in the arena of social problems, this process generates policies that for a variety of reasons are inherently vague.[4] In dealing with complex problems it is impossible to specify in advance either precise goals or the exact course of action to be followed because sufficient knowledge of cause and effect does not exist. Congress possesses neither the time nor the staff to create precise policy. Language itself is insufficiently precise, with laws always subject to some degree of interpretation. And it is often beneficial within implementing organizations, especially if the environment is characterized by instability, complexity and uncertainty, to avoid being locked in by a fixed set of goals and strategies.

All of these factors no doubt contribute to the dilemma. But by far the most persuasive reason behind vague social policy rests in the simple fact that legislators find it politically expedient to intentionally avoid clear statements of policy. Abstract thinking about problems and their solutions is one thing, but the legislative adoption of written policy often requires the establishment of coalitions with different and conflicting interests; vague written policies offer the advantage of allowing each actor in the coalition to *interpret* the policy (both individually and on behalf of his constituents) as promoting his own interests. Thus, much more may be lost than gained by attempting to formulate clear legislation, because such efforts may easily upset the delicate balance and fragile associations that permit the legislature to act.

At some point, however, vague intentions must be translated into concrete actions, oftentimes discretionary actions undertaken by persons responsible for policy and program implementation. But the exercise of such discretion leaves the implementing organizations vulnerable to scrutiny and challenge by interests who claim that discretionary decisions are not consistent with *their* interpretation of policy intent. Written policy and implementing procedures may be altered as a result and challenged by another group; and the process continues. The result is that policy is not *made* but rather *emerges* through the process of implementation, and a key factor in understanding this process is the notion of accountability.

When organizations, programs, and organizational actors are responsive to legitimate sources of authority and influence it is said that their behavior is *accountable*. When organizations, programs, and organizational actors are unresponsive to legitimate sources of authority it is said that their behavior is *unaccountable*. If no legitimate source of authority exists or none chooses to exercise its influence, it is said that behavior is *discretionary*. Although sometimes used interchangeably, the terms *accountability* and *responsibility* are not the same and should not be confused. Whereas the organizational actor may be responsible *for* the performance of a task, the actor may also be accountable *to* some group or individual possessing legitimate authority over its performance. Accountability, then, explicates a specific source of power, authority, or influence.

For a *given aspect* of organizational performance, the analysis of accountability raises two questions. First, what groups and individuals have legitimate authority over that aspect of organizational performance? And second, through what mechanisms do they exercise authority and control? If the program is seen as a complex series of interrelated activities, the issue of accountability raises a third fundamental question. What effect does a multitude of legitimate authorities, each focusing upon a particular aspect of organizational performance, have upon the integrity of the program as a whole?

Volumes have been written in regard to the first issue, and the various views on what constitutes a legitimate source of authority in the American political system will not be recounted here.[5] In a sense, however, we are captives of our perspective, for if the social program is viewed as an open system, it is presumed that groups and individuals having control over the resources necessary for program operations and survival—or other groups who are able to influence them—possess legitimate control over program operations. Simply, those who can influence its resources—its legal mandate, its finances, its clients, its personnel, and its information— can influence the program. Given this, our interest here is with the second and third questions regarding accountability.

the external locus of accountability

The combination of vague policy mandates and a multitude of groups and individuals possessing legitimate authority over some aspect of program performance—frequently providing program decision makers with mixed and conflicting signals as to what shall be considered accountable program behavior—requires a revision in the way we normally think about organizational and program goals. In the real world, it seems far less appropriate to assume that behavior is governed by a singular, official goal that is revealed by mandate, than by a complex set of contending influences that will "emerge as a set of constraints defining acceptable performances."[6] Moreover, as Graham Allison has noted:

> [t]he set of constraints emerges from a mix of expectations and demands of other organizations in the government, statutory authority, demands from citizens and special interest groups, and bargaining within the organization.[7]

Few of us as individuals, much less as members of large complex organizations, are able to accommodate simultaneously multiple constraints upon our behavior. Rather our attention is selective; we tend to do the work, to accommodate the constraints that seem most immediately pressing. Likewise, it has been noted that an organization's multiple but competing goals and constraints can be made somewhat compatible by treating them *sequentially* in response to continuously changing demands. Allison comments:

> As a problem arises, the subunits of the organization most concerned with that problem deal with it in terms of the constraints *they* take to be most important. When the next problem arises, *another* cluster of subunits deals with it, focusing upon a different set of constraints.[8]

Note that the organizational leadership does not tell its membership that, for example, "This week we will abandon efficiency and focus upon equity as our major constraint"; neither people nor organizations are so malleable. Rather, leadership shifts authority and responsibility to various organizational sub-groups known to be in support of, and possibly better able to implement, the constraint of current importance.

Alice Rivlin has noted that the beginning of the newfound concern with accountability coincided with the many social program reforms that occurred during the 1960s.[9] This seems natural in view of the nature of those reforms, many of which were based upon new and unproven theories of societal and individual change, many of which were designed to alter traditional power relationships, and most of which were accompanied by only the vaguest of Congressional mandates. Using some of these reforms as a backdrop, in this section we shall investigate three political and administrative mechanisms used to insure program accountability: the formal rules and guidelines that emanate from social legislation; the constraints provided through the process of citizen participation; and those issued by the courts.

LEGISLATION, RULES, AND GUIDELINES

Any social program will be embedded somewhere in a bureaucratic hierarchy, and thus various aspects of its performance will be held accountable to various rules laid down by hierarchically superior authorities. The program is thus the object of a bureaucratic mode of control, involving a process that Anthony Downs has summarized as follows:

1. An official issues a set of orders.

2. He allows his subordinates time to put each order into effect.

3. He selects certain orders to evaluate his subordinates' performance.

4. He seeks to discover what has actually been done at lower levels as a result of the orders he is evaluating.

5. He compares the effects of his orders with his original intentions.

6. He decides whether these results are effective enough to require no more attention, ineffective but unlikely to be improved because of severe obstacles encountered, or partially effective and capable of being improved by further orders.

7. In the last case, he issues further orders, starting the cycle again.[10]

American society is predicated upon the existence of laws to which the actions of all citizens and institutions are to be held accountable. The supreme body of law, the common law, is derived from a variety of diverse sources including, of course, the American Constitution as amended periodically by action of state legislatures and reinterpreted continuously by the courts. The common law reflects what is sometimes called "judge-made" law.[11] But it is the set of laws called statutes, created by duly elected federal, state, and local government officials, that is of greatest interest to the administrative agencies responsible for implementing social policy.

Within the legalistic model, the implementation of policy is centered upon the creation of a set of rules which serve two important functions: to ensure that administrative actions are equitable and nonarbitrary and to ensure further that those actions are in compliance with the statutory provisions in the legislation. With the possible exception of military and foreign affairs or times of national emergency, the Constitution legitimates no inherent administrative authority over persons or property; only legislative bodies are empowered to exercise such authority.[12] This constraint is satisfied by a set of administrative rules and procedures designed to ensure compliance with statutory directives. Compliance—both that administrative guidelines comply with policy directives and that administrative actions comply with the guidelines—is enforced by the courts.

The purpose of these rules and procedures is to limit agency discretion, which in the context of administrative law may be seen to have two sources.[13] First, the legislature can grant to the responsible administrator in the implementing agency (usually the secretary in a federal agency and the director or administrator in a state or local agency) the statutory authority to make specific kinds of rules. The granting of statutory authority confers formal law-making powers upon the administrative agency, and the administrative guidelines that result from this grant of authority are called *legislative* rules. An alternative is for legislators to retain law-making authority by issuing statutory directives that limit agency discretion in certain areas, but that will likely leave wide latitude to agency practices. The administrative guidelines formulated within these statutory constraints are called *interpretative* rules and do not necessarily have the power of law. Interpretative rules comprise the main body of rules an agency lives by, and in addition to interpreting statutes, they may be used to interpret "a legislative rule," "another interpretive rule," "judicial decisions," "administrative decisions," "administrative rulings," "any other law or interpretation," "any combination of items on this list," "or nothing."[14]

Within the provisions of the Administrative Procedures Act of 1946, the principal difference between legislative and interpretative rules concerns the authority of the courts to pass judgment on agency decisions. Legislative rules have force of law, and the courts possess no authority to alter their content (just as the courts have no authority to pass judgment on the content of a statute, as long as it is not in violation of the common law) provided they meet three conditions: (1) they are within the legislature's statutory grant of authority, (2) they were issued in accordance with proper procedure, which generally means sufficient public notice, and (3) they are reasonable, in the sense that Congress is assumed to "avoid the delegation of power to act unreasonably."[15]

Interpretative rules, however, are quite another matter. Unless it is expressly prohibited by the legislative body, the *content* as well as the process by which an interpretative rule is formulated may be subject to review by the courts.[16] Following review of an interpretative rule, the court may choose to give the force of law to it, rescind the rule and substitute its own interpretation in the form of a court decision, or adopt the middle-of-the-road strategy of granting some intermediate degree of authority to the rule.

Rules are key elements in the implementation of national policy through state and local governmental operations; as we saw in the previous chapter, various rules often accompany the grants-in-aid that are a primary source of funds in the social welfare enterprise. To understand the difficulties in formulating clear, concise rules through which to control the behavior of state and local implementing organizations—especially when the policies governing rule generation are vague—the recent history of the federal government's attempt to establish a national social services policy is especially instructive. Of particular significance are the rules implemented in an effort to control the actual implementation of both the need and the allocation parameters of social programming.

Absolved of blame during the Depression, the poor once again became the object of public scrutiny during the relatively prosperous years following World War II. By the mid-1950s it had become clear to policy makers that the public assistance rolls were not about to "wither away"[17] as had initially been assumed by the framers of the Social Security Act. Despite greatly expanded social insurance benefits and coverage during the two decades following passage of the act, public assistance, but especially the AFDC program, had not proven to be residual; contrary to expectations, the rolls did not gradually decline after the social insurance program had been phased in.

Little substantive change in public assistance would occur during the Eisenhower years of the fifties; a balanced federal budget and the maintenance of state autonomy were the orders of the day. John F. Kennedy took office in 1961 in a period of relatively severe economic recession, and among his first acts was the establishment of a number of task forces and committees to investigate the problem of the continually expanding relief rolls. Virtually all members of these advisory groups had strong ties to the social work profession,[18] and among the committee reports' major recommendations was the need to supplement the cash assistance programs with programs providing social and rehabilitative services to welfare recipients. The behavior of recipients must be altered, they maintained, if dependency was to be reduced. From one influential report:

> Financial assistance to meet people's basic needs for food, shelter and clothing is essential, but alone is not enough. Expenditures for assistance not accompanied by rehabilitative services may actually increase dependency and eventual costs to the community. The very essence of a vital program should be full use of all rehabilitative services including, but not confined to, provision of financial assistance. The ultimate aim is to help families become self-supporting and independent by strengthening their own resources. Achieving this requires the special knowledge and skill of social workers with graduate training and other well-trained specialists.[19]

Kennedy's staff initiated and Congress ratified what were popularly known as the Public Welfare Amendments of 1962. These amendments created a distinct category of grants to the state for caseworker-provided services, an adjunct to the grants for cash assistance already in existence under the original public assistance programs. Neither the statute nor the administrative guidelines, however, clearly specified what "services" were to qualify for the 75 percent matching federal funds to be made available to the states under the amendments. Instead, both bureaucratic and legislative decision makers were prepared to let the definitions "emerge from experience."[20] This was accomplished by giving the Secretary of HEW, the agency responsible for implementation, the statutory authority (i. e., discretion) to define what services were to be funded under provisions of the new law. Policy was initially vague because the definition of services was vague.

A second goal of the amendments was to *prevent* dependency. To implement the preventative strategy, eligibility for federally supported services was extended to include, not only current welfare recipients, but also former and persons "likely to become"[21] welfare recipients. By implication, the authority to determine who was "likely to become" a welfare recipient was vested in the state and county welfare bureaucrats already implementing the AFDC program, particularly the intake workers. Eligibility determination had always allowed intake workers substantial discretion within the state-operated programs; the vague statutory specification of potential recipients further increased it.

Finally, as was federal practice with respect to the grants to states for cash assistance under the public assistance programs, Congress placed no ceiling on the federal dollars to be allocated to the states for services. Provided that the states submitted a general plan, and provided that services were judged by HEW to qualify for funding, the federal government would match $3 for every $1 the states spent.

Almost immediately both administrative and congressional leaders realized that the strategy of using services to reduce dependency had been oversold. Despite dramatically improving economic conditions, the welfare rolls continued to grow; the service strategy, whatever good it might be achieving, was not reducing public dependency. In 1967, under the leadership of House Ways and Means Chairman Wilbur Mills, Congress moved to further tighten the definition of services and to further strengthen work requirements.

A major result of the 1967 amendments was the creation of the Work Incentive Program (WIN), in which the Congress *attempted* to condition welfare benefits on the recipient's willingness to work. Under the provisions of WIN, HEW was required to refer all welfare recipients to the Department of Labor to register for work. This was implemented by giving HEW the authority to require state and county welfare offices to refer recipients to state employment service agencies, the latter the responsibility of the Department of Labor. There welfare recipients would receive job counseling, would be referred to training programs, or would receive on-the-job training in federally subsidized jobs.

The law did not require, however, that *all* individuals be referred. Those whom Congress deemed "inappropriate" for referral, nonetheless, were rather well defined under statutory provision. Nevertheless, HEW and a large number of states *interpreted* the statute far more liberally than was apparently intended; as a result, state welfare offices were actually required to refer comparatively few recipients. Additionally, the Department of Labor, through its guidelines issued to the state employment offices, did not require its state counterparts to accept the referrals if there was "good cause" for refusing.[22] The net result was that between October 1968, when the program began, and September 1971, slightly more than 300,000 persons had been enrolled in WIN projects.[23] In one not atypical month during that period, WIN enrollees represented less than 8 percent of the total adult AFDC population.[24]

In an effort to further strengthen the specific nature of services that would be federally supported, Congress also required in the 1967 amendments the states to make child care and family planning services available to AFDC recipients. The new law also divested HEW of its statutory authority to specify and prescribe services as had been its prerogative under the 1962 amendments. Instead, Congress tried its hand at defining social services, specifying in the new law that funding would be available for

> services to a family or any member thereof for the purpose of preserving, rehabilitating, reuniting, or strengthening the family, and such other services as will assist members of a family to attain or retain capability for the maximum self-support and personal independence.[25]

Note that Congress did not define the services eligible for funding, merely the *purposes* of those services. Though the definition of qualifying services remained vague, the fact that they were now specified in statute created a significant change in HEW's discretionary posture. The service guidelines generated by HEW were no longer statutory rules carrying the force of law, but were now interpretative rules that were open to challenge. While the degree of discretion remained potentially great, the change effectively left HEW without much protection when pressures—principally from the states—developed. Whereas the earlier law had allowed HEW to place the burden of proof upon the states to demonstrate that services were consistent with the purposes of the law, the new law effectively placed upon HEW the burden of proof that the claims were invalid.[26]

A final change created by the 1967 amendments is of greatest significance, although it received little attention at the time. The new law allowed the state and county welfare agencies to purchase services from other governmental and private service agencies. In conjunction with the earlier provision that the federal government would fund services to those persons likely to become welfare recipients and the still vague definition of eligible services, this new law greatly increased the states' opportunities to support a wide variety of nonwelfare service programs with federal funds. Thus, the federal government might easily fund a corrections program, a halfway house, or a drug treatment program, all perhaps worthwhile, but most of whose beneficiaries were not welfare recipients.[27]

The effect? When the new law took effect in 1967, social service expenditures totaled $248 million on 607,000 children. In fiscal year 1971, four years later, expenditures totaled $1.6 billion on 12 million chidlren.[28] If the theory that services would reduce dependency had not been refuted earlier, it certainly was now. In 1972 Congress attempted to further strengthen the work requirement; still the welfare rolls continued to grow and service expenditures for the following year were projected to reach $4.7 billion.[29] In exasperation, Congress succeeded in curbing the growth of social service expenditures by doing what it had never done in the history of the public assistance grants; it placed a yearly ceiling of $2.5 billion on grants to the states for social services.

Ultimately, HEW and the Congress got out of the business of attempting to define and to implement a national social service policy through the states. With the exception of some child family planning, and job-related services, grants to the states for social services are now governed by the provisions of Title XX of the Social Security Act adopted in 1975. The central thrust of Title XX maintains that federal social service dollars will be allocated to the states on the basis of a population formula. The exact nature of services the states will provide with these dollars is to be a state decision to be based upon and accountable to the implementation of a state-wide needs assessment process. That process will be discussed in greater detail in a later chapter.

There are many explanations for the astronomical growth of both the welfare rolls and social service expenditures during the late 1960s and early 1970s; some are attributable to government policy and operations, others to factors beyond its control. Some say that the growth of welfare rights organizations and an advocacy-oriented social work profession increased the enrollment of those already eligible for but not claiming benefits.[30] Others argue that an increasingly attractive combination of benefits with interrelated eligibility provisions—AFDC cash payments, food stamps, Medicaid, and other social services—helped to induce dependency.[31] Some will argue that the growth in service expenditures, especially during the latter period, was the result of the Family Assistance Plan, which most expected to become law; within that legislation, grants to states for services were to be tied to 1971 spending levels, thereby providing states with a strong incentive to spend as much as possible.[32] The fact is, the lack of reliable statistics and sound accounting procedures reduce these explanations to the status of speculation. Nonetheless, the policy did not fulfill public or congressional expectations that dependency would be reduced.

While it is tempting to look for a scapegoat, to isolate the blame, it is not as simple as it might seem. Let's look at the results; were the results accountable to the "intent" of Congress? There are differing opinions as to what the intent of Congress really was. It has been noted, for example, that conservative congressional decision makers intended that the service strategy would reduce the welfare rolls, while liberals saw it as a means of providing greater benefits to the poor, regardless of their impact upon the rolls.[33] On the one hand, it does not appear that the conservative expectations were fulfilled, since the welfare rolls continued to increase despite ever-increasing expenditures for services. Conversely, it has been argued that the welfare increase during that period might actually have been greater had not a substantial amount of federal "social and rehabilitative" service dollars gone to support "administrative" services. The vague definition of services allowed states to use federal dollars for such administrative procedures as eligibility determination, thereby helping to keep the rolls down.[34] Nonetheless, that is small consolation for those who expected a dramatic decline, rather than merely a slowed rate of increase in the number of welfare dependents.

Certainly, you may argue, the service strategy at least produced the results expected by those desiring to provide greater benefits to the poor. Not necessarily so, for it has also been argued that the policies merely shifted the funding base for services the states would probably have provided anyway, not to mention that much of the funding was used in support of administration.[35]

One can "blame" the states for being unaccountable to congressional statutory provisions, especially as they became more clearly specified toward the end of the period. Yet the new regulations and implementing guidelines were often garbled, the states receiving one interpretation from one of ten HEW regional offices, and quite another from its Washington, D.C. headquarters. Moreover, just as a state agency was getting settled into its new routine, a new set of guidelines would emanate from Washington.

Additionally, there are a variety of more general reasons why the implementation of a national social services program through the states failed to achieve national purposes. Alterations in federal funding practices that require a state match, like those of the social service program, frequently require legislative as well as administrative actions at the state level; thus, program implemention must be accountable to state as well as national interests. Yet the lines of authority and responsibility between the federal and state governments have never clearly been drawn; only the courts have had consistent success in achieving state compliance with federal policy. In addition, HEW's enforcement powers and methods are often ineffective. Their power is often diluted by political pressures from state officials and congressional representatives (meaning that the sanction of withholding federal funds, even if state practices deviate substantially from established federal guidelines is often politically untenable); their methods for achieving conformity are cumbersome and ineffective; and their enforcement staff is in short supply.[36]

ACCOUNTABILITY AND CITIZEN PARTICIPATION

In 1963 planning was begun on another set of programs, which were to become a second major element of welfare strategy for the ensuing decade; the result was the Economic Opportunity Act of 1964 (EOA). Together with the 1960s' Model Cities legislation—which established programs aimed at curbing physical deterioration in declining neighborhoods —the EOA was to become the major strategy in America's war on poverty. The war on poverty was government's official attempt to make its welfare efforts *accountable to the poor* through a strategy of citizen participation. And in apparent response to the tenet that policy makers can overcome resistance to change by constructing alternative parallel institutions that can do the job better, the philosophy, the principal actors, the structure, and the vast majority of programs that comprised the EOA differed substantially from those of the Public Welfare Amendments. Yet, the EOA retained one characteristic that was identical: the policy was extraordinarily and intentionally vague.

The Public Welfare Amendments were based upon a loosely specified theory, which stated that the welfare rolls and dependency could be reduced through a strategy of social and rehabilitative services. The EOA planners were less concerned with the reduction of the welfare rolls, per se, than with the social, human, and family conditions that accompanied poverty, especially poverty in urban settings. Although widely accused of lacking a causal theory, EOA planning was dominated by the "opportunity theory" of sociologists Richard Cloward and Lloyd Ohlin.[37] Developed after exhaustive research on the problem of juvenile delinquency, Cloward and Ohlin's theory concluded that much deviant social behavior could be explained by a lack of opportunity to conform in socially acceptable ways to a variety of materialistic social norms. The result was alienation and deviant behavior; the cure was to create the opportunity to share in the fruits of mainstream American life.

As ratified by Congress in 1964, the Equal Opportunity Act adopted a dual strategy for dealing with poverty. First, the EOA contained six titles which embraced a number of new service programs:[38] the Job Corps, Volunteers in Service to America (VISTA), work study, Neighborhood Legal Services, and Head Start. It also provided for the expansion of then existing programs: work training, adult education, special programs for rural areas and promotion of urban-rural cooperation (concessions to rural interests in what was a predominantly urban-oriented bill), and work experience. It is noteworthy that the last of these—work experience— represented the only significant programmatic overlap with the service strategy adopted in the welfare amendments only two years earlier.[39]

In addition to authorizing funding for services, requiring only a 10 percent local match, the EOA promoted a number of major structural changes as well. A new federal agency, the Office of Equal Opportunity, was created. Federal funds were to bypass the states completely (at the time there was widespread sentiment among urban officials that the rural-dominated state legislatures didn't care about and state bureaucracies were incompetent to deal with pressing urban problems)[40] and go directly to the local community. Traditional categories of individuals were to be *neither* the target of different benefit packages *nor* a defining characteristic of programs, but rather *problem areas* and areas of opportunity were to serve as the object of funds.

If the statutory directives governing the nature of services were vague in the welfare amendments, those outlined in the EOA were no less so, stating only in the most ambiguous terms the desired ends of the various programs—to provide "education," "training," "useful work experience," and for VISTA volunteers to "combat poverty."[41] But this was not inconsistent with the major structural innovation of the act. Under Title II, the EOA provided funds for the establishment and operation of local Community Action Agencies (CAAs) which were to be responsible for all phases of program design, planning, and implementation embraced by the Act. Moreover, these were not to be agencies of local government, accountable to established local interests. Rather they were to be accountable to the poor through a *process* (not a set of rules or guidelines) emphasizing "maximum feasible participation" of the poor. From the Community Action Program Guide:

> A vital feature of every community action program is the involvement of the poor themselves—the residents of the areas and members of the groups to be served—in planning, policy making, and the operation of the program.[42]

The manual goes on to state in more precise terms, the intended structure of the CAA governing boards. Each was to be a "three-legged stool," with local board membership comprised of representatives from three groups: public agencies, including social service agencies, local government, and school districts; business, labor, religious, and established minority groups; and the poor in the areas to be served by the programs. To further widen the scope of participation, the guide encouraged local CAAs to hold neighborhood meetings, conduct community surveys, and to provide jobs for the poor within the agency.

Because the operation of the CAAs was locally controlled, there was much variation in the specific programs adopted, their methods of operation, and their pattern of expenditure and of raising external funds. The framers' idea was that the local CAAs would pick and choose from the menu of service programs offered through the funding provisions of the act. Most communities adopted a set of core programs, including educational programs like Head Start, "storefront" service centers, Neighborhood Legal Services, and so on; beyond these basics there was wide variation.[43]

Almost immediately two sources of tension emerged, because there was great uncertainty concerning to whose interests the local CAAs were to be held accountable. If the CAA boards adopted low-profile strategies closely aligned with established interests, they were often accused by the poor of "selling out." Other community action agencies—notably those in San Francisco and Syracuse—adopted the strategy of confronting the established interests, to the obvious disenchantment of those interests. Martin Rein has suggested that it was this variation in political styles and political allegiance that caused different CAAs to interpret the OEO implementing guidelines differently; as the political climate became more radical, the demand for political *involvement* by local CAAs quickly escalated to a demand for *control* of policy and program decisions.[44]

However, the major conflict was not between the various local interests but the accountability conflict created by local control of federal funds allocated in pursuit of national policy. In an attempt to reestablish accountability, the 1967 amendments to the EOA restricted local discretion by earmarking funds for some of the more popular, apparently successful, and least controversial programs like Head Start and Neighborhood Legal Services. Congress in the same year also adopted the Green Amendment, which gave local governments the option of bringing the CAAs under their control. Over the years, congressional and popular support for OEO declined, a war in Southeast Asia replaced the war on poverty on the list of top national priorities, and the activist Democratic philosophy of the Great Society was replaced by a more passive Republican policy of the New Federalism.

Many observers contend that the war on poverty failed because neither the federal policy makers nor local decision makers were able to resolve the inherent conflict between national priorities and local discretion.[45] When local priorities, even local political and administrative "styles," failed to match federal expectations—priorities and styles that might have existed in the minds of policy makers, but that were seldom articulated in the law or the guidelines—it was natural that such conflict would ensue. A national goal creates the expectation that a national problem will be solved, and indeed, as we have seen with both the EOA and the Public Welfare Amendments, it is the creation of such expectations that allows the program to be sold to the Congress and to the American public.

Others claim that the program failed because of a more fundamental reason: simply, we knew very little about poverty or its causes, much less its cure. Daniel Moynihan, for one, has stated bluntly that "government did not know what it was doing."[46] Moreover, as Samuel Krislov has suggested, this lack of knowledge was, at least in part, reflected in the adoption of what he calls the "flexibility of ambiguity" inherent in the policy.[47] A principal source of this ambiguity lay within the rationale underlying the participatory strategy for achieving accountability.

Moynihan contends that maximum feasible participation was included in the act only to ensure that the federal government maintained leverage over those communities that might use the funds for programs to the nonpoor. If this was in fact the reasoning, it was only one of many competing interpretations that pervaded the planning community, ranging from "organizing the power structure" to "confronting the power structure" to "expanding the power structure" to "assisting the power structure."[48] The result was that the participatory process was expected to do something that has not been achieved in even the most carefully planned policy and program strategies. Participation was supposed to be a means of achieving mutual accountability to a variety of interests—to the poor, to local interests, and to national expectations.

More recently, citizen participation has become a central component of a large number of federally funded, locally administered social programs, including those under the Housing and Community Development Act, the Older Americans Act, the Rehabilitation Act, and Title XX of the Social Security Act. Within the provisions of Title XX, citizen participation is one method of defining and enumerating a community's social service needs. Indeed, Title XX implementing guidelines require that the needs assessment process include community forums, preceded by substantial advance publicity to ensure widespread participation and thus accountability to community-wide interests. Nonetheless, as Peter O'Donnell, staff associate with the National Governors' Association, has noted:

> much of the information collected at open meetings has to be discounted due to the skewed population that attended—often the most vocal advocacy groups, such as those interested in day care and aging. Although it was a genuine attempt to make the outcome of the planning process more reflective of the needs of the citizens, most of the involvement on the part of the general public would be hardpressed to qualify as a technically sound "needs assessment."[49]

The reality, as the welfare amendments, the Economic Opportunity Act, and Title XX amply demonstrate, is indeed that participation is an integral part of the processes surrounding both policy making and implementation. But even if provided with a forum and substantial resources, it is not the ordinary folk, participating in structured "participatory processes," who will influence the key decisions. These decisions have already been influenced and made by "blue ribbon" committees of experts, and interest group spokesmen in the upper echelons of the federal implementing organizations; in the budgetary recommendations submitted by the

President, the governors, and the mayors; and by the congressmen, legislators, and council members who must authorize public expenditures. Nonetheless, as Murray Edelman has noted, citizen participation, although exerting little substantive influence in comparison to that exerted through traditional channels, may still provide some degree of symbolic reassurance that government is responsive and accountable to the citizenry.[50] It is with apparent understanding of symbol over substance—and its potential dangers—that O'Donnell, with no apologies, concludes with respect to Title XX:

> For interest groups and individuals to ignore these traditional channels and expect to have their function replaced by a formalized process is inviting disappointment in the outcome and frustration with the process.[51]

ACCOUNTABILITY AND THE COURTS

Among the most significant developments in social policy during the past two decades has been the increasing use of the courts as a vehicle for promoting social change and for shaping social policy. Normally, we think of only the U.S. Supreme Court as a powerful force of change through such decisions as that in *Brown v. Board of Education,* which brought about major federal efforts to end racial segregation in the schools. Yet even the lower courts have become significant institutional settings for the creation of social policies and for ensuring that those policies are accountable to the public interest.

An often overlooked development in the evolution of the congressional-judicial-administrative triumvirate occurred with the passage of the Administrative Procedure Act (APA) of 1946. Pushed through Congress on a wave of conservative reaction to Roosevelt's New Deal (and the increase in uncontrolled administrative power that some foresaw), the APA gave the judiciary—principally through the geographically decentralized federal district courts of appeal—substantial control over the administrative process. The provisions of the APA were minimally exercised during the first twenty years of its existence, since the courts were specifically prohibited from reviewing, in Donald Horowitz's words, "matters 'committed to agency discretion.' The courts were not to second-guess wholly discretionary judgments."[52] Instead, the APA was applied as a means of ensuring that agencies followed appropriate *procedures* in carrying out their responsibilities; significantly, the substance of decisions was not an issue.

> The intention was to make the procedures of the agencies *predictable,* to confine them to decisions that had some demonstrated basis in fact,

and to prevent them from acting in disregard of statutory law or fundamental constitutional principles. The courts were *not* to have a central role in formulating public policy, and for quite some time they did not seek such a role.[53]

One area in which the courts have been particularly active in enhancing predictability, in reducing arbitrary discretion, concerns client eligibility and entitlement decisions; these are the judicial procedures commonly known as fair hearings. The established procedure in virtually all public welfare programs, fair hearings may be requested by persons who feel they have been unfairly denied benefits to which they are entitled. Once requested sparingly for fear of bureaucratic reprisal, the frequency of requests for fair hearings and other judicial proceedings has grown considerably in recent years, largely because of the increased availability of legal services to the poor and the activist stance taken by advocate groups like the welfare rights organizations.

Normally, we think of a fair hearing or similar judicial appeal proceeding as a means of limiting arbitrary, discretionary behavior by administrative officials. But in recent years, the influence of the courts has moved beyond protecting the aggrieved party against the discretionary behavior of *individuals* to one of protecting against discretionary *agency* practices. An interesting example of this movement is provided by the "medical disability" criterion used to determine eligibility for social security benefits. Recall that in the early sixties the Social Security Act was amended to enable persons who are disabled after having worked a minimum number of quarters to be eligible for Disability Insurance benefits; the benefits levels are the same as if the claimant had worked until retirement and are financed from the Social Security trust fund. Persons who have *not* accumulated a sufficient work history but are disabled, are eligible for lesser benefits under the Supplemental Security Income program, funded from general revenues. Although benefit levels and eligibility criteria differ, the statutory definitions of disability under the Social Security and Supplemental Security Income programs are substantially the same. Congress has made the purpose of the disability programs quite clear in statutory language by limiting benefits to those not merely unwilling, but unable to engage in

> . . . any substantial gainful activity by reason of any medical determinable physical or mental impairment which can be expected to result in death or has lasted or can be expected to last for a continuous period of not less than 12 months. Substantial gainful activity is any level of work performed for remuneration or profit that involves significant physical or mental duties, or a combination of both.[54]

Eligibility determination in either program is made by a state agency, which has the primary responsibility for assembling any medical, vocational, and other evidence, evaluating that evidence in light of the available criteria; and rendering a decision. Medical, vocational, and other necessary criteria are provided to the state agencies by the Social Security Administration, although to date these criteria have proven insufficiently clear to result in uniform eligibility determination among the states.[55] It is important to note that unlike the many grant-in-aid welfare programs, in which the state bears some fraction of the costs of providing benefits, the federal-state relationship in the disability programs is contractual. The states merely provide an administrative support service to the federal government, which in turn pays all individual benefits and reimburses the states for the full costs of program administration. Our interest here, however, is not with the federal-state relationship, but the relationship between program administration and the courts.

Suppose that you and I both suffer from the same rare blood disease, call it alpha-gamma. Armed with evidence from our respective physicians, we both apply for disability benefits at the local Social Security office. Without explanation, you are denied benefits. But because of my wit, charm, good looks, and only incidentally because the person processing the claims is my cousin, I am designated as eligible to receive benefits. Learning of this, you cry foul and request a fair hearing to appeal the decision. In the process, it is learned that the Social Security Administration has no clearly defined rules or procedures for defining disability; the courts intervene.

To cease such clearly arbitrary decision making, the Social Security Administration is ordered by the courts to adopt less discretionary procedures, and the SSA subsequently establishes a more rigid and formal set of rules for determining who is medically disabled and thus who is eligible for benefits. Research is conducted, physician testimony assembled, and a list of all injuries and illnesses that are "medically determinable" to be disabling is compiled. Like the law itself, the purpose of these rules is to ensure that similar cases are treated similarly within the administrative processes for determining disability. As it turns out, the decision is that alpha-gamma is not determined to be disabling, and you and I are both denied benefits under the new rules.

But you argue, again supported by medical documentation, that yours is not a typical case of alpha-gamma, and that for reasons unknown its impact upon your ability to work has been especially severe. Assuming that this is indeed the case, do you have recourse? Until the last decade or so, probably not. As long as the rules were applied equally and impartially —as long as administrative decisions were predictable—the courts would probably not reverse the administrative decision.

The use of such heavy-handed rules, notes Lance Liebman, promotes a "certain sort of fairness by regularizing discretionary determinations."[56] But these rules, like many rules designed to limit program eligibility to various categories of individuals, contain a serious flaw from the court's point of view. The flaw is this: administrative rules are based upon the implicit assumption that the *reaction* to any particular injury or illness (or any objectively verifiable condition, for that matter) will be *identical* for all individuals. If you and I both are inflicted with alpha-gamma, all the unmeasurables—the pain experienced, the psychological trauma endured, the residual physical impairments, all those factors that might differentially affect our ability to work—are implicitly assumed to be identical. For a *group* of people, the rules might indeed apply. On average, a person with alpha gamma might easily be able to work. But the courts are not concerned with groups or averages in this case; the courts are concerned with the individual instance.

If the court rules for a reversal of the administrative decision (as they have been known to do in a high proportion of disability appeals), they do not do so by appealing to their own set of rules; they have none. Rather they employ the technique of finding, in the particular instance, that there was insufficient evidence to support the administrative conclusion that the medical condition was not disabling.[57] The judicial process shifts the burden of proof from the individual claimant to the administrative agency. Liebman comments on the implications of this shift:

> Attempting to implement Congress' clear purpose that benefits be provided to only those persons in fact medically disabled, the Secretary [of Health, Education and Welfare] establishes hurdles that make it difficult for someone to qualify solely on the basis of a persistent assertion that he is physically incapable of work or able to work only with great pain. Judges, on the other hand, need not consider the program as a whole or its annual budget. Their inquiry is normally focused upon an individual claimant, whose story is often sympathetic, whose perseverance in carrying the case so far is evidence of a sincere claim, and who will not be on Easy Street even if he wins the appeal.[58]

In essence, the judicial appeals process enhances accountability to the individual by its ability to identify legitimate *exceptions* to established administrative rules. If a sufficient number of exceptions are granted, say, for alpha-gamma, administrative rule makers have two choices: either they can place alpha-gamma on the list of disabling diseases, or if it is still believed that many cases of alpha gamma are not disabling, they can further refine the illness category, creating alpha-gamma 1 which is not disabling and alpha-gamma 2 which is. This process of rule generation will continue until the established rules conform more closely to possible different reactions to the illness.

Eligibility appeals are not the only judicial check on administrative discretion and accountability. Particularly in recent years the

> courts have become a more prominent part of the process of administrative decision making. They have moved beyond the protection of the rights of parties aggrieved by administrative action to participation in problem solving and protection of more general public interests against agencies accused of indifference to public interest. Judicial review has passed from matters of procedure to matters of *both* procedure *and* substance. . . . Far from eschewing discretionary judgements, some meliorist judges today see themselves as warriors in the "fight to limit discretion" on the part of administrative agencies.[59]

The newfound activist role of the courts has created new standards for and new methods of achieving administrative accountability. But the use of judicial power for reconciling matters of policy implementation is not without its drawbacks. Although the judicial process is seen as the guardian of such important principles as "justice," "rights," "equity," and strict adherence to the facts, its use to achieve accountability to the public interest is often cumbersome, expensive, and time-consuming. More important, the judicial decision-making process often creates policy that is reactive and inflexible. The courts cannot propose policy, but can only respond to a grievance, the particular facts of which may be atypical but the results all-encompassing, and neither judges nor the courts are well equipped to appreciate the nuances of program operation or the relationship of program to the total welfare structure.[60] And through the establishment of numerous precedents and ever more complex sets of rules, the exercise of discretion—what James Thompson has called "the essence of the administrative process"[61]—is ultimately stifled. Unlike the judiciary, "the administrator is expected to treat experience not as a jailer but as a teacher."[62] Perhaps the significance of the courts' involvement in matters of policy is evidence that this expectation has not been fulfilled.

accountability and the service provider

While external sources of accountability impinge in various important ways on the social welfare enterprise, only indirectly do they influence the task-related behavior of organizational participants. The constraints imposed must still be translated into some effective means for ensuring that the behavior of individual service providers is made predictable and accountable, for it is here—in the user-provider transaction—that social policy is truly implemented. It is here as well that provider norms and practices will come into conflict with other norms and other views regarding what constitutes accountable program behavior.

While the distinction is not always clearcut, it is necessary to distinguish between professional and nonprofessional service providers because the principal norms and forces to which each will be held accountable are different. In view of their mastery of a body of specialized and often esoteric knowledge, and the skills necessary to apply that knowledge in solving problems people cannot solve themselves, until recently at least service professionals have enjoyed a degree of autonomy and authority not normally shared by nonprofessionals. And although the degree of autonomy varies with the profession—clearly physicians enjoy greater autonomy than schoolteachers or caseworkers—it traditionally has extended to embrace the two most fundamental decisions in the user-provider transaction: the authority to determine client needs and the authority to determine appropriate treatment.[63] This authority is controlled, moreover, by the dominant ethic of the social service professions: the professional will be accountable to the client.

In the sixties, it was common for some professionals—planners, social workers, academics, and to some extent members of the legal profession and public administrators—to respond to the demands for greater accountability to the client by adopting an advocacy posture. In essence, and consistent with the rhetoric of the day that espoused, "If you're not part of the solution, you're part of the problem," client advocacy became one of only two possible modes of professional behavior. Richard Cloward and Frances Fox Piven, two of the foremost proponents of client advocacy in the social work profession, describe the mood of the time.

> The issue was whether we were going to take sides with the agencies and further our careers, or with the victims of an aggressively cruel capitalist society. Were we in our daily work going to defend the practices and policies of the hospitals, courts, prisons, foster care agencies, welfare departments, and mental institutions for which we worked, or were we going to use our jobs to defend and protect the poor, the sick, the criminal, and the deviant against these agencies?[64]

But advocacy has its other side, especially if it is viewed as a *political* and not a professional response to unmet needs, a view which is likely if the legitimacy of the profession itself is in question. Even in the best of professional times, with the professional mandate on firm ground, Heinz Eulau has noted that the role of the advocate professional raises fundamental questions.

What will happen if things go wrong? To whom will the advocate professional be accountable? His clients, his peers, his employers, or only his own conscience? What would accountability imply? Would it imply making restitution? Risking censure or suspension of license? Dismissal from the job? Most of these questions have yet to be answered.[65]

Lacking a client-orientation that has been conditioned by professional affiliation, nonprofessional providers nonetheless do not behave as individuals, but rather are accountable to service users, as Michael Lipsky puts it, "on behalf of their agencies and the public purposes they represent."[66] Despite the existence of controls to ensure that provider behavior is indeed representative of agency purposes, however, most social welfare agencies demonstrate, as James Q. Wilson has observed, the paradoxical quality that "discretion increases as one moves down the hierarchy"[67] to the level of the direct service provider. And indeed, some contend that a high degree of discretion at the level of the direct worker is *the* defining characteristic of social welfare organizations.[68] This is striking because it is increasingly the nonprofessional worker who shoulders most of the responsibility for direct contact with service users and frequently presides over a transaction—normally in one of a variety of intake processes—that has been characterized as follows:

On the one side of the desk sits the applicant for service with all the needs, experiences, and idiosyncratic characteristics that combined to bring him or her there. On the other side of the desk sits a person whose function it is to determine the validity and appropriateness of the presenting request, the goodness of fit between it and the franchise, policies, and resources of the organization, and thus the entitlement of the applicant to service. The conversation may be brief, although the preliminaries are often lengthy. It ends with a decision, or a referral, which may satisfy or deny the presenting request. Any sympathy or antipathy that the agency representative may feel for the applicant is supposed to have no effect on the outcome of the episode. The resources of the agency and its formal policies regarding their use are expected to define the eligibility of the client for service.[69]

Oftentimes provider behavior in this transaction is guided less by formal agency policy and procedure than by the simple necessity of coping with a stressful situation. Placed in the situation of dealing with numerous people with countless problems that have little probability of solution, where they are continuously exposed to physical and psychological threat, where working conditions are poor, and where there are neither the organizational nor the human resources to perform the job adequately—service workers are forced to invent what Richard Elmore has called, "routines for mass processing," including the use of "formal procedures of the organization to strike an impersonal balance between oneself, as an individual, and the client."[70]

But how might administrators help ensure that providers are accountable to users on behalf of the agency? First, agency decision makers must know how they want providers to behave; they must be able to identify a preferred provider response for each identifiable contingency, and, if the agency or program is the instrument of multiple objectives, they must be able to rank order preferred provider responses. Second, administrators must be able to document provider behavior and to compare this with established agency preferences. And third, administrators must be in possession of various incentives and sanctions that can be applied to induce desirable patterns of provider behavior.[71]

If the needs and problems of service users were not unique, not idiosyncratic, there would be a finite number of user types, and it would be theoretically possible for administrators to create a set of preferred responses for each presenting situation. But the needs of individuals are unique and idiosyncratic and not readily susceptible to preprogrammed and rigid decision criteria; thus substantial discretion in matching services to needs is required. The problem here is one of striking a balance between discretionary and controlled behavior, to know when the clarification of program goals and preferred provider response "is desirable because continued ambivalence and contradiction is unproductive, and when it will result in a reduction in the scope and mission of public services."[72]

When this dilemma has been resolved, administrative attention turns to the methods by which provider behavior is controlled, a task based upon a very simple principle: administrators can exert control only over those aspects of behavior they know something about. In general, knowledge about provider behavior may be obtained in three principal ways: through analysis of written records compiled by the provider, by direct observation, or by inferring what that behavior was from an analysis of numerical performance measures.

Of the methods of knowing about provider behavior, probably the most important derives from written records maintained by the individual provider. In general, these will contain two types of information: (1) information pertaining to the individual's presenting situation, and (2) of the actions initiated or taken by the provider. Records are of extreme importance and value when the bounds of the user-provider transaction can be well specified, for example during the intake process when certain questions must be asked, verified, and recorded for all applicants. The answers are then matched with standardized criteria to determine eligibility and benefit levels. In addition, records may be useful for ensuring that process standards of service quality are adhered to, requiring that providers record whether or not specific tasks (for example, the provision of a referral or the administration of a test) were carried out. If records are maintained on standardized forms, moreover, it can help to ensure that provider decisions and actions have been uniform across the total range of service users.

Caution must be exercised in using standardized records to audit provider accountability, however, for it is all but impossible to create forms which can accommodate all of the intangibles and all of the contingencies that will influence the provider's response in a particular situation. Interpretation and recording especially of the presenting situation is highly discretionary, often dependent upon the provider's prevailing state of mind;[73] the written record guarantees neither an unbiased interpretation nor an appropriate response to the user's needs.[74]

Direct observation may be a way for administrators to evaluate the intangible factors that pervade the user-provider transaction, provided of course that the administrator knows what to look for and has some set of criteria for judging the transaction. (These attributes are among the major benefits derived from the common practice of drawing administrative personnel from the ranks of providers.) The administrator can, for example, observe whether a procedure is properly carried out, whether the provider behaves courteously, and whether the provider's interpretation of the presenting situation and action taken is consistent with his or her own judgment. Of course, the mere presence of an observer is likely to distort the transaction, since most seasoned providers already know what their supervisors want to see. Moreover, continuous observation is expensive and runs counter to the dominant expectation—held by both user and provider alike—that the transaction is to be conducted in private.

Quantitative measures of performance—the number of cases processed, accepted, rejected, or referred, the number of persons successfully completing a training program, and so on—may be useful for inferring whether provider behavior is accountable to the desired results of a transaction. But quantitative measures of performance are at best only crude indicators of actual behavior. The absence of statistical controls makes it difficult to establish relationships between results and the myriad factors —including provider behavior—that might have caused them. Moreover, the establishment and monitoring of numerical measures can create criterion behavior, behavior that may be accountable to the measure but not to the service user. Such behavior may inordinately highlight the importance of one dimension of the transaction at the expense of all others, particularly those that relate to service quality. Indeed, the greater the degree of provider discretion, "the less one can infer that quantitative indicators bear relationship to service quality."[75]

The best approach to achieving provider accountability to agency preferences is, for the most part, dependent upon the model of organization one chooses to adopt for describing participant behavior. Research has shown, however, that the appropriateness of various methods for achieving control is largely dependent upon the nature of the provider task being performed. Where tasks can be well defined and where the preferred response is known—like that of eligibility determination—it is likely that centrally issued rules and guidelines, supplemented by standardized reporting requirements, will have substantial impact upon provider behavior.[76] In essence, behaviors that are simple and come closest to being preprogrammable and readily evaluable, as one might suspect, are most easily controlled by rules.

Tasks that are not well defined or for which agency preferences are not well developed, but that are observable—for example, providing users with information about alternative courses of action—are less readily controllable through rules. Rather, close supervision is required. Supervisors should be recruited for their understanding of the transaction, trained in its intricacies, and sufficiently motivated to ensure that the agency provides the highest possible level of service to its users. Finally, for those aspects of the user-provider transaction that are indefinable, not readily observable, and primarily evaluable only from a user standpoint—like the provider's apparent attitude, responsiveness, and "style"—some combination of supervision and provider training seems the most appropriate means of control.[77]

Like the various ways of generating the necessary *knowledge about* provider behavior, the quickest, cheapest, and apparently most easily implemented methods for generating *control over* provider behavior—centrally issued rules and procedures, for example—may only strike at the periphery of the transaction. What is seldom mentioned and never researched is the *residual* effect of these rules and procedures, not their effect upon the benefits rendered or denied, but upon interpersonal dimensions of the encounter itself and upon the consequential behavior of the service user.

accountability
and social program
administration

Stated policy goals as we have seen may not prove to be the principal determinants of program decision and action, which arise instead in sequential response to various constraints imposed by external and internal forces. If a newspaper article appears proclaiming high levels of welfare fraud, administrators will probably respond by requiring that providers more closely scrutinize new applications and the family and income status of current recipients. If cumulative program expenditures are substantially higher than those of the budget time-line or if a budget reduction appears imminent, administrators may demand that eligibility procedures be tightened, caseloads increased, or that services previously provided individually now be performed in groups. Conversely, if it appears that a budgetary surplus will exist at the end of the fiscal year, the exact opposite—perhaps supplemented by a vigorous outreach campaign—may become the preferred program response. Or a federal judge may decide that state governments are no longer required under federal statutes to provide funding for abortions and, under strong pressure from a citizens' lobby, the state legislature restricts funding to only those cases where the mother's health is in question; administrators respond with revised program eligibility guidelines. A county-wide needs assessment indicates that a high proportion of children from poor families have serious dental problems, necessitating a revision in child welfare priorities, a shifting of funds, and a new set of preferred responses. Operators of a state mental health program are accused of abuse and neglect of their patients; an investigation by the State Mental Health Commission reveals that patients' quarters are filthy and that patients are periodically beaten and denied food as part of their "therapy." New standards of service quality are drafted, the patient care staff reorganized, and the administrator fired; a new set of preferred responses is in order.

As we have also seen, social program implementation requires a perspective that is inherently multi-organizational in nature, one in which different sources of authority exert varying degrees of control over different aspects of program operations. Some will control funds, others the qualitative characteristics of the service delivered, others the specific eligibility criteria in use, and still others the process of service delivery. Some forces may be governmental, but in a different level than that responsible for implementation, others may be nongovernmental and within the local community itself. Some will be highly organized and well financed; others, but loose, temporary coalitions of community interest groups. In this concluding section of this chapter, we shall investigate the impact of these separate forces on the integrity of the whole program and investigate the possible roles of the program administrator in guiding its implementation.

AN OPEN SYSTEMS MODEL OF SOCIAL PROGRAM IMPLEMENTATION

Throughout this book, we will often rely upon conceptual models to help simplify and clarify complex concepts and issues. Among the more

FIGURE 3.1:

logic flow and measurement models

(a) **Logic Flow**

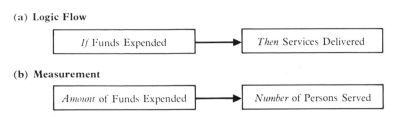

(b) **Measurement**

useful general class of models, one that can be used to describe the implementing process, is known as a *logic flow* model.[78] The general pattern of any logic flow model, as Figure 3.1(a) shows, is a series of "if-then" statements. For example, *if* resources are expended *then* services will be delivered; *if* services are delivered *then* certain outcomes will occur. In addition to clearly describing the logic of a process, the logic flow model possesses another valuable attribute. If the events are capable of quantification (and data are available)—for example, the *amount* of resources expended, the *number* of persons receiving services—the logic flow model can easily be converted into a measurement model, a model particularly useful for program analysis and evaluation. A simple measurement model is shown in Figure 3.1(b).

Using the general logic-flow framework, an open system model of a typical social program is shown in Figure 3.2. Justified politically as an instrument for remedying an undesirable human or social condition, the events that comprise the logic of the program's implementation are governed by specific decisions taken within the four parameters of social programming—eligibility criteria and procedures, the amount and type of the allocation provided, the mode of delivery, and the type and level of program resources. Loosely specified in the program plan, each of these parameters is assumed to be the object of three general sources of control during the implementing process: (1) the other parameters in the process, since all are logically interrelated, i.e. without resources there can be no allocations, (2) forces in the program's external policy environments, and (3) internal forces generated by program personnel. The heavy arrows impinging upon the parameters indicate that external forces will often exert greater control over the implementing process than will internally generated decisions and controls.

The circular shape of the model is consistent with the fact that program implementation is an on-going process, with no logical beginning and no logical end. Within the process, alterations in one parameter will generate ramifications throughout the entire program. If, for

FIGURE 3.2:

the ongoing process of implementation

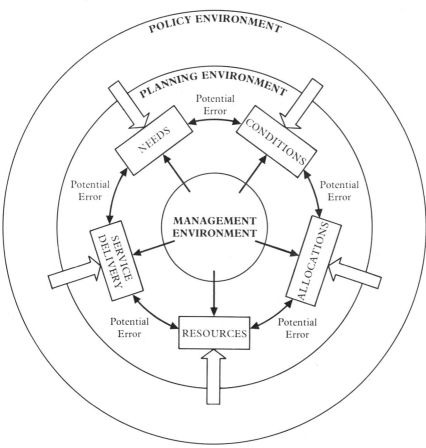

example, the definition or magnitude of need is changed, it will undoubt-edly affect both the types and numbers of persons requiring access to the program, the type and level of resources required, the type of allocation deemed appropriate, and the specific nature of the human or social condition addressed. Alter the level of resources available and a different set of disturbances will permeate the entire process, and so on. If the process is left undisturbed these ramifications will continue until the parameters are once again compatible with one another; at this point the process of program implementation will have reached a state of equilibrium. Seldom, however, will such quietude and stability exist in the implementing process.

A major reason for this is found in the dynamic and often contradictory impulses emanating both from within the program and from its various policy environments. Note that the program is considered not to have a singular, homogeneous "environment" but rather is immersed in a *series of different environments or policy arenas*, created by and focusing upon the parameters.[79] Significantly, *seldom will a single force within the program's multiple policy environments consider the integrity of the whole program, but will more often adopt a more limited focus.* That is, each parameter has the potential to become a major policy issue in its own right. For example, a legislative committee may desire to reduce an aging program's level of funding as part of a general cost-cutting measure, while another group, say the Gray Panthers, is in the process of promoting wider program utilization. These contradictory forces, if left alone, will generate changes incompatible with one another, creating logical errors within the implementing process and greatly limiting the program's potential effectiveness.

ACCOUNTABILITY AND THE ADMINISTRATOR: ROLES AND OPTIONS

If the programs of the social welfare enterprise are largely influenced by divergent and contradictory external forces, what are the possible roles and options available to persons in positions of administrative responsibility? It depends, say Jeffrey Pfeffer and Gerald Salancik, upon the perceived relationship among external constraints, administrative action, and organizational outcomes. In particular, they have identified three functional roles that might plausibly describe administrative behavior in organizations that are confronted by myriad external constraints: the symbolic role, the responsive role, and the discretionary role.[80] Each of these, in turn, promotes a distinct conception of administrative accountability.

Certainly the most iconoclastic of these roles, at least in terms of more traditional conceptions of administrative responsibility and behavior, derives from the view that administrative actions will have little or no effect upon organizational outcomes. Since there is no relationship between administrative action and organizational outcomes, administrative behavior is largely *symbolic,* designed to promote only the *appearance* of maintaining accountability to external forces. The role is, they note, not lacking in importance, for it perpetuates the valuable illusion that causation exists, rational action is being taken, and that someone is in control.

> As a symbol of control and personal causation, managers and organizational leaders can be used as scapegoats, rewarded when things go well and fired when they go poorly. The knowledge that someone is in charge and that the fate of the organization depends on that person offers the promise of change in organizational activities and fortunes. When problems emerge, the solution is simple and easy—replace the manager.[81]

Closely related to this role is the symbolic conception of accountability itself—accountability that is "divorced from any systematic efforts to promote actual attainment of the desired values."[82] The promotion of symbolic reassurance through the use of verbal slogans, visible shifts in key administrative personnel, the establishment of blue ribbon investigation committees, the adoption of rules with no expectation nor any means of enforcing compliance, and other symbolic gestures, as Murray Edelman has noted, often enhance the short-run survivability of the organization by mollifying unorganized political groups, thereby making political self-mobilization more difficult. In the long run, however, simple symbolic reassurance may backfire, with the eventual realization that they have been manipulated providing a rallying point around which groups may organize and become potent forces in extracting substantive organizational response to their demands.[83] Such was the case in many Community Action Agencies.

The second or *responsive* role posits that the administrative function is one of processing, assimilating, and implementing appropriate responses to various external demands, usually by altering aspects of program operations that are not *currently* the subject of controversy. For example, to accommodate potentially greater program utilization in the face of an impending resource reduction, administrators may decide to provide a less expensive form of allocation by converting from professional to non-professional personnel, or alternatively from individualized to group services. These "new" allocations, however, may prove less effective in alleviating the undesirable conditions that are the program's ultimate reason for being; thus a new set of logical disturbances may upset the program's integrity. Moreover, their implementation might be resisted by legislative, professional or other forces having a stake in the nature of the allocation provided; what was originally a non-issue—the nature of the allocation—now becomes an issue of crucial importance.

The critical decision within the responsive role is, of course, to determine which of the often contradictory set of demands to heed and which to ignore.[84] The problem with this purely reactive posture, as Amitai Etzioni recognizes, is that "by and large, groups with more status, income, and education have more power and hence make the system relatively more 'accountable' to them."[85] An additional problem arises when the administrator uses the reactive posture as a means of abrogating his or her discretionary authority, as in, "But I was just following standard procedure."[86]

The third administrative role is consistent with the notion that the relationship between administrative actions and externally imposed constraints is reciprocal. This leads to the administrator's *discretionary* role, one in which the administrator actively seeks to shape the organization's external environment.[87] Considering the potential conflict between reduced resources and expanded utilization, for example, the program administrator might seek to open channels of communication and help to identify areas of possible compromise between the two opposing interests.

Central to an understanding of the discretionary administrative role is the view, first posited some time ago by Richard Cyert and James March,[88] that organizations are internally comprised of and are also more or less powerful participants in external bargaining coalitions. The most important aspect of the conflict-bargaining model—one that makes it especially attractive for use in the social welfare enterprise—is that organizational action need not be framed in terms of a clear, concise statement of organizational goals. Indeed, the organizations and organizational actors need share no commonality of purpose whatsoever, only the willingness to bargain and compromise; the result is a set of organizational outcomes that are temporarily bargained solutions implying no overall agreement on a single purpose. As in the responsive role, it is of utmost importance that the administrator be able to identify critical internal and external interdependencies; in addition, however, the administrator must seek to cultivate and preserve the bargaining arena within which differently valued ends will occur. This implies, as Thomas Schelling has noted, that "there is a powerful common interest in reaching an outcome that is not enormously destructive to both sides.[89] Schelling also notes that convergence upon a mutually acceptable outcome is largely dependent upon the ability of each actor in the conflict-bargaining process to discover the often implicit "rules of the game," or the expectations held by each party for the other.[90]

Significantly, these expectations may differ substantially from those implied in the law, written guidelines, labor agreements, or other formal demands made upon the program; what is important is whether administrators anticipate being forced to comply with those demands. In programs requiring substantial intergovernmental interaction, for example, an increasing body of research suggests that action in state and local agencies is largely dependent upon the expectation that federal officials will or will not enforce compliance with written policy.[91] If federal officials deem that state and local actions are not accountable to prevailing policy and initiate attempts to enforce compliance, state and local administrators will respond in part with greater compliance and in part with counterattempts to alter the policy; the process will continue until some temporary, but mutually acceptable compromise is achieved. And then it will start again. Thus, a system of centralized planning and decentralized implementation appears to work when administrators are able to negotiate a compromise between federal and local interests, creating as Martha Derthick has noted, "programs that are neither 'federal' nor 'local' but a blend of the two."[92]

An expansion of the discretionary administrative role creates what

Etzioni has called the "guidance" approach to accountability, which he considers as having both a power and a moral base.[93] Within this view, the administrative role is neither one of symbol, of responsiveness, nor one of actively shaping the organization's external environment, but one of exercising what he calls "creative leadership." The principal difference between Etzioni's creative leadership role and the other possibilities discussed is that—while still maintaining accountability to the widest possible set of internal and external constraints on program operations—the administrator actively seeks to promote values *other* than simple organizational survival.

With respect to social programs in particular, Simon Slavin's observations regarding this often risky and difficult balancing act are of great value. He contends that the governing ethic of professional administrative behavior in the social welfare enterprise ultimately derives from a fundamental concern for clients and their needs. This ethical posture, however, requires political skills that transcend those associated with single-minded and heavy-handed advocacy, which may only weaken the administrator's professional credibility and may also heighten political conflict to a level at which no program change becomes possible. Rather, as Slavin notes, professional skills are concerned "precisely with the ways in which the administrator balances and orchestrates the interests of divergent constituencies, but from a client perspective as an organizing principle."[94] To do so requires first and foremost knowledge about clients, especially how the organizational and administrative technology of the enterprise both denies and fulfills their needs. It is to this all-important set of influences that we now turn our attention.

notes

1. Woodrow Wilson, "The Study of Administration" (1887) reprinted in *Political Science Quarterly*, 56, no. 4 (December 1941), 481–82.

2. See, among others, Wallace S. Sayre, "Premises of Public Administration," *Public Administration Review*, 17, no. 1 (Spring 1958).

3. Theodore Lowi, *The End of Liberalism* (New York: W. W. Norton & Co., Inc., 1969), p. 388.

4. Richard B. Stewart, "The Reformation of American Administrative Law," *Harvard Law Review*, 88, no. 8 (June 1975), 1,077.

5. For an excellent summary of these differing views, see Thomas R. Dye, *Understanding Public Policy* (Englewood Cliffs, N.J.: Prentice-Hall, Inc., 1975), Ch. 2.

6. Graham T. Allison, "The Power of Bureaucratic Routines," in Francis E. Rourke, ed., *Bureaucratic Power in National Politics*, 2nd ed. (Boston: Little, Brown, 1972), p. 85, emphasis added.

7. Ibid.

8. Ibid, emphasis added.

9. Alice M Rivlin, "Social Policy: Alternate Strategies for the Federal Government," in Randall B. Ripley and Grace A. Franklin, eds., *National Government and Policy in the United States* (Itasca, Ill.: F. E. Peacock, 1977), pp. 305–14.

10. Anthony Downs, *Inside Bureaucracy* (Boston: Little, Brown, 1967), p. 144.

11. Lon Fuller, *Anatomy of the Law* (Middlesex, England: Penguin, 1968), p. 34.

12. Stewart, "The Reformation of American Administrative Law," 1,672.

13. See Kenneth Culp Davis, *Administrative Law and Government* (St. Paul, Minn.: West Publishing Co., 1960), pp. 121–29.

14. Ibid., p. 125.

15. Ibid., p. 121.

16. Ibid.

17. Gilbert A. Steiner, *Social Insecurity* (Chicago: Rand McNally, 1966), p. 18.

18. Ibid., pp. 37–38.

19. Ad Hoc Committee on Public Welfare, *Report to the Secretary of Health, Education and Welfare* (Washington, D.C., September 1961), p. 13. Cited in Ibid. p. 38.

20. Martha Derthick, *Uncontrollable Spending for Social Services Grants* (Washington, D.C.: Brookings Institution, 1975), p. 9.

21. Social Security Act, Sec. (403) (a) (3) (A) (iii) and Sec. 1603(a) (4) (A) (iii), *Compilation of the Social Security Laws*, pp. 135, 212.

22. Joel F. Handler, "Federal-State Interests in Welfare Administration," in Joint Economic Committee, Studies in Public Welfare, Paper 5, pt. 2, pp. 20–24.

23. Ibid., p. 75.

24. Monthly Status Reports for WIN (May 31, 1971) cited in Stephen F. Gold, "Comment: The Failure of the Work Incentive Program," *University of Pennsylvania Law Review*, 119 (1971), 495.

25. Cited in Derthick, *Uncontrollable Spending*, p. 12.

26. Derthick, *Uncontrollable Spending*, p. 13.

27. Handler, "Federal-State Interests in Welfare Administration," p. 74.

28. Joseph Heffernan, "Public Assistance and Social Services," in Joint Economic Committee, *Studies in Public Welfare*, Paper 5, pt. 2, p. 109.

29. Ibid.

30. Heffernan, "Public Assistance and Social Services," p. 114.

31. Frederick Doolittle, Frank Levy, and Michael Wiseman, "The Mirage of Welfare Reform," *The Public Interest*, no. 47 (Spring 1977), 65.

32. Joseph Heffernan, "Public Assistance and Social Services," p. 115.

33. Derthick, *Uncontrollable Spending*, p. 13.

34. Irene Lurie, "Legislative, Administrative, and Judicial Changes in the AFDC Program, 1967–71," in Joint Economic Committee, *Studies in Public Welfare*, Paper 5, pt. 2, p. 95.

35. Derthick, *Uncontrollable Spending*, p. 2.

36. Peter Sitkin, "Welfare Law: Narrowing the Gap between Congressional Policy and Local Practice," in Joint Economic Committee, *Studies in Public Welfare*, Paper 5, pt. 2, p. 52.

37. Richard A. Cloward and Lloyd E. Ohlin, *Delinquency and Opportunity: A Theory of Delinquent Gangs* (New York: Free Press, 1960).

38. Not all programs were in the original act.

39. Lowi, *The End of Liberalism,* p. 234.

40. See, for example, Frank P. Grad, "The State's Capacity to Respond to Urban Problems," in Alan K. Campbell, ed., *The States and the Urban Crisis* (Englewood Cliffs, N.J.: Prentice-Hall, 1970), pp. 27–58.

41. Cited in Lowi, *The End of Liberalism,* p. 235.

42. Office of Economic Opportunity, *Community Action Program Guide,* Washington, D.C., October 1965.

43. Robert L. Lineberry and Ira Sharkansky, *Urban Politics and Public Policy* (New York: Harper & Row, Pub., 1971), p. 206.

44. Martin Rein, *Social Policy* (New York: Random House, 1970), p. 366.

45. See, for example, Samuel Krislov, "The OEO Lawyers Fail to Constitutionalize a Right to Welfare: A Study in the Uses and Limits of the Judicial Process," *University of Minnesota Law Review,* 58 (1973), 213–14.

46. Daniel Moynihan, *Maximum Feasible Misunderstanding* (New York: Free Press, 1969), p. 170.

47. Krislov, "The OEO Lawyers," pp. 214–15.

48. Moynihan, *Maximum Feasible Misunderstanding,* pp. 87, 168.

49. Peter S. O'Donnell, *Social Services: Three Years after Title XX* (Washington, D.C.: National Governors' Association, Center for Policy Research, 1978), pp. 38–39.

50. Murray Edelman, *The Symbolic Uses of Politics* (Urbana: University of Illinois Press, 1964), Ch. 2.

51. O'Donnell *Social Services: Three Years after Title XX,* p. 42.

52. Donald L. Horowitz, "The Courts as Guardians of the Public Interest," *Public Administration Review,* 37, no. 2 (March/April 1977), 150.

53. Ibid., emphasis added.

54. Comptroller General of the United States, *A Plan for Improving the Disability Determination Process by Bringing It under Complete Federal Management Should Be Developed* (Washington, D.C.: U.S. General Accounting Office, August 31, 1978), p. 2.

55. Ibid., pp. 11–25.

56. Lance Liebman, "The Definition of Disability in Social Security and Supplemental Security Income: Drawing the Bounds of Welfare Estates," *Harvard Law Review,* 89, no. 5 (March 1976), 846.

57. Ibid., 845.

58. Ibid.

59. Horowitz, "The Courts as Guardians of the Public Interest," p. 150.

60. Ibid., p. 152.

61. James D. Thompson, *Organizations in Action* (New York: McGraw-Hill, 1967), p. 51.

62. Opinion of Judge Wyzanski, *Shawmut Association v. SEC,* (1st Cir. 1945) cited in Davis, *Administrative Laws and Government,* p. 323.

98   social program implementation

63. Heinz Eulau, "Skill Revolution and Consultative Commonwealth," *American Political Science Review,* 67, no. 1 (March 1973), 183.

64. Richard A. Cloward and Frances Fox Piven, "Notes toward a Radical Social Work," in Roy Baily and Mike Brake, eds., *Radical Social Work* (New York: Pantheon, 1975), p. xii.

65. Eulau, "Skill Revolution," p. 188.

66. Michael Lipsky, "The Assault on Human Services: Street-Level Bureaucracy, Accountability and the Fiscal Crisis," a paper presented at the Conference on Public Agency Accountability in an Urban Society, Urban Research Center, University of Wisconsin–Milwaukee, Milwaukee, Wisconsin, April 3–5, 1977, p. 34 (emphasis deleted).

67. James Q. Wilson, *Varieties of Police Behavior* (New York: Atheneum, 1973), p. 7.

68. This is the position taken in Joel F. Handler, *Protecting the Social Service Client: Legal and Structural Controls on Official Discretion* (New York: Academic Press, 1979).

69. Robert L. Kahn, Daniel Katz, and Barbara Gutek, "Bureaucratic Encounters—An Evaluation of Government Services." *Journal of Applied Behavioral Science,* 12, no. 2 (May–June 1976), 181–82.

70. Richard F. Elmore, "Organizational Models of Social Program Implementation," *Public Policy,* 26, no. 2 (Spring 1978), 203.

71. Michael Lipsky, "The Assault on Human Services," p. 3.

72. Ibid., p. 16.

73. If you've not worked in a welfare office, Frederick Wiseman's film, *Welfare* provides a powerful portrait of the user-provider transaction.

74. Lipsky, "The Assault on Human Services," p. 12.

75. Ibid., p. 20.

76. Tana Pesso, "Local Welfare Offices: Managing the Intake Process," *Public Policy,* 26, no. 2 (Spring 1978), 326.

77. Ibid., 327.

78. For excellent discussion of logic flow and measurement models, see The Urban Institute, *The Development and Use of Measurement Models* (Washington, D.C.: The Urban Institute, undated).

79. See Jeffry Pfeffer and Gerald R. Salancik, *The External Control of Organizations* (New York: Harper & Row, Pub., 1978), Ch. 4.

80. Ibid., 262.

81. Ibid., 263.

82. Amitai Etzioni, "Alternative Conceptions of Accountability: The Example of Health Administration," *Public Administration Review,* 35, no. 3 (May–June 1975), 280.

83. Edelman, *The Symbolic Uses of Politics,* Ch. 2.

84. Pfeffer and Salancik, *The External Control of Organizations,* p. 266.

85. Etzioni, "Alternative Conceptions of Accountability," 281.

86. Thompson, *Organizations in Action,* p. 119.

87. Pfeffer and Salancik, *The External Control of Organizations,* p. 267.

88. Richard Cyert and James March, *A Behavioral Theory of the Firm* (Englewood Cliffs, N.J.: Prentice-Hall, 1963).

89. Thomas Schelling, *The Strategy of Conflict* (London: Oxford University Press, 1963), p. 219.

90. Ibid., p. 220.

91. See for example Helen Ingram, "Policy Implementation through Bargaining," *Public Policy,* 25, no. 4 (Fall 1977).

92. Martha Derthick, *New Towns in Town: Why a Federal Program Failed* (Washington, D.C.: Urban Institute, 1977), p. 98.

93. Etzioni, "Alternative Conceptions of Accountability," pp. 284–85.

94. Simon Slavin, "Editor's Introduction to Part II," in *Social Administration,* ed. Simon Slavin (New York: The Haworth Press, 1978), pp. 39–42.

Needs assessments are methodologies for identifying and quantifying the level of human need within a defined geographical area. They are generally conceived and implemented to achieve one or more of four primary objectives: (1) to establish service priorities, (2) to provide the basis for funding allocations, (3) to evaluate existing service arrangements, and (4) to better understand the interdependencies among service providers.

There is no single universally accepted approach to the assessment of need. A variety of factors, including its purpose, the agency or jurisdiction undertaking the assessment, the availability of data, and the degree of measurement sophistication possible, will largely dictate the needs assessment format adopted. All needs assessments must, however, deal with three dimensions of analysis: situations or problems, individuals or groups of people, and services or strategies of intervention. Depending upon which of these is adopted as the primary focus, needs assessments may be classified as community-based, client-oriented, or service-oriented respectively.

While one may identify a multitude of stages in any needs assessment process, they all incorporate two principal activities, need identification and need enumeration. Need identification is the act of defining the human and social conditions that call for organized intervention on the part of the community. Need enumeration may incorporate a variety of statistical and nonstatistical methodologies for counting the persons in need and the number of service units required.

assessing need

4

Needs assessments reflect formal attempts to identify and quantify the levels of various needs existing within a defined geographical area. While they have only recently become the basis for social planning and decision making in the social welfare enterprise, the rationale underlying their conduct is certainly not new. In Acts it is written that some of the disciples had become concerned about the problem of hunger among a group of widows. They approached the problem rationally by first determining the magnitude of the problem, performing a needs assessment designed to determine the number of widows who were hungry. They then explored the feasible means for solving the problem, and selected the most suitable alternative. The result was that the widows were to be fed at special tables.

More recently, in the late nineteenth century, Dorothea Dix performed an extensive nationwide survey of the incidence and treatment of mental illness, which became the basis for legislation aimed at improving the conditions of the mentally ill.[1] The Hill-Burton Act of 1946 established nationwide standards for hospital construction based upon the geographic and population characteristics of a community, both rough indicators of the need for hospital services and new facilities. The original UWASIS taxonomy developed by the United Way encouraged the development of needs assessment research to guide the funding of social welfare programs.[2] But no doubt the greatest stimulus underlying the concern with needs has been provided by regulations that accompany federal grants-in-aid, regulations that increasingly require a needs assessment as a precondition for obtaining funds. Needs assessments are now required by twenty-eight of the largest federal grant-in-aid programs administered by the Department of Health and Human Services (formerly the Department of Health, Education and Welfare), including social services funded under Title XX, health planning and resources development, community mental health centers, and a variety of aging programs.[3]

As methods of generating information useful in program decision making, needs assessments are still in their infancy; as yet, there is no single approach that would qualify as the best means of assessing human and community needs. Nonetheless, if the idea of need is to serve as the basis for planning and evaluation in the social welfare enterprise, a number of crucial questions must first be addressed. First, is there a single, identifiable need or set of needs that somehow relates to an individual's well-being? Second, through what process or set of processes do needs become identified as such? And third, how are needs measured and incorporated into the decision-making process?

the concept of need

The concept of *need*, like *goal*, *objective*, or *policy* is a device that orients perception and eventual analysis. Unlike the others, however, the concept of need is a term that has meaning in the experience of the individual. Individuals do not ordinarily possess fixed goals, objectives, or policies; rather they possess problems, wants, and needs. Logically, a statement of need is a conditional statement, which may explicate but usually only implies the desirability of a higher order end. The statement, "I *need* a pencil," implies that it is needed to fill some higher order desire, presumably that I *want* to write. In other words, given that I want to write, I need a pencil. The logic of need can easily be expanded to include higher order ends. "Given that I want to survive, I need a job, I need to publish, I need to write, and therefore I need a pencil." Of course, jobs, publishing, writing, and pencils represent but one of many strategic alternatives or "need hierarchies" that could lead to survival.

THE PSYCHOLOGY AND THE SOCIOLOGY OF NEED

The psychology of need, as might be expected, focuses upon certain fundamental characteristics of the human condition, independent of cultural setting, that are assumed to affect every individual's quality of life. The assumption that universal human needs exist and can be identified is well stated by anthropologist Clyde Kluckhohn.

> Some values are as much given in human life as the fact that bodies of certain densities fall under certain conditions. These are founded, in part, upon the fundamental biological similarities of all human beings. They arise also out of the circumstance that human existence is invariably a social existence. . . . There are important variations, to be sure, in the conception of the extent of the in-group and in-conditions. But the core notion of the desirable and the undesirable is constant across all cultures.[4]

Certainly the best known treatment of human need from the psychological perspective of individual constants is that of Abraham Maslow.[5] Within Maslow's view, human existence and human behavior are assumed to revolve around the individual's attempt to meet certain needs as arranged in hierarchical sequence, with successively higher order needs indicative of the individual's increasing mastery over himself and his environment. Presumably, progression through this hierarchy is also indicative of an improving quality of life for the individual. Only when the needs of one level have somehow been met is the individual assumed to become aware of and in a position to derive well-being from meeting those within the next higher level. Maslow's hierarchy of needs is shown below in Figure 4.1.

What should be immediately apparent from the figure is that Maslow's higher order needs are successively more abstract than those lower. Thus, it is relatively easy to attach some universal meaning to physical needs or those of protection; it is also relatively simple to achieve substantial agreement upon some of the strategies by which these needs can be met, for example through food and shelter. At the lowest level, at least, Kluckhohn's contention that human needs are universal seems plausible. Successively higher order needs, however, such as "self-actualization" or "self-direction and control," do not so easily yield to simple, universal definition, nor to an obvious strategy for meeting them.[6]

While psychologists have concentrated their efforts upon developing a variety of need typologies characteristic of all individuals, the sociological approach emphasizes the importance of cultural forces in the creation and identification of human needs. Like the psychological approach, the sociology of need draws a fundamental distinction between *biological* needs and *acquired* needs, the latter conditioned by culture.[7] The cultural determinants of need have been of particular interest in analyzing an individual's decision to voluntarily seek help for problems he cannot solve himself.

For example, in the health care field, individual perception of need is considered a primary factor in the individual decision to seek medical care,[8] and these perceptions are directly related to the existence of readily identifiable symptoms of illness, such as severe pain, fever, or shortness of breath. Yet, research has shown that, in addition to the existence of manifest symptoms, the individual's perception of need is highly dependent upon cultural factors and group membership. In one well-known study, researchers demonstrated a strong relationship between social class membership and the recognition of the symptoms requiring medical attention.[9]

FIGURE 4.1:

Maslow's hierarchy of human needs

Highest	Self-actualization
│	Esteem
│	Belongingness and love
Lowest	Security, physical survival
Order	

In another study, Irving Zola concluded that an individual's cultural background, ethnic group, or other reference group were powerful mediating factors in the recognition of symptoms and the perception of need for medical care. In a comparison of Irish and Italian patients at the Massachusetts General Hospital, Zola found that among the Irish patients there were four times the number of complaints involving eye, ear, nose, and throat symptoms than all other parts of the body combined. Although there was no significant difference in the two groups from a clinical standpoint, these same complaints comprised only one-half the total among the Italian patients.[10]

Within the mental health field, a study performed by Eaton and Weil provides substantial evidence that certain social groups are more tolerant in their expectations of individual behavior, particularly what constitutes deviant behavior; consequently fewer mental health care needs will be identified.[11] Prior to their in-depth study of the fundamentalist Hutterite communities, there was thought to be a lower prevalence of mental illness among Hutterites than among comparable groups. The research indicated, however, that the actual prevalence of mental illness as medically determined was no different than among other comparable groups. Rather, by culturally normalizing the medically defined symptoms of neurosis and psychosis, the subculture had effectively masked the existence of mental illness to outsiders.

In sum, while psychologists look for commonalities, sociologists look for the source of differences in human need; in reality the answer probably lies somewhere between the two views. The sociology of need emphasizes the fact that different groups will perceive needs differently, a product of mutual expectations existing between the individual and the collective. This applies to needs within groups and the perceptions of those in other groups. Inevitably, there will arise conflict over what human condition constitutes a need and what level of resources will be applied to meet it. These questions concern the politics and economics of need.

THE ECONOMICS OF NEED

The *economics of need* may, in fact, be a non sequitur, as indeed the very idea of need is alien within the context of microeconomic theory. From an introductory graduate level economics text:

> We know of no more common denial of the law of demand than the repeated talk of "vital needs." At best such talk is the result of ignorance that goods are scarce. At worst, it is a calculated attempt to confuse the reader or listener into paying the costs of what the speaker wants. Yet, do not conclude that you should never speak of your

"critical, urgent, crying needs." As a matter of practical, good advice, you may find it worthwhile to speak that way in a self-serving attempt to con others into paying for what you want. But do not confuse yourself with your own language or be confused by others who talk of "critical needs."[12]

Nonetheless, the concept of need does have economic *implications.*

The reason for this pervasive treatment of need by economists is that their primary interest is the *act* of consumption, not its underlying motivational factors. And while the demand for services is sometimes called an expressed need by students of social welfare (just as it is called a revealed preference by economists), what economic theorists are telling us is that if the optimal *economic* allocation of scarce resources is to be achieved, people must be willing to pay a fair market price for the goods and services they consume. Within the tenets of microeconomic theory, individual consumption is based upon personal wants and the price each consumer is willing to pay. For a total society of consumers, all else equal, the lower the unit price the more consumed. But the unit price of a good or service is also dependent upon the price that must be received to induce production; in general, and again all else equal, a higher price will induce a higher level of production. What happens if the price people are willing to pay is lower than that required to induce consumption? The market will be in disequilibrium and nothing will be produced or consumed. To achieve equilibrium, either the demand schedule (the relationship between unit price and quantity consumed) or the supply schedule (the relationship between price and quantity produced) must somehow be altered.

Were the production of a specific service to be based solely upon the equilibrium of supply and demand, Figure 4.2(a) shows that a quantity of this service, Q_e, would be produced and sold at a unit price, P_e. Suppose, however, that it is determined *politically* by some group in society such as service professionals that the total quantity of services *needed* is substantially greater than that determined by the interaction of market forces. Call this quantity Q_n. How might these market forces be altered such that the needed quantity is produced and consumed?

If policy makers attempt to increase consumption by the simple expedient of reducing price they confront an immediate dilemma; the market will no longer be in equilibrum. If price were reduced to P_c, Figure 4.2(a) shows that the needed quantity would in fact be consumed. Note in the figure that this is a negative price; as is sometimes found to be the case with some services in developing countries (e.g., birth control), one might actually have to pay people to consume the needed service. But even this won't help matters because producers will have long since ceased production; to produce the needed amount they must receive a price P_n for

FIGURE 4.2:

need and the economic theory of demand

(a) The Disparity Between the Equilibrium and the Needed Quantity

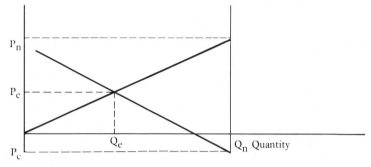

(b) Reconciling the Disparity by Inducing an Upward Shift in the Demand Schedule

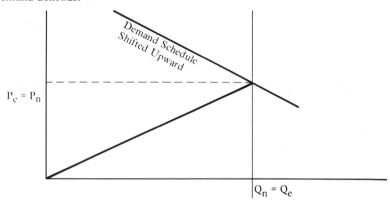

(c) Reconciling the Disparity by Inducing a Downward Shift in the Supply Schedule

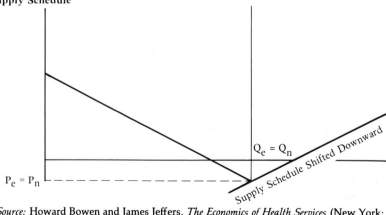

Source: Howard Bowen and James Jeffers, *The Economics of Health Services* (New York: General Learning Press, 1971), p. 11. Reprinted by permission of Silver Burdett Company.

the service. In short, the market is in an intolerable state of disequilibrium at the needed quantity of service.

Basic microeconomic theory considers only the relationship between two variables, the quantity produced and consumed at equilibrium (these are equal) and the unit price of a good or service, which is called the market clearing price. With the exception of price, all other factors that might influence the quantity produced and consumed—wealth, tastes, technological developments, the costs of other goods and services, and so on— are assumed constant; this is the well-known *ceteris paribus* (all else equal) assumption. This assumption must now be relaxed.

To induce the needed quantity produced and consumed and still maintain market equilibrium, the supply and demand schedules must be shifted so that equilibrium occurs at the quantity needed. Some set of forces must somehow induce either a shift in the demand schedule upward and to the right, a shift in the supply schedule downward and to the right, or some combination of both. In almost all cases this will require intervention in the marketplace by some external agent possessing sufficient resources to alter prevailing market equilibrium.

One strategy used to shift the demand schedule is aimed at altering consumer preferences; this is the effect of *marketing.* Marketing strategies may be used to either retard or expand consumption. In the fifties, for example, it was common to promote greater use of health care services by educating individuals to be aware of, say, the "telltale signs of cancer"; in the seventies with health care services in short supply and at increasingly high cost, quite the opposite seems the case with a variety of promotional efforts—led by medical insurance carriers in particular—aimed at reducing health care consumption by encouraging, for example, "self-care."

A primary device used by government to effect shifts in prevailing market equilibrium is the subsidy, provided either to producers or consumers. Indeed, as we previously saw in chapter 2, government action directed at subsidizing the consumption of certain goods and services through the tax system—medical care, housing, food, child care, and so on —is a major element of American social policy. Because consumer subsidies lower the effective price paid by individual consumers—government picks up the tab for the difference between the price required by producers and the price people are willing to pay—the result is an upward shift in the demand schedule. The equilibrium quantity, as Figure 4.2(b) shows, is now identical to the needed quantity.

In addition to subsidies, a second strategy also involves intervention in the marketplace by an external agent, but is less direct than the implementation of producer or consumer subsidies. Simply, its premise is that the demand schedule will shift upward and to the right as personal income is increased; consumption will increase with an increase in general economic prosperity. Since it is assumed that financial barriers represent a major cause of underutilization of needed services, it can also be assumed that utilization, at least among the poor, will increase by redistributing wealth from the rich to the poor.

Unlike the subsidy approach in which direct incentives are provided to produce and consume a specific service, a redistribution of wealth does not *guarantee* that income redistributed to the poor will necessarily result in the utilization of the needed good or service. All of the increase, some, or nothing may be spent on basic needs, depending upon the preferences of each individual consumer. Economists call the percentage increase in consumption of a good or service resulting from an increase in income the *income elasticity of demand.* Although it will vary with one's income, the income elasticity of demand for most goods and services, even such necessities as housing, food, and health care is quite small, generally averaging less than 25 percent even for the poor. That is, on average we can expect that an increase in income of $1,000 will result in something less than an additional $250 being spent on, say, housing. If the income elasticity of demand is in fact 25 percent, then it will cost four times more using the indirect method of redistribution by cash transfers to induce the needed level of consumption of a specific service than it would were government to provide credits or in-kind services to those in need.

Note from Figure 4.2(b), however, what has happened to the total price (the price paid by the consumer *plus* the cost of the subsidy) under either the subsidy or income transfer strategy. Since no simultaneous alteration has been made in the supply schedule, the price has risen dramatically to P_n. This is the identical phenomenon that has created skyrocketing costs of many subsidized social welfare services. For example, with respect to medical assistance to the poor, Martin Rein and Hugh Heclo conclude:

> The dramatic increase in Medicaid is best understood as the natural outcome of increasing the chances for effective demand to be expressed, while failing to alter significantly the supply of medical services or to impose adequate constraints on the medical fees charged.[13]

The imposition of price controls will force the supply schedule downward and to the right thus creating, as Figure 4.2(c) shows, a lower price at the needed level of consumption (at least temporarily). In the social welfare enterprise, price controls are often implemented by specifying what particular service activities will be subsidized or funded by government or a third party, rather than directly controlling the price of each activity. Thus, government and the insurance companies may claim that certain tests, routinely taken upon admission to a hospital, for example, will no longer be reimbursed; the fewer the activities performed, the lower the price. Providers will doubtless argue, however, that not only is this an intrusion upon professional prerogatives, but that such controls ultimately lower the quality of the care provided.

If price controls are levied upon the specific activities performed, say the fee charged for a hernia operation, most providers will argue that the long-term effect will be one of decreasing the supply of services—fewer persons will enter the ranks of a price-regulated profession, less money will be spent upon the construction of facilities and the development of new technologies, and so on. This aspect of price controls should be of great interest to students of social welfare. If the long-term effect of price controls is that of decreasing supply—an argument made for years not only by the medical profession but by the petroleum industry as well—then the result will be the creation of black markets for controlled goods and services. The net effect will likely be a "different" set of higher quality services for those who can afford to pay the black market price—different service systems for the rich and the poor.

Government can also provide incentives to increase the supply of services, as for example in medical care, by increasing the supply of trained professionals through the construction of more medical schools. However, this may prove politically infeasible in light of professional vested interests and (contrary to the instantaneous flow of resources assumed in perfectly competitive markets) it takes time. The supply schedule can also be shifted downward if goods and services are produced more efficiently. Especially in labor intensive service industries, improvements in the efficiency with which services are delivered are difficult to come by, often involving in the case of the medical, legal, and social work professions, the introduction of paraprofessionals. Such strategies may, however, confront substantial resistance from professional traditionalists, they take time to implement, and they may *reduce* consumption if equivalent quality is not maintained.

Although the economics of need is a useful framework for assessing the implications of inducing alterations in existing patterns of supply and demand, particularly with respect to costs and who will bear those costs, it assesses only one dimension of the concept of need. Specifically, the problem with the economic view of need is embodied in the general character of economic theory itself: economic theory deals with consumer *wants* and *aggregate* consumption, not with the specific needs of individuals or communities and the manner in which they are defined. A perspective that does is the political economy of need.

THE POLITICAL ECONOMY OF NEED

Within a political-economic framework, need is seen as the basis for allocating scarce resources among members of society. In contrast to the psychological and sociological views, which focus respectively upon the intrinsic and cultural determinants of human need, the political economic perspective focuses upon need as a distributive concept, and social institutions are seen as existing to meet some defined set of human needs. According to J. A. Ponsioen,[14] the first responsibility of contemporary society is to meet the basic survival needs of its members; included in his list of basic survival needs are both biological and nonbiological needs. Within his view, each society or a dominant group in the society will identify a level of individual well-being below which no individual or group of individuals would be allowed to fall. Failure to achieve these levels of well-being, which continuously change over time, is attributable to a lack of access to needed goods and services by these disadvantaged groups.

In common discourse, *need* is used in two quite different ways. First, it has become common to speak of *individual* or *group needs,* the needs *of* minorities, of the elderly, of the poor, and so forth. A second usage is oriented to the identification of specific *consumption needs,* such as the need *for* food, the need for shelter, health care, day care, and many others. In analyzing need as a political-economic concept, it is useful to understand both dimensions, for what is needed by whom exists as a restatement of the classic political question, "Who is to get what?"

Implicit in the two dimensions of need is the existence of a set of causal relationships that link a particular service to defined categories of individuals. The variable through which causality flows is some condition or set of conditions calling for outside intervention in the life of the individual. It is common to refer to these conditions as "states of deprivation" or barriers to the achievement of individual and group well-being.[15] That is, there is a representative set of conditions or states of deprivation associated with ("caused by") being elderly, handicapped, or unemployed. There is also a representative set of conditions of interest to ("capable of being solved by") health care services, rehabilitative services, child care services and so on.

The second dimension of need, the need for goods and services, implies the existence of conditions best met by specific types of intervention. Thus, the *need* for medical care implies the *condition* of illness. While the existence of service organizations might be seen as a response or reaction to the identification of conditions requiring intervention, it is equally likely that the opposite is true, with existing service technologies, agencies, and programs serving as powerful forces in defining what conditions will call for intervention; in short, it is in the interest of the service organization to identify needs that are capable of being met within its menu of services.

It is the *institutional perception* of these conditions—how they are identified, how they are defined, how they are understood, and how they come to be labeled as problems requiring intervention—that creates the relationships between the two dimensions of need. The way in which conditions are perceived, as Perlman and Gurin have noted, will greatly influence policy and programmatic response. First, the perceived *magnitude* of conditions and needs can lead to an expansion or a contraction in the level of *existing* services; second, the condition may be interpreted as calling for the identification of a *new* need calling for a new type of allocation; or third, the condition may be interpreted as not being amenable to resolution via the provision of cash or service allocations to those in need, but as one calling for more fundamental institutional reform.[16]

Needs are *both* natural and created, the product of some set of mutual expectations existing between the individual and the collective. By itself, however, the presumed existence of a state of deprivation experienced by a group or an individual is insufficient basis for the identification of need; nor does the identification of need necessarily reflect a commitment to allocate resources to meet it. Still required are the political and organizational processes that permit its identification and that provide a legitimate rationale for resource allocation.

need identification

In developing the procedures, methodologies, and data bases that will permit the comprehensive assessment of need, we discover that the overall needs assessment process is comprised of two separate but interdependent activities—need identification and need enumeration. *Need identification* is the determination of those social, economic, and human conditions that are seen to call for some kind of organized intervention. *Need enumeration* is simply the process of counting the number of persons in need or the number of service units required to alleviate those conditions.

Although the general purpose of the needs assessment process is to guide the allocation of resources, one may identify four distinct ways its results may be incorporated into program decision making. First, the results may be used in the establishment of *priorities,* either among similar programs in different geographical areas, or among different programs in the same area. Second, when combined with estimates of service utilization, they provide a basis for determining *budgetary requirements.* Third, they can be used to aid *evaluation* of existing service programs. And fourth, they may provide a basis for improving interprogram and interorganizational *coordination.*[17]

THREE APPROACHES TO THE IDENTIFICATION OF NEED

The purpose of the needs assessment and the institutional setting in which it is conducted will determine which of three possible approaches will guide the initial identification of needs. Recall that the concept of need possesses two dimensions: needs of individuals and groups, and needs related to particular social allocations. Recall further that some human or social condition, some state of deprivation, is seen as the variable both rationalizing and linking together these two dimensions of need. As Figure 4.3 demonstrates, the three approaches to assessing need differ primarily in respect to which of these three orientations is adopted as a starting point, which in turn depends upon the type of agency or program for which they are conducted.

One possible orientation is concerned with the needs possessed by individuals or groups. These *client-oriented* needs assessments are generally undertaken by a program or agency that exists to promote the interests of specific subgroups of the larger population—for example, children, the elderly, or the handicapped. The process begins with a definition of a specific constituent group or a "population-at-risk," then identifies the problems prevalent within the group, and finally attempts to enumerate the level of specific services that will alleviate these problems.

A second approach, the *service-oriented* needs assessment, is generally conducted by an agency responsible for the provision of a particular service. Assumed given in the initial stages of the needs assessment is the existence of a service technology that is capable of resolving certain problems; for example, medical technologies are assumed to resolve health problems. At this point, decision makers will attempt to identify the populations-at-risk in which there is a high prevalence of such problems, and from the populations at risk enumerate the level of need for service.

While the client-oriented and service-oriented approaches to the assessment of need are useful for planning and evaluating the operations of existing agencies and programs, neither is able to provide the comprehensive perspective that is the prerequisite of systemwide, coordinated priority-setting, planning, and decision making. Agencies specializing in client needs are often able to promote more and better services for their

FIGURE 4.3

three approaches to the assessment of need

Service	Problem or Condition	Groups or Individuals
	Client-Oriented Needs Assessment	
	Service-Oriented Needs Assessment	
	Community-Based Needs Assessment	

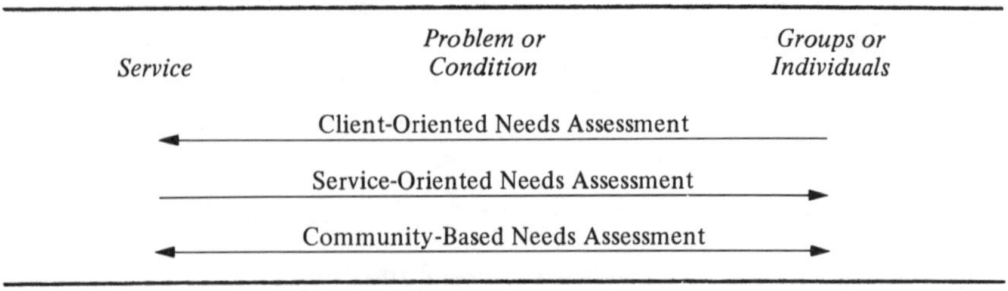

constituents, but they generally cannot further the integration of services for a variety of client categories. Even worse, agencies that provide specialized services often cannot concentrate upon the interrelationships of these to other services and agencies, and "services that are fragmented force the consumers to fragment their problems."[18]

The third approach, the *community-based* needs assessment, provides a solution to this dilemma but is the most general and most difficult to perform, for it reflects a synthesis of the client-oriented and service-oriented approaches. The community-based approach focuses first upon the total range of undesirable human and social conditions or *problems* existing within a geographical area, quite independently of any prior definitions pertaining to needy groups of people or needed types of services. Given these problems, the process is geared to determining the priorities of problem resolution, the size of the appropriate populations at risk, and the magnitude of services or interventions appropriate to the resolution of these problems.

To appreciate the significance of the needs identification process in the overall conduct of needs assessments, one must recall that beyond those basic requirements for physical survival, the definition of problems and hence needs are culturally and socially determined. Three primary factors, derived from its political and cultural history, appear to affect the definition and identification of acquired needs in the United States. First, needs must reflect conditions that can feasibly be altered within existing resource levels and technology; no agency or political jurisdiction will contract to do an impossible job. Second, the need must reflect some condition that the pluralist political process has identified as calling for organized intervention. And third, to ensure accountability, needs must reflect states or conditions that are capable of objective definition and measurement.

RESOURCES, TECHNOLOGY, AND THE IDENTIFICATION OF NEED

It is unlikely that human and social problems that do not *apparently* lend themselves to resolution by available technology and resources will be identified as needs. In fact, in the absence of apparently feasible methods of solution and an attendant level of expectations, many conditions will not even be labeled as problems. Consistent with former television newscaster Eric Severeid's frequent comment that "solutions create problems," consider yaws, a disease once rampant in much of the less developed world.

In many cultures yaws, which results in the entire body being covered by lesions by middle age, was considered an undesirable but inevitable aspect of the aging process. A technology of intervention, however, was available and immediately following World War II the World Health Organization initiated a vigorous campaign against the disease, which was rather easily cured by a single dose of penicillin. Only then was yaws considered a "problem" by the health care *institutions* of societies in which it previously had been considered merely one irreversible aspect of the human condition.[19]

Other examples abound, and the importance of technology as the *creator* of problems and needs becomes increasingly significant with each new technological development; this seems especially true in the health care field. One can easily imagine for example, that the need for genetic modification is not far off, provided that the technology is readily available and that it is politically propitious to use it.

THE POLITICS OF NEED IDENTIFICATION

Inquiry is a political process and the identification and definition of problems calling for organized intervention is the most important result of this process. Clearly, the conditions identified as calling for intervention and the way in which they are defined are prime factors in ultimately determining tentative solutions and needs.

Some problems, such as hunger, may call for organized community intervention on the basis of purely humanitarian grounds, at least in affluent societies such as our own. With other problems, such as illness, our lack of knowledge stipulates that we yield the definition of needs to the expertise of professionals. Still others, such as unemployment, may call for intervention to reduce the possibility of undesirable externalities, for example, crime, that may result from such conditions. Each of these is a substantive justification for the identification of problems that may ultimately lead to needs.

The identification of still other problems and needs may reflect the self-interest of groups or individuals who stand to profit by their resolution. They may reflect the interests of either the groups experiencing the problems—for example, the poor—or those organized interests in a position to provide solutions. One needn't be a cynic to marvel at the sound marketing strategy adopted recently by the Textile Workers Union of America in calling clothing a "major necessity of life" and asking that apparel be included in the food stamp program.[20]

In still other cases, the identification of needs will invite a clash between economic interests and those which are ideological in nature, as seems the case with current debate regarding day care. The day care services subsidized by some federal programs are formally justified in legislation as social interventions on the grounds that they will decrease unemployment among single mothers of young children. Such programs are obviously supported by those mothers and the potential providers of day care services as well. In vocal opposition to the idea of day care services to solve this problem is a group having no economic or professional interest in the issue of day care, but rather opposing it on the ideological grounds that it only contributes to the problem of family decay.[21]

Pluralist politics invokes no substantive rules for reconciling the myriad conflicts surrounding the identification of needs. Instead it depends upon the participation of individuals and groups having an interest in the identification, definition, and resolution of human and social problems. To ensure that the process is equitable, such groups must be given both the opportunity to organize and to participate. Regarding the former, it has been previously noted that large amounts of government funding have been made available to enhance the organization, and hence the opportunities, of disadvantaged groups. In the case of the latter, Title XX and many Office of Equal Opportunity programs require that substantial publicity surround the conduct of needs assessments and plans in order to ensure participation by those who stand to be affected by their results.

NEED IDENTIFICATION AND DEFINITIONAL CONSTRAINTS

In chapter 2 we saw that social program eligibility was confined to various categories of individuals. People were eligible for program allocations because they were poor, because they were disabled, because they were young, because they had been denied opportunities, and so on. We have also seen that much of the effort that attends the definition and redefinition of specific eligibility criteria, for example what conditions are to be considered disabling, is designed to achieve some degree of consistency and fairness in the assignment of individuals to either "eligible" or "ineligible" categories. Likewise the identification of abstractions like problems, conditions, and needs is constrained by the demand for consistency. Simply, if problems, conditions, and needs are to be the basis for more rational decision making, they must be defined in a way that permits the more or less objective assignment of individuals to the categories they define. Only if various definitional constraints can be satisfied can appropriate measures be developed and valid and reliable quantitative estimates of conditions and needs be made.

Viewed as an analytical process, the assessment of need involves two distinct steps. First is the identification and labeling of *qualitative* states of human and social existence that are considered important to individual and social well-being. As has been previously noted, these states tend to be defined as states of deprivation, or barriers to the achievement of individual or group expectations, and are the result of the political process and the expectations engendered by technology. For example, the lack of shelter, the lack of health, the lack of food, or the lack of income are all states of deprivation that could plausibly lead to the identification of human needs.

It is doubtful, however, that the truly difficult political decisions in any developed society will concern states of deprivation that are absolute. It is unlikely that the crucial decisions will pertain to anyone who *totally* lacks income, skills, health, and so on. Rather, the states of deprivation are generally identified in reference to some set of politically or professionally determined *standards* that define an *adequate* level of existence—adequate food, adequate shelter, adequate income. Thus, the second task in the analytical process of identifying problems is the establishment of a political, not a natural or biological, dividing line, often expressed in *quantitative* terms, between adequacy and deprivation. Indeed, what level of income separates those labeled as poor from the nonpoor, has been at the center of social welfare debate for years. The needs identification process merely extends this notion of a dividing line between adequacy and deprivation to a much wider range of human and social conditions and needs, many of which are even less susceptible to precise definition.

The decision to adopt formal, analytical methods for enumerating the conditions upon which estimates of need will be based forces decision makers to confront a number of common measurement problems. How they are resolved will directly affect the value of numerical results in planning and decision making. Generally, these issues concern the inevitable disparity between the meaning of a term, the information required, and the raw data available for analysis. In particular, C. West Churchman[22] has identified four problems that will be confronted in any measurement activity: the problem of language, the problem of specification, the problem of standards, and the problem of accuracy. The first three of these problems will affect a measure's *validity*, while the last refers to its *reliability*.

The problem of *language* is one of reconciling the need for precision in measurement on the one hand, and the equally important need to communicate the results to a variety of disparate groups and individuals on the other. Language is inherently imprecise; yet measurement requires precise definitions of the phenomenon under investigation. Inevitably there will be a disparity between the conceptual definitions used in popular discourse, those used by professionals and other experts, and those that will enable precise measurement. As has been argued with respect to the scientific and the professional communities, the problem of language can be overcome if the members of a group can agree on the meaning of an abstract concept.[23] In measuring and evaluating social conditions and problems, however, the large number of interested groups with different and continuously changing perspectives makes it virtually impossible to create measures that will enjoy universal acceptability as valid representations of the phenomenon under investigation.

Valid measurement of a human or social condition requires that the condition which is the subject of investigation be *precisely specified.* As an illustration of the importance of precise specification, consider two surveys of the sixties that were designed to determine the needs of the American elderly. Each was expressly concerned with determining the rates of "impairment" among members of the population classified as "elderly," defined in both surveys as those seventy-five years of age and older.[24] One study concluded that some 62 percent of those surveyed were limited in their normal activities, while the other concluded that the rate of impairment was only 30 percent. Both studies used the *same* abstract terms, "impairment," "limitation," and "capacity" in reporting their research findings, but each used *different* instruments for measuring these conditions. While the former relied heavily upon respondents' answers to questions regarding their impairment (for example, questions such as, "Are you able to walk to the bus stop?"), the latter study actually had survey participants undergo a series of physiological tests.

Undoubtedly the results of the two studies were different largely because they implicitly used different *definitions* of impairment, reflected in the different *measurement* instruments. The latter study conceived of impairment as a physical condition, while the former implicitly included in its measurement of impairment attitudinal and motivational factors as well. The physiological study was probably more objective, since it relied less on the subjective impressions of respondents. But unless we know whether the meaning of impairment is to include behavioral as well as physiological attributes, it is impossible to say which has the higher degree of validity.

To further develop the important idea of validity, consider a final examination score as a measure of your knowledge in a given subject area. A properly constructed examination should adequately measure knowledge and understanding in all aspects of the subject matter under study; it should also permit the instructor to determine, on the basis of some standard, whether or not a student possesses adequate knowledge of the subject matter. These two attributes of a well-constructed exam are, respectively, its *content* and its *criterion* validity.

Now apply the same analysis of validity to a common measure of a human or social condition that might give rise to the identification of needs. Family income, for example, is a common measure of poverty. But does income measure *all aspects* of the condition of poverty as it is generally understood? Does the measure possess a high degree of content validity? Probably not, because it measures only the condition's monetary aspects; it can tell us little about its *behavioral* implications: the poverty of health, the poverty of education and skills, the poverty of spirit. Second, does the measure possess criterion validity enabling one to accurately categorize families and individuals as "poor" and "nonpoor"? Can the measure be compared to a set of *standards* that allows the analyst to classify individuals and families as either "poor" or "nonpoor"? Again, probably not. While we may *politically* establish a "poverty line" we do so with little assurance that all those below the line are behaviorally "poor," while all those above are "nonpoor." As would be expected in the face of such uncertainty, different organizations and groups will invoke different definitions of the poverty line; and as of 1975, using different measures and different criteria, the measured number of poor in the United States ranged from 6.4 to 17 million individuals.[25]

Unfortunately there are no clear guidelines for assessing the validity of a numerical measure, because this depends so heavily upon the subjective interpretation or the meaning of the phenomenon in question. One approach then is to appeal to common sense; does the measure make sense intuitively? Another approach involves evaluating the measure in light of the prevailing theory surrounding the phenomenon; does the measure make theoretical sense? A third approach is to look at the behavior of the measure and to compare it with others that are supposedly measuring the same phenomenon; is it consistent with other measures? A fourth approach to assessing the validity of a numerical measure is to compare the predictions based upon it to actual occurrences; is the measure a good predictor?[26]

Even if the measure is valid, however, predictive accuracy also depends upon the *quantitative fit* between the measure and the phenomenon in question; this quantitative fit is referred to as the measure's *reliability*. The most important factor affecting the reliability of any measure is its sensitivity to changes or variability in the phenomenon of concern. Unlike validity however, which is extremely difficult to evaluate analytically, reliability can be evaluated and improved through the use of a variety of statistical techniques.

The principal factors affecting a measure's validity and reliability are shown in Figure 4.4. As the figure shows, a measure's validity will largely depend upon the group context in which it is used. Ideally, the measurement process is one in which the perceptions of all affected groups are somehow incorporated into a single measure or, more realistically perhaps, multiple measures of the same phenomenon. Yet measurement depends not only upon perceptions and analytical definitions, but upon the types of data available for analysis. Significantly, rather than responding to an ideal definition of a phenomenon, it is often the case that the data will *create* the measure. The dynamic between available data and the conceptual definition is especially critical in needs assessment research because

FIGURE 4.4:

validity and reliability in measurement

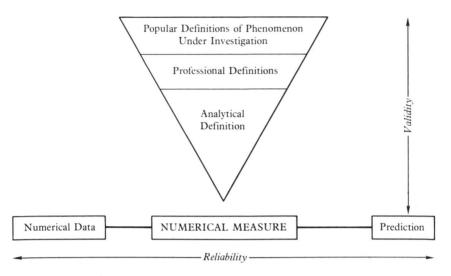

much of the most readily available data is collected and tabulated for purposes other than enumerating need.

need enumeration

Although it is common to speak of approaches useful in enumerating needs, the focus of these efforts is, in fact, upon the enumeration of *conditions* from which numerical estimates of needs will be derived. As we have seen, the identification and definition of a specific need reflects an (often implicit) assumption that by meeting that need, one will *also* alleviate an undesirable condition. It is entirely possible, however, that the same condition can be alleviated by meeting one of a large variety of different needs. The effect is that *needs cannot be measured directly;* instead one first enumerates conditions, one then establishes relationships between the various needs that if met will alleviate those conditions, and *then* one enumerates needs. Michael Scriven provides a useful illustration of the extremely important difference between measuring and enumerating conditions and the enumeration of needs.[27] He cites the example of illiteracy, a condition that is commonly measured by administering one of a variety of standardized literacy tests. One then counts the number of individuals scoring below some professionally established literacy norm to determine

119

the number in need. Technically, however, this approach is incorrect, for as Scriven notes, "Nobody has any *need* at all to score at norm level on a standardized non-functional literacy test."[28] Instead, he notes, one should look at all the reasons *why* people truly need to read. Said another way, individuals should look at the specific conditions that will be improved if a need is met—their mobility is improved because they are able to read maps and street signs; their safety is enhanced because they are able to read the word *poison;* their employability is enhanced because they are able to read blueprints, and so on. If it is determined that persons truly need to read the comics, a Harold Robbins novel, or the Greek tragedies, fine. The point is that we must understand the conditions that will be altered by meeting a specific need.

Often the relationship between conditions and needs is only implicit, but it is sometimes possible to determine its substance by noting *who* is conducting the needs assessment process and the sources of *data* used to generate numerical estimates. The four primary sources of data, each reflecting a distinct approach to enumerating needs, are: the participatory needs assessment forum, social indicators, community surveys, and utilization data derived from social service agencies.[29]

PARTICIPATORY STRATEGIES IN THE ASSESSMENT OF NEED

The conceptual difficulties in producing needs assessments that are based upon analytical definitions and hard data, not to mention the time and costs involved, are frequently surmounted by adopting one of two procedural, participatory strategies: the *key informant* approach and the *community forum* approach. Rather than emphasizing the generation of objective numerical data to achieve validity, the participatory strategies adopt what Karl Popper has called the "intersubjective" definition of objectivity[30] in which *agreement on the results of analysis* by affected individuals is the prime test of validity. The participatory methodologies thus rely upon the authority of persons, experts and nonexperts alike, to generate estimates of community problems and needs.

Both methodologies are conducted in a similar manner, the principal difference being that the key informant approach uses professional, provider, and other expert judgments to generate data, while the community forum involves a representative cross section of community members, attitudes and opinions. Clearly, a major disadvantage of the former is its built-in bias in favor of existing institutional arrangements, and although the key informant approach tends to be more structured in design than the community forum, George Warheit and others[31] have identified a number of activities common to both processes.

1. *The establishment of a steering committee* to guide the needs assessment process. Generally the committee should be comprised of professionals, providers, administrators, and informed citizens familiar with the community, the purposes of the needs assessment and, the uses to which it will be put. The committee will have responsibility for the following major activities.

2. *Determining the objectives of the needs assessment process* is the first task to be undertaken by the steering committee. Is it to be a simple preliminary inventory of community problems and needs, or is it to provide the basis for resource allocation, evaluation, or improved interorganizational coordination?

3. *Determining the format for gathering information* is the second task undertaken. In the key informant methodology, the information-gathering format generally centers around a questionnaire, whch deals with problems, populations-at-risk, and existing and required services. The community forum design is intended to encourage "spontaneity and candor on the part of participants,"[32] and is therefore less structured than the key informant approach.

4. *Determining who will participate* is the third task of the steering committee. In the key informant approach an attempt is made to select participants who reflect a variety of perspectives on community problems, services, and needs. The community forum methodology is purposely less structured in its means of selecting participants, calling for the widest participation possible and relying upon publicity and convenient meeting times to achieve this objective; it is the basis for needs assessments conducted on behalf of Title XX programs.

5. *Conducting the meeting and interpreting the results* are the fourth and fifth tasks of the steering committee. While the community forum approach does not discriminate against participation by professionals and service providers, experience suggests that while such individuals may attend the forum, their actual participation in discussion and debate may be minimal. Defensiveness or self-interest in maintaining the service status quo are human traits even among professionals, and nonparticipation seems to be a way of disguising these traits. Furthermore, the freewheeling, relatively unstructured format of the community forum approach may result in perspectives and metaphors that are alien to the professional's way of looking at things. Indeed, this is a valuable outcome of the forum, provided it can be translated into useful information for service providers.

The presence of providers or professionals may also detract from the purpose of the forum. Some individuals may be intimidated by the presence of "the experts," while others may focus upon the provider as the symbol of what's wrong with the world. The steering committee must also attempt to accommodate the fact that some individuals or groups are more polished in group situations; they have learned how to present an excellent case for *their* problems and needs. Again, this is often the case for service providers and professionals, vis-à-vis those whose livelihood does not depend upon their success in the politics of articulation, negotiation, and compromise.

A strategy that may overcome some of these difficulties and the inherent bias in the key informant approach is to adopt both participatory methodologies, in which the steering comittee or some other body acts in the role of interlocutor, mediating between the two processes and attempting to synthesize their often divergent results. A series of alternating meetings conducted in sequence—community forum, key informant, community forum, and so on—may ultimately result in the necessary degree of convergence upon problems and needs. Such a process, called *convergent analysis,* is based upon two key assumptions surrounding the assessment of need.

> First, no single set of stake holders or informants (i.e., administrators, program managers, advocacy groups, policy board members, clients, etc.) can offer a comprehensive view of the health and social needs of a particular community. Second, each methodology of gathering and assembling information will portray some unique aspect of the needs of a particular community or target group. Convergent analysis is thus perceived as a *dynamic process* of integrating information and perceptions generated by various needs assessors and methodologies over time to produce a constantly evolving portrait of conditions and needs.[33]

The idea of convergent analysis can be extended to help reduce the principal disadvantages of either of the two participatory approaches even if they are combined: the data are often impressionistic and not susceptible to systematic analysis, and there is little guarantee of their accuracy.[34] It is quite common in the participatory approaches, for example, to overestimate the level of need because of the simple accounting dilemma of double counting, the result of inconsistent definitions of problems, conditions, and needs. For this reason, it is useful to consider the participatory methodologies not as self-contained needs assessments in their own right, but as part of the larger convergent process that incorporates hard data and statistical methodologies as well.

SOCIAL INDICATORS

Broadly speaking, an indicator is an observable surrogate or symptom of something that cannot be observed directly.[35] IQ is an indicator of intelligence; grade point average is an indicator of learning; wealth is an indicator of personal well-being; Gross National Product is an indicator of national economic well-being; the height of a column of mercury is an indicator of temperature; and the population-at-risk is an indicator of the incidence of problems. Although not all indicators involve numerical measures (the color of litmus paper is an indicator of acidity), quantification does allow a rigorous basis for comparing various phenomena over time, from place to place, or from group to group.

A social indicator is a quantitative measure pertaining to certain aspects of a collective of individuals. To date, most social indicators have concerned phenomena and quantitative measures that are territorially or spatially defined—national indicators, metropolitan indicators, neighborhood indicators, and so on.[36] Indeed, we have already seen that such indicators are the basis for formulas used to allocate federal grant-in-aid funds to state and local jurisdictions.

The principal reason for adopting a territorial focus is certainly the ready availability of reasonably accurate and consistent spatial data from which quantitative measures and indicators can be developed. From census and other regularly collected data it is possible to construct a variety of statistical measures that characterize a defined geographical area. Among the most important for needs assessment research are the sociodemographic characteristics of a community, such as age distribution and the number of female heads-of-household; aggregate population characteristics, such as spatial distribution, population density and population mobility; additional characteristics of individual, social, and environmental well-being, including income distribution, housing, illness morbidity and mortality rates, crime rates, and pollution indices; and the spatial distribution of institutions, such as schools, churches, and hospitals.[37] A summary of phenomena of concern to most communities and the statistical measures that serve as indicators of these phenomena is shown in Table 4.1.

As Table 4.1 clearly demonstrates, social indicators are merely aggregate measures such as rates and averages that characterize a community and certain aspects of its total population. While all the indicators relate to problem areas, e.g., the unemployment rate, none specifically relates to the problems as experienced by selected individuals, e.g., the individual problems brought on by unemployment. This points out an often overlooked limitation of social indicators in needs assessment research. *By themselves, social indicators cannot be used to enumerate individual needs.* Rather they must be used in conjunction with other supporting data pertaining to individuals be they judgmental, derived from surveys, or from service statistics. The social indicator approach is an indirect means of enumerating need, and a critical assumption underlying the approach is that valid and reliable relationships can be established between the aggregate charac-

TABLE 4.1:

areas of social concern and selected indicators

Areas of Social Concern	Selected Social Indicators
Economic Base	Retail Sales: % per 1,000 population
Education	Number of seniors taking college board entrance exams (SATs) Average per pupil expenditures
Employment Opportunity	Occupational Distribution: Number and % of census tract heads of households employed in various job categories % of heads of households within census tract claiming no occupation Unemployment Rate: % of total work force
Health and Well-Being	Suicide Rate: Number of suicides per 100,000 population Communicable Disease Index: Number of cases of VD, TB, and Hepatitus reported per 1,000 population Infant Mortality Rate: Number of deaths of children under 1 year per 1,000 births
Housing	Vacancy Rate: % housing units in an area which are vacant or abandoned Median assessed value of single family units
Personal Income Distribution	Number of assistance payment welfare cases Number of Income Tax Returns Claiming Adjusted Gross Income: Under $3,000; $3,000 to $5,000; $5,000 to $10,000; $10,000 to $15,000; $15,000 or more
Pollution	% increase or decrease in concentration of particulate matter suspended in air % increase or decrease in concentration of atmospheric NO_2 and SO_2
Public Safety and Justice	Type I Crime Rate: Number of cases of murder, forcible rape, robbery, and aggravated assault reported per 100,000 population Type II Crime Rate: Number of cases of burglary, larceny ($50 and over), and auto theft reported per 100,000 population General obligation bond rating
Sense of Community	% voting in most recent local election compared to % voting in most recent state election Household Turnover: Number % census tract housing units with new residents
Transportation	% public street miles served by public transportation Number of traffic accidents per 100,000 population

Source: An Introductory Set of Community Indicators *(Austin: University of Texas, 1973), p. 3.*

teristics of a *collective* and the problems and needs of its *individual* members.[38]

Social indicators are of greatest value in helping to define successively refined populations-at-risk, which are smaller subgroups of the population in which certain social and human problems are likely to be concentrated. That is, we assume that the majority of these problems are not uniformly or randomly distributed throughout the entire population, but rather vary predictably from subgroup to subgroup. In general, the more detailed the specification of the problem, the more complex the set of characteristics that will define the population-at-risk. For example, if a problem is simply stated as "unemployment," the logically appropriate population-at-risk would be "all those members of the population who are of working age." If the problem is defined as "excessively high levels of unemployment," one might need to define populations-at-risk by multiple characteristics, for example, "black teenage males living in urban areas."

Note that the population-at-risk is a qualitative idea, involving the establishment of observable sociodemographic, geographic, and other population categories, that can in turn be related to defined problem categories. Quantification is achieved by enumerating the people, or if appropriate, the families, that fall within each of these categories. Statisticians would say that they determine the number of times or the *frequency* with which a statistical *event,* defined by the category, is found to occur. Each event may be defined in terms of various populations-at-risk, e.g., a "low-income family," or an "elderly individual"; or as problems, a "unit of unemployment," a "case of measles," or a "divorce."

Statistical relationships are established when the frequencies of two or more events are found to vary in roughly the same way. For example, the presence in neighborhoods of both high unemployment rates and large numbers of black teenage males, would give reason to suspect a relationship between that sociodemographic class and the problem, thus permitting one to identify the appropriate population-at-risk. Consequently, in formulating the experimental design that determines what data are to be collected, the analyst must consciously introduce variability into the data base, and this is done in one of two possible ways. The analyst may introduce variability by collecting the same data at the same time for different communities or different groups of people; this approach is called a *cross-sectional* or latitudinal analysis. Or the analyst may collect the same data for the same group or community over a period of time, yielding a *time series* or longitudinal analysis.

The most reliable source of social indicator data in the United States is that collected at ten-year intervals and updated periodically by the Bureau of the Census. For any Standard Metropolitan Statistical Area (SMSA) or community, census data will be collected, tabulated, and published (in tables and also on computer tapes) for a number of smaller geographic subdivisions of that community. Census tracts are the largest of these subdivisions, followed by block groups (contiguous city blocks having a combined average population of roughly 1,000) and blocks. In general, one can assume that the smaller the geographical subdivision, the more homogeneous its population. For every tract, block group, and block, some 900 data elements are available from the most recent 1970 census. An example of 40 such elements is shown in Table 4.2.

TABLE 4.2:
forty selected data elements from the 1970 census

Socio-Economic

% Population 45 and over with one or more years of college
% Population 45 and over with eight years or less of school
% Population 30 to 34 enrolled in college
% Families with income below $3,000
% Families with income between $3,000 and $7,000
% Families with income between $7,000 and $10,000
% Families with income between $10,000 and $15,000
% Families with income $15,000 and over
% Females 16 and over in labor force
% Labor force unemployed
% Employed in services and public administration
% Employed in construction and manufacturing
% Employed as professionals and managers
% Employed as clerical and sales workers
% Employed as skilled and semi-skilled workers
% Employed as service workers
% Employed as non-farm laborers
% Employed as farmers and farm workers

Demographic

% Population rural farm
% Population white
Mean household size
% Population 0 to 4 years old
% Population 5 to 17 years old
% Population 18 to 24 years old
% Population 25 to 44 years old
% Population 45 to 64 years old
% Population 65 years old and over
% Families with a female head with children
% Population 5 years and over in same house in 1970 as in 1965

Housing

% Housing units in structure built before 1940
% Housing units in structure built between 1950 and 1960
% Housing units with central heating
% Housing units with public water supply
% Occupied units with more than one person per room
% Occupied units with 4 to 6 rooms
% Occupied units owner-occupied with value $15,000 and over
% Occupied units owner-occupied with value under $15,000
% Occupied units renter-occupied with rent $100 and over
% Occupied units renter-occupied with rent under $100
% Housing units in 5-or-more unit structures

Source: Cited in Bureau of Governmental Research and Service, Oregon Social Area Classification *(Eugene: University of Oregon, 1977), p. 15.*

FIGURE 4.5:
a census map combining multiple population characteristics

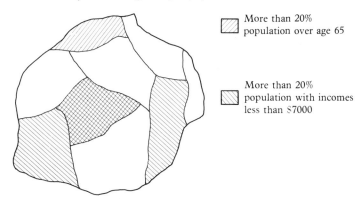

More than 20% population over age 65

More than 20% population with incomes less than $7000

Perhaps the easiest way to begin analyzing these and other cross-sectional data is to construct a map which pictorially summarizes the spatial distribution of population characteristics in the community. Such a map may reflect single population characteristics (e.g. the percentage of persons over sixty-five years of age in each tract, block group, or block) or it may reflect multiple characteristics. Multiple characteristics are easily presented using clear plastic overlays that incorporate a variety of symbols to denote specific characteristics of a geographic subunit. Figure 4.5 gives an example of this technique, combining an age characteristic with one of income.

The advent of high-speed computers, the availability of census data on computer tape, easily used "canned" programs or software such as computer graphics packages, the Statistical Package for the Social Sciences (SPSS) or Interactive Data Analysis (IDA), are largely responsible for the increasing use of social indicators and sophisticated statistical analysis in needs assesssment research and practice. The significance of these developments is that statistical techniques are able to reflect the complexity of many pressing social problems, but the danger arises that interpretation of the results will overstep the inherent limitations of the data and techniques. Recall that the method of social indicators is an indirect method of establishing the relationships between regional characteristics and individual characteristics that are essential to assessing need; they cannot, however, establish causality. One common problem with this approach is that correlations between aggregate statistical measures for a defined geographical area, sometimes called ecological correlations, need not necessarily reflect the characteristics of the *individuals* in those areas. A related problem, called *ecological determinism,* results from attributing the popula-tion characteristics to defined geographical areas. "While the spatial char-acteristics of an area obviously influence and limit the social conditions found in them, they do not determine what these *must* be."[39] Finally, most current indicators are simply too gross, too insensitive to permit the estab-lishment of reliable statistical relationships between indicators and human and social problems. They are too insensitive to permit reliable predictions of problems and needs. With few exceptions, given the current state of the art in social indicator theory and practice, it is probably best to consider them as just that: indicators of the *possible* existence of and interdependen-cies among problems, people, and needs.

COMMUNITY SURVEYS

Surveys represent the first of two sources of direct needs assessment data. Because they are geared to establishing information about *individuals,* community surveys avoid many of the limitations associated with the indirect social indicator approach. However, they tend to be much less general, less flexible, and far more expensive to perform than needs assess-ments conducted on the basis of aggregate indicator data.

Most surveys (with the notable exception of the census) are con-ducted for samples, subsets of the larger population of interest. Standard techniques of statistical inference are then used to infer characteristics of the larger population from those of the sample. The accuracy or reliability of statistical inferences drawn from surveys depends upon three major factors: sample design, sample size, and survey or questionnaire design. As with virtually all statistical approaches, increased levels of reliability or accuracy will be reflected in the increased time and expense of conducting the survey. Hence one must have some idea of the degree of accuracy required.

The reliability and validity of statistical inferences is directly affected by errors introduced into the analysis, and the two kinds of errors of general concern to statisticians are systematic errors and sampling or ex-perimental error. *Systematic* errors result from improperly designed statisti-cal studies; the most common of these in the conduct of surveys is a failure to achieve conformity between the sample and the population of interest. Hence, when inferences are drawn, they will apply to a population other than the analyst intended; the result is an invalid inference. The classic polling errors made during the presidential election of 1948 provide an excellent example of systematic errors introduced by an improper specifi-cation of the sample.

Truman won an election that the theretofore highly accurate pollsters had given to Dewey, and following the election the reason for the error was discovered. In performing their last minute survey of voters (most likely to reflect the way people will actually vote in the election) the pollsters had used telephone surveys. Unfortunately, in 1948 a large percentage of the American voting public, primarily those of lower income, did not own telephones; and that segment of the population was more likely to vote for Truman, the Democrat, than for the Republican. The pollsters thought they were taking a representative sample of the total voting public, when in fact they were sampling from the population of the voting public who owned telephones. In view of the continued popularity of telephone surveys, it is noteworthy to add that even today in some regions of the country as many as 20 percent of the population either do not own phones or have unlisted numbers.

In addition to problems of systematic error are problems of *sampling* or experimental error, error introduced by the inherent uncertainties in selecting individuals that are representative of the larger population. Since all legitimate sampling procedures involve some means of randomized selection, sampling errors are those that are caused by the "luck of the draw." In contrast to systematic errors, which are extremely difficult to identify and evaluate, the effect of sampling errors upon the reliability of statistical inferences can be predicted and to a large extent controlled by the appropriate sample design.

In theory, the most common method for controlling and predicting sampling error is through the technique of pure *random sampling,* a sample drawn in such a way that each and every individual in the population has an equal probability of being selected. In practice, however, it is extremely difficult to select a true random sample. The most important reason is that seldom can a community population be defined so that the analyst will know its total membership, a prerequisite for everyone's having an equal opportunity of being selected. Common population lists from which samples might be drawn—voter registration lists, property taxpayers, telephone listings, postal directories, lists of utility hookups (probably the best of the available alternatives)—seldom contain all persons in the general population. About the only thing the researcher can do is to try to avoid lists that it is suspected will introduce systematic errors into the survey.

Random sampling is used by many of the television rating organizations, which often survey a great many communities at fixed intervals by telephone. Unless there is reason to believe that people without telephones or those with unlisted numbers will have substantially different viewing patterns than those with phones, this method is quite reliable. At the time of the survey, they will simply tell their interviewers to telephone the "fourth listing on page 22 of the directory, the eighteenth listing on page 87," and so on, until the desired sample size has been achieved. Each of the numbers involved, the page number and the listing on the page, is selected randomly.

An easier approach, especially when population lists are long, is *systematic* sampling. This approach entails selecting individuals at fixed intervals on the list until the correct sample size is achieved. For example, if one wanted to select a sample of 100 from a population of 10,000, then he would select every hundredth person on the list. To ensure that bias is not introduced, it is common to randomly select the first person to be included in the sample.

There are a number of sample designs which attempt to control for sampling error and costs by controlling the elements to be included in the sample. The two most common methods are stratified and cluster or area sampling. *Stratified* sample designs attempt to control the types of persons included in the sample, if there is reason to believe that different types of people will respond differently. For example, a survey might be designed to discover attitudes about social welfare expenditures by local government. Since it could easily be presumed that one's income would have a significant effect upon the nature of the response, a stratified sample would be constructed such that the proportion of persons selected would reflect the income distribution of the community. The general procedure for constructing a stratified sample design includes: first, the stratification of the population into two or more subgroups defined by one or more characteristics (cross stratification); and second, randomly selecting a sample of persons from each of these strata such that the size of the samples is in proportion to the size of their respective strata.

A second controlled sampling procedure is *cluster sampling,* probably the most widely used method in marketing analyses and polling studies because of its relatively lower unit cost. Cluster sampling is a sequential sampling method in which a population is broken down into subpopulations, a number of these subpopulations is selected at random for further analysis, and then elements of these subpopulations selected at random. For example, if we were interested in obtaining a sample of high school teachers representative of all high school teachers in the United States, we might first randomly select a number of states. Within the states, we would randomly select a number of school districts; from the school districts, a number of high schools; and from the high schools, a number of teachers. Cluster samples that are based upon such geographically defined subpopulations are often referred to as *area samples.* Their lower unit cost is obviously a result of limiting the actual conduct of the survey to confined geographic areas.

There are a variety of additional sampling procedures that are often referred to as *nonprobability* or *nonrandom* samples. *Quota samples* often result when a stratified sample design is poorly implemented. Instead of randomly selecting individuals within a particular stratum, surveyors merely locate enough individuals to satisfy the proportionality requirements. In *haphazard sampling*, another nonrandom design, the interviewer merely finds enough individuals to reach the desired sample size. A good example is the sampling done by a TV reporter standing on a street corner and interviewing anyone (preferably someone articulate, representative, and interesting looking) who will talk to him about the latest public issue. While convenient, generally inexpensive, and frequently yielding interesting and plausible results, nonprobability sampling procedures do not lend themselves to formal techniques of statistical inference; there is no formal means for evaluating either the reliability or the validity of the generalizations that might be drawn from them.

A second major factor affecting both survey cost and reliability is the size of the sample selected. A fact that is often misunderstood is that unless population is quite small it is the absolute size of the sample that is important, *not* the percentage of the population surveyed. Using extremely careful design procedures, the Gallup and Harris polls have historically achieved remarkable levels of reliability nationally by sampling only a few hundred individuals (a very small percentage of better than 200 million people).

Needs assessment surveys are generally conducted for one of two purposes: (1) to estimate the number of problems or needs in the total population, or (2) to determine the existence of relationships having significance in the identification of problems and needs. An example of the first use would be to estimate the *number* of persons in need of financial counseling. The second is exemplified by surveys designed, for example, to establish the *relationship* between an individual's income and his need for financial counseling. The express purpose for which the survey is designed—estimating numbers or estimating relationships—will have a profound effect upon the size of the sample that must be selected to ensure reliable results, with the latter requiring a substantially larger sample. Note, however, that a survey designed to establish relationships is the type of instrument that would allow social indicators to be used in estimating need. These problems and opportunities are best illustrated with an example. Suppose that a simple survey instrument is designed to identify the relationships and interrelationships among race, income, sex, age, and the need for dental care. The questionnaire might look like that shown in Figure 4.6.

In this very simple survey instrument there are 320 possible questionnaire profiles or different sets of responses (4 categories of race multiplied by 4 categories of income multiplied by 2 of sex, and so on). Assuming that a sample of ten of each profile will yield reliable results (highly unlikely) and that sample design procedures will evenly distribute

FIGURE 4.6:

dental care need questionnaire

Race (check 1): Anglo_____; Black_____; Spanish-American_____; Other_____

Income (check 1): $0–3,000_____; $3,001–7,000_____; $7,001–11,000_____;

$11,001 +_____

Sex: (check 1): Male_____; Female_____

Age (check 1): 0–15_____; 16–30_____; 31–45_____; 46–60_____; 60+_____

Need for dental care (check 1): Yes_____; No_____

---

those interviewed across all necessary respondant categories (even more unlikely) then the minimum sample size dictated by this very simple questionnaire is 3,200! Even at the extremely nominal cost of $3 per individual (for $3 and some ready volunteers you *might* get a telephone survey) for interviewing, processing, and analysis, this questionnaire will cost nearly $10,000!

In addition to demonstrating why surveys can be so expensive, this example illustrates two additional points. First, when direct relationships are a desired outcome of the survey instrument, stratified sampling procedures are generally in order. This method is one way to ensure that the racial, income, and other characteristics of those interviewed will, in fact, be distributed equally across all questionnaire categories. Were these attributes not distributed equally, the sample size needed to ensure statistical reliability might easily have to be doubled or even tripled, resulting in a proportionate increase in survey costs.

The second point is that sample size and cost escalate dramatically when the questionnaire is made more complex. For example, if "diet" were included, as measured by, say, four categories of daily caloric intake, the sample size required and the cost of the survey would quadruple. Conversely, it might be determined that the existing questions are adequate, but that the categories for each response are too "fine." Although it would reduce reliability significantly, each question could be limited to two possible responses: "white," or "nonwhite," "less than $10,000 income" or "greater than $10,000 income," and so forth. While providing less elegant results, such a modification would reduce the required sample size and cost by a factor of ten. These possible changes in sample size and costs demonstrate a point that cannot be overemphasized: clearly define the purpose of the survey and use the successes (and mistakes) of others in determining the kind of information that is absolutely required and that the instrument is expected to yield.

A final consideration in conducting community needs surveys is the design of the survey instrument. This is more of an art than a science and the intricacies of that process will not be covered here in detail. Whether it is to be in the form of a questionnaire or some kind of physical test or examination, the way in which questions are phrased, the order in which they occur, and the degree to which they may rely upon the respondent's memory, for example, are significant factors that affect a survey's validity and reliability. These choices are best left to the experienced researcher who is versed in the art of survey design, but who is also aware of the specific purposes of the community needs survey.

In general, there are two types of survey schedule items or questions, the *open-ended* or unstructured and the *fixed-alternative* or structured schedule item. In open-ended survey instruments, as the name implies, no predefined pattern of responses is specified. A frame of reference is supplied by the interviewer, but few restraints are placed upon the length or content of the answers. The value of the open-ended questionnaire in community needs surveys is primarily confined to exploratory research, research conducted to determine the meaning and definition of human conditions and needs as expressed by individual respondents. Also, open-ended surveys are frequently used in conjunction with the community forum approach to assessing needs.

Because open-ended schedules are flexible and have possibilities of achieving great depth, a skilled interviewer is often able to probe, to clear up misunderstanding, and to make better estimates of the individual's beliefs, attitudes, and general state of being.[40] As an exploratory instrument, open-ended surveys may also lead to responses that suggest possibilities both of hypotheses and relationships not previously anticipated.[41] While valuable in exploratory research, open-ended schedules are extremely costly to perform, and because the answers so often lack uniformity, are difficult to analyze.

The structured questionnaire is the most frequently used survey instrument. Figure 4.6 demonstrates the primary characteristics of the structured survey instrument: all questions are posed in the same way to every respondent and the answers are limited to very specific possibilities. Because of uniformity in response, interviewers need not be as well trained as in the open-ended approach, and the analysis of both relationships and numerical estimates is far simpler and more amenable to traditional statistical procedures.

A final survey instrument that is of value in community needs surveys is the *funnel* schedule,[42] one that combines both unstructured and structured survey items. The funnel is an instrument designed to channel the initial response to an open-ended question to a single or related set of topics. Oftentimes, the "trigger" which determines how the channeling process is to be directed by the interviewer is the repeated use of a key word in the respondent's answer to an open-ended item. The following example will illustrate.

Q_1: "How would you describe your outlook on life?"

A_1: (The respondent mentions the word *depressed* several times during the answer to this open-ended question.)

Q_2: "Everyone feels depressed from time to time, you know—the kids, bills, the weather." (this is designed to put the respondent at ease) "How often do you feel depressed?"

A_2: (check 1): Always____; Daily____; Weekly____; Seldom____

Q_3: "Who do you talk to when you're depressed?"

A_3: (check 1): Spouse____; Family member____; Friend____; Other____; No one____

Q_4: (if "no one") "Would you like to have someone to talk to from time to time?"

A_4: (check 1): Yes____; No____ (If yes, a possible need for, say, counseling services has been identified.)

Clearly, the key to the use of the funnel approach in need surveys is the translation of the problem ("depression") into a solution and a need ("someone to talk to") and the appropriate service.

Other than relying upon general rules of survey design, the best guarantee of a useful, valid, and reliable survey (even one designed by an expert) is the pretest administered to a small sample of respondents. Although the pretest may add both time and expense, its cost is small compared to an untested, full-scale survey whose results are useless.

RATES-UNDER-TREATMENT

A fourth source of data for enumerating needs is that compiled by service organizations pertaining to their clients; these are often called rates-under-treatment data. As part of monitoring and intake procedures, most social welfare organizations will normally obtain and maintain records which include the following information: selected sociodemographic characteristics of clients, the problem or need, the service or services provided, the frequency or duration of the service, the source of referral, and possibly the outcomes of the intervention.[43]

As we shall see in a later chapter, such information is essential to sound management control and program evaluation. Because it reflects direct information about individuals, it can also provide a valuable source of needs assessment data, provided a number of major obstacles can be overcome. First, for obvious reasons such records may be considered confidential and therefore useful only in the conduct of an agency-based needs assessment. Unless a guarantee of complete anonymity and confidentiality is possible, it is unlikely that such records will be released to other organizations engaged in the assessment of needs.

A second major obstacle concerns the manner of record keeping in many social welfare agencies. Data are collected for purposes of accountability and management control, not the assessment of need. Generally, there is no standardized reporting system governing all agencies in the community, and as a result, the data categories will not be uniform from agency to agency. Moreover, many of the records useful in the assessment of need may not be easily accessible to agency employees, much less to outsiders. Rummaging through dusty files in the basement is a time-consuming means of gathering needs assessment data.

A third and final obstacle is conceptual; service records, obviously, pertain only to service users, not to the total need population. Substantial research has shown, moreover, that there are a great many differences between the characteristics of service users and those of the general need population.[44] That is, there is a great deal of difference between the statement, "Half our clients are elderly," and "Half the elderly in this community are in need of our service." There is no logical reason to believe that the latter necessarily follows from the former.

Nonetheless, is one can overcome the problem of confidentiality and design and maintain consistent, accessible records, rates-under-treatment data can provide an extremely valuable source of needs information. Especially if a convergent approach to needs enumeration is adopted, an approach that incorporates community and expert forums, social indicators, surveys, and rates-under-treatment data, the overall validity and reliability of the need enumeration process can be greatly enhanced. It is the development of procedures and methodologies for achieving this convergence that will likely determine the future value of the needs assessment process as the basis for allocative decisions in the social welfare enterprise.

the symbolic nature
of needs assessments

The espoused purpose of needs assessments is to provide a more rational basis for allocating resources among the various agencies, programs, and contending interests in the social welfare enterprise. At present, however, the needs assessment process must be seen as largely symbolic. In part, this is the result of an inadequate data base from which to estimate the number of persons in need, but more important is the indisputable fact that they have had no truly significant impact upon state and local decision making. The translation of conditions into needs that will be met by the enterprise is a political decision, and no amount of data and analysis can disguise the fact that—since they will help determine who is to get what—needs assessments are essentially political instruments.

Earlier in this chapter, four potential uses for needs assessments were identified: (1) to aid in the establishment of priorities, (2) to assist in determining budgetary requirements, (3) to provide a basis for evaluating the network of existing services, and (4) to assist in program coordination. Several years of experience with needs assessments under Title XX permit the drawing of tentative conclusions with respect to each of these functions.

Even if the data and necessary expertise are available, the needs assessment process provides no rules or procedures for determining needs priorities, a necessary activity since there are insufficient resources to meet all needs. Are decision makers to concentrate on conditions and needs that are found to occur at highest frequency, or those that are the most apparently "pressing"? If the latter, how do they assign weights to indicate the relative importance of different needs? And even if they can, political and bureaucratic inertia must still be overcome because any systematic attempt to investigate and to assign priorities among the total range of needs of the population will generate resistance and "hostility on the part of the program managers, providers, and advocacy groups . . . since this is often seen as a possible threat to the status quo."[45]

To be useful in evaluating the existing network of services, it is common to focus upon "unmet" needs, needs currently unaddressed by existing programs. The approach proceeds as follows: first, identify and enumerate conditions and needs; second, assess available resources; third, compare needs and resources and identify the "gaps" or unmet needs; fourth, establish priorities among the unmet needs; and fifth, allocate resources accordingly.[46] But there are many possible needs and only limited resources, and "in actual practice, . . . agencies are thrown into the position of assessing only partial needs—those that are covered by categorical programs."[47] Indeed, in this use of needs assessments, one never even confronts the problem of setting priorities; "stranded on its first step, the 'gap' model is interesting but of little use."[48]

In program planning and coordination, the needs assessment process fares a bit better; indeed, it is considered by state and local decision makers the most positive impact of the needs assessment process under Title XX.[49] This does not mean the needs assessment process actually results in the establishment of linkages among programs, but rather the process helps identify those programs that should be linked. When an agency or a program is forced to announce, "These are the conditions and needs that we see as important, and this is how we intend to address them," it is, in effect, "positioning" itself in the total realm of service programs. This positioning, we have previously seen with respect to UWASIS, helps to identify sources of duplication, overlap, and programs whose activities should be coordinated.

Needs assessment procedures may be useful in forecasting the future need population and, hence, for estimating future budgetary requirements; normally, these use a defined population-at-risk as the basis for generating forecasts. The model (usually a time series model developed from historical data) might indicate, say, that a ten percent increase in the population-at-risk will result in a five percent increase in the number of needy individuals; with estimates of a future population-at-risk one is then able to estimate the future need for services. Knowing the per-unit service cost, one is then able to estimate future budgetary requirements. Most human and social problems, however, arise from a complex series of factors that are poorly understood, factors that because of poorly developed theoretical explanations and the lack of an adequate data base are not usually reflected in the population at risk upon which the forecasts are based. That is, simple populations-at-risk—"the number of children" for example—are used to forecast the incidence of problems with complex causes, for example child abuse. The most frequent result is highly unreliable forecasts. But there is an even more fundamental barrier to using needs assessment techniques as a budgetary tool.

Budgetary allocations, as we shall see in a later chapter, are usually but incremental changes upon the previous year's level of funding; they are not based upon newly identified need or newly assigned priorities. Dramatic increases in needs are more often indicative of an "overzealous" needs assessment process than the existence of needs themselves. In the case of Title XX, moreover, a federally imposed ceiling upon grants to the states for social services, and the fact that most states have long since reached the limits of their formula allocation, mean that the needs assessment process merely helps the states maintain—not alter—their federal funding status quo.

Is it possible to go beyond the symbolism inherent in the needs assessment process? Is it possible to transcend the idea that the only purpose of needs assessments is to make social welfare decision making *appear* economically and administratively rational, not the object of the meandering, apparently aimless push and pull of a pluralist, political rationality? Probably not, but this does not mean that the process is worthless from a decision-making standpoint. In particular, the needs assessment process can provide a structure for problem solving in the social welfare enterprise, a structure that forces decision makers to clarify the problems and conditions to be addressed and the crucial assumptions underlying the strategies to be used in their resolution. Wayne Kimmel, for example, suggests as a first step in any needs assessment process the preparation of an "issue paper" in which are addressed in tentative terms:[50]

*The structure of the human or social problem

*Likely causes or sources of the problem

*Identification of the population at risk

*Objectives that might be achieved were the problem alleviated

*The identification of evaluative criteria that would indicate progress toward alleviating the problem

*An overview of existing programs—public and private—currently focusing on the problem, including an assessment of their cost and effectiveness

*Identification of major constraints that might limit problem alleviation

*Identification of major data and analytical barriers to better understanding of the problem, and a general outline—including cost and time estimates—of desirable analysis.

The approach taken here is significant, because it does *not* pretend to *replace* the political rationality of social welfare decision making with the analytic rationality of needs assessments. Rather it is designed to supplement it by focusing the decision maker's attention upon areas of disagreement among different perceptions of important conditions and needs and the gaps in information, which if eliminated, would promote community consensus regarding desirable directions of program change.

notes

1. Norman A. Polansky, "Research in Social Work," in *The Encyclopedia of Social Work,* 16th Issue, Vol. 2 (New York: National Association of Social Workers, 1971), 1,100.

2. United Way of America, *UWASIS: A Taxonomy of Social Goals and Human Service Programs* (Alexandria, Virginia: United Way of America, 1972). The emphasis upon need was more pronounced in this version of UWASIS than in the later version, *UWASIS II* discussed in chapter 1.

3. Wayne A. Kimmel, *Needs Assessment: A Critical Perspective* (Washington, D.C.: Office of Program Systems, Office of the Assistant Secretary for Planning and Evaluation, Department of Health, Education and Welfare, 1977), p. 3.

4. Clyde Kluckhohn and others, "Values and Value-Orientation in the Theory of Action," in *Toward a General Theory of Action,* eds. Talcott, Parsons and Edward A. Shils (Cambridge: Harvard University Press, 1951), p. 418.

5. Abraham Maslow, *Motivation and Personality* (New York: Harper and Row, Pub., 1954), pp. 80–106.

6. The universal hierarchy of needs is of course merely a way of looking at human well-being; its existence has never been proven emphatically.

7. Alfred J. Kahn, *Social Policy and Social Services* (New York: Random House 1973), pp. 61–63.

8. John B. McKinlay, "The Help-Seeking Behavior of the Poor" in *Poverty and Health,* eds. John Kosa and Irving K. Zola (Cambridge: Harvard University Press, 1975).

9. Cited In Ibid., p. 230.

10. Cited In Ibid., p. 231.

11. Cited In Ibid.

12. Armen Alchian and William Allen, *University Economics,* 3rd ed. (Belmont, Calif.: Wadsworth, 1972), p. 67.

13. Martin Rein and Hugh Heclo, "What Welfare Crisis?," *The Public Interest,* no. 33 (Fall 1973), 63.

14. J. A. Ponsioen, *Social Welfare Policy: Contributions to Theory,* Publications of the Institute of Social Studies, Series Major, Vol. 3 (The Hague: Mouton & Co., 1962).

15. Brian D. Jones and Clifford Kaufman, "The Distribution of Urban Public Services," *Administration and Society,* 6, no. 3 (November 1974), 346.

16. Robert Perlman and Arnold Gurin, *Community Organization and Social Planning* (New York: John Wiley, 1972), p. 172.

17. George J. Warheit, Roger A. Bell, and John J. Schwab, *Planning for Change: Needs Assessment Approaches* (Washington, D.C.: National Institute of Mental Health, undated), *passim.*

18. Robert M. Moroney, "Needs Assessments for Human Services," in *Managing Human Services,* eds. Wayne F. Anderson, Bernard J. Frieden, and Michael J. Murphy (Washington, D.C.: International City Management Association, 1977), p. 139.

19. Personal correspondence with J. L. DeVries, M.D., former Assistant Director of Health Services, South-East Asian Regional Office, World Health Organization.

20. *Christian Science Monitor,* Feb. 3, 1975, p. 50.

21. B. Bruce-Biggs, " 'Child Care': The Fiscal Time Bomb," *The Public Interest,* no. 49 (Fall 1977), 101.

22. C. West Churchman, "Why Measure," in *Measurement: Definition and Theories,* eds. C. West Churchman and P. Ratoosh (New York: John Wiley, 1959), pp.83–94. See also John P. Van Gigah, *Applied General System Theory* (New York: Harper & Row, Pub., 1974), Ch. 6.

23. Thomas S. Kuhn, *The Structure of Scientific Revolutions,* 2nd ed., (Chicago: University of Chicago Press, 1970).

24. Moroney, "Needs Assessments for Human Services," pp. 142–43.

25. John Bishop, "The Welfare Brief," *The Public Interest,* no. 53 (Fall 1978), 175.

26. Fred N. Kerlinger, *Foundations of Behavioral Research,* 2nd ed., (New York: Holt, Rinehart & Winston, 1967), pp. 467–72.

27. Susan Salasin, "Exploring Goal-Free Evaluation: An Interview with Michael Scriven," *Evaluation,* 2, no. 1 (1974), 9–16.

28. Ibid., 9, emphasis added.

29. Warheit and others, *Planning for Change.*

30. Karl Popper, *The Logic of Scientific Discovery* (New York: Science Editions, 1961), pp. 32–33.

31. Warheit and others, *Planning for Change,* pp. 27–38.

32. Ibid., p. 33.

33. Minnesota State Planning Agency, *News Assessment: A Guide for Human Service Agencies* (St. Paul: Minnesota State Planning Agency, 1977), p. 11.

34. Warheit and others, *Planning for Change,* p. 38.

35. Mario Bunge, "What Is a Quality of Life Indicator?" *Social Indicators Research,* 2, no. 1 (1975), 66.

36. Karl A. Fox, *Social Indicators and Social Theory* (New York: Wiley-Intersciences, 1974), p. 104.

37. Warheit and others, *Planning for Change,* p. 48.

38. Ibid., p. 47.

39. Warheit and others, *Planning for Change,* p. 59.

40. Kerlinger, *Foundations of Behavioral Research,* p. 484.

41. Ibid.

42. Ibid.

43. Warheit and others, *Planning for Change,* p. 41.

44. Ibid., p. 45.

45. Peter S. O'Donnell, *Social Services: Three Years after Title XX* (Washington, D.C.: National Governors' Association, Center for Policy Research, 1978), p. 39.

46. Kimmel, *Needs Assessment,* p. 56.

47. Ibid.

48. Ibid., p. 57.

49. O'Donnell, *Social Services: Three Years after Title XX,* p. 40.

50. Kimmel, *Needs Assessment,* pp. 62–63.

The provision of access to services reflects a primary strategy through which social policy is implemented. This chapter explores the multitude of societal values, perspectives, assumptions, institutional arrangements, and administrative techniques that together conspire to make access among the most complex and controversial of topics in social program administration.

Access strategies are invoked in an attempt to control who utilizes what services. If services are to be distributed to all citizens the problem is said to be one of achieving universal access. Conversely, and more typical of American views of social welfare, access may also be seen as a problem of selectively distributing goods and services to individuals meeting one or a variety of eligibility or need criteria.

Fundamental to controlling either universal or selective access systems is an understanding of factors that comprise an individual's propensity and ability to seek assistance in the morass of programs, organizations, and services that define the social welfare enterprise. Service utilization is seen as a process within which the potential user encounters a series of barriers, which must be overcome if the search for assistance is to be successful. The management of access involves the selective manipulation of each of these barriers in an effort to match the right service to the right person at the right time.

assessing barriers to utilization: the problem of access

5

Thus far, need has been discussed as an allocative concept, and the philosophy of need and methods of conducting the needs assessments which together provide a rationale for these allocations have been outlined. It is important to emphasize that to this point the perceived existence of a need, even if it has achieved the stature of a legal right to services, may but reflect an *intent* to allocate resources. Still required is a means of ensuring utilization by those in need, of providing access to goods and services. If need is an abstract political statement of who is to get what, then access refers to the structures, processes, programs, and institutions for meeting those needs. Access ultimately concerns all those factors that affect an individual's utilization of a particular service or benefit, and the number of strategies that might be invoked to manage this complex set of psychological, sociological, economic, and physical variables is virtually endless.

A state welfare department finds that its budget is insufficient to meet the needs of all potential users of child care services, and responds by "tightening up" on eligibility requirements.

The Department of Health, Education and Welfare initiates an extensive television campaign to inform senior citizens of their right to social security benefits.

A local not-for-profit agency receives a grant from the federal Urban Mass Transit Administration to establish a dial-a-ride bus system for the elderly and the handicapped.

A large city government initiates a well-publicized, vigorous campaign to cut down on the numbers of welfare cheaters in the ranks of service users and providers alike.

A local government establishes an information and referral center designed to help its citizens cut through the bureaucratic maze of red tape surrounding the delivery of social services.

A health maintenance organization initiates a screening procedure for separating the "worried-well" and others without need from potential users with symptoms of actual illness; at the same time one of the largest medical care insurers initiates a publicity campaign designed to reduce the number of unnecessary visits to the doctor.

A state welfare agency establishes a voucher system for providing homemaker services to the elderly.

A local counseling center hires a Spanish-speaking American to provide outreach services to members of that ethnic community.

All of these represent but a small sample of the many possible strategies for managing access, of purposefully erecting and removing barriers to individual utilization patterns in an attempt to match the right service to the right person at the right time.

understanding
the problem of access

Originally established as a price subsidy device to assist farmers (it is still administered by the U.S. Department of Agriculture) as well as an effort to assist the poor, the food stamp program is one of the federal government's "Big Three" welfare programs (along with Aid to Families with Dependent Children and Medicaid), distributing nearly $4.5 billion in benefits during 1975.[1] Significantly, the food stamp program was the first of the major governmental transfer programs to include the working poor;[2] persons in households not receiving public assistance (welfare) are also eligible.

Eligibility to participate in the food stamp program is determined using a complex set of means-tested criteria including family income (adjusted for some necessary expenditures for medical expenses, shelter, and fuel costs), assets, and family size (by law this maximum entitlement must be changed every six months to account for inflation). As family income increases the monthly allotment of food stamps declines.

Recently, the U.S. General Accounting Office initiated a study of *errors* in the administration of the food stamp program. Among the significant findings of a six-month survey of participating households not also receiving public assistance were: 18 percent of participating households were actually found to be ineligible for food stamps; 11 percent of those who were eligible were overcharged for the stamps; 26 percent of those who were eligible were actually undercharged; and 7 percent of the eligible were improperly and completely denied benefits.[3] Lastly and most important in terms of its magnitude, the Senate Select Subcommittee on Nutrition estimated that in 1975 of the 38 million eligible households, only 19 million (50 percent of those eligible) were actually participating in the program.[4] The problem is not confined only to the Food Stamp program, but is characteristic of a large number of publicly funded social programs. The Social Security Administration, for example, estimated that in 1974 fully half of the elderly poor who were eligible for Supplemental Security Income benefits failed even to apply.[5]

From these and similar studies, one can see that administrative errors involving social program allocations are expressed in two different ways, either as errors in determining *benefit levels* or errors in *utilization*. If one centers on benefits that are less or greater than those allowed by law, one must consider internal administrative techniques for correcting those errors—better control over benefit determination. If, on the other hand, one focuses upon errors in utilization, one is forced to confront the interaction of human beings and organizations from a much broader perspective, allowing for the total range of factors—not simply eligibility criteria—that can influence the process of service utilization. This is the dilemma of providing and managing access to services.

A MODEL OF SERVICE ACCESS

At the most general level, the problem of managing access to services can be seen as one of achieving a correct match or, in analytical terms, congruence between two sets of individuals, the set representing the target or need population and that representing the population that actually utilizes the needed service. Perfect congruence, or a total overlap between the two sets, is indicative of a perfectly effective, or as it is sometimes called, a perfectly target-efficient access system. Typically, however, there is both a quantitative and a qualitative discrepancy between the two sets as shown in Figure 5.1; that is, the sets are of different size, and they contain different individuals.

Four distinct subsets of a total regional population, each an output of the broadly defined access system, are apparent in the Venn diagram description of Figure 5.1.

FIGURE 5.1:
the relationship between the need and user populations

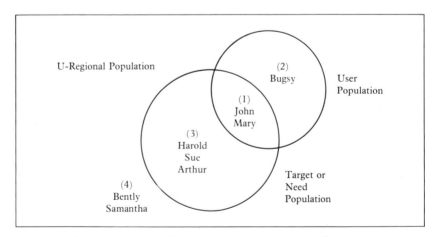

Source: Bruce L. Gates, "A Model of Service Access," in Managing Public Systems: Concepts and Methods, *ed. Ross Clayton and others © 1980 by Wadsworth, Inc., Belmont, Ca. 94002. Reprinted by permission of the publisher, Duxbury Press.*

1. The subset of the total population, John and Mary, that is determined to need and also utilizes the service. With respect to these two individuals, the access system is functioning properly. (region 1)

2. The subset of the total population, Bugsy, that does not fall within the defined criteria of need, but that utilizes services. (region 2)

3. The subset of the population, Harold, Sue, and Arthur, that falls within the defined criteria of need, but does not for any number of reasons utilize the service. (region 3)

4. Finally, the subset of the total population, Bentley and Samantha, that neither needs nor utilizes the service. (region 4)

The first thing that should be apparent from the figure is that a *quantitative* difference exists between the need and user population; the two sets are not the same size. Five persons are in need (John, Mary, Harold, Sue, and Arthur), but only three actually utilize the service (John, Mary, and Bugsy).

The figure also depicts a *qualitative* difference in the need and user populations as well. As is shown, only a partial overlap will generally exist between the need and user populations for a given service or program, resulting in two possible types of *access error*. The first of these errors, *underutilization*, results from the failure of some individuals in the need population (Harold, Sue, and Arthur) to utilize the service. In cases where service capability exists, such underutilization is a primary cause of what are called *unmet needs*.

A second error in access is *overutilization;* the utilization of services by persons not needing them, in this case the unit of service utilization represented by Bugsy. Although sometimes associated with "ripping off" the welfare system, overutilization does not necessarily involve malice of intent. It may be, as currently seems the case with medical care utilization patterns, that individual expectations of service capabilities and individual perceptions of need simply differ from those held by professionals or other groups charged with identifying and defining the appropriate user population.[6] That is, *expressed needs,* which are the product of individual perception and motivation, may differ in definition from those that the program is formally charged with satisfying.

With respect to this example, it is easy to see that the access system is not particularly effective at matching services to needs. Only 40 percent (John and Mary) of the need population actually utilize the service, and fully 33 percent of the users (Bugsy) are found not to be in need of the service. These results can be combined into a useful quantitative index of access effectiveness as given by the following:

$$\text{Index of access effectiveness} = \frac{\left(\begin{array}{c}\text{number of individuals in}\\\text{need who also utilize}\end{array}\right) - \left(\begin{array}{c}\text{number of}\\\text{overutilizers}\end{array}\right)}{\text{total number in need}} = \frac{2-1}{5} = 20\%$$

Suppose that service administrators were to initiate a set of strategies designed to improve the operation of the access system, strategies that will be discussed in some detail later in this chapter. The result of these modifications in the access system is that Sue and Arthur now become service users, but the strategies are still ineffective in eliminating Bugsy's overutilization. It can be seen that these new access strategies result in a threefold increase in effectiveness, the new value given by:

$$\text{Index of access effectiveness} = \frac{4-1}{5} = 60\%$$

Finally, it should be noted that 100 percent access effectiveness can be achieved only if Harold is encouraged to utilize and we can somehow eliminate Bugsy's unit of overutilization. The simultaneous elimination of under- and overutilization errors is the essence of selectively managing access to services.

Associated with the management of the access system are three basic costs. First are the *costs of underutilization,* the costs associated with a human or social problem not resolved (or an entitlement denied) because the access system incorrectly filtered out a needy individual. The costs of underutilization are borne by the needy individual and the society at large. Second are the *costs of overutilization,* opportunity costs or potential individual and *societal benefits foregone* because available resources were not expended more productively, presumably on behalf of those in genuine need. Overutilization costs are borne by needy individuals denied benefits and society at large. And third are the *administrative costs* or the costs associated with selectively stimulating or retarding program utilization with reference to some definition of need—the costs of manpower, transportation, information systems, judicial proceedings, and so on. These costs are borne by society at large (in the form of increase agency and program budgets) and the seeker of services.

Although the behavior of these costs is poorly documented, note in particular that the costs of underutilization are the most abstract; unlike overutilization and administrative costs they involve no direct expenditure of funds, but are merely imputed as the costs of unresolved problems. Note as well that the three elements of cost are highly interdependent. It is probably true, for example, that if administrative costs and efforts increased, both under- and overutilization errors and their associated costs could be reduced. It is also probable that the errors and costs associated with under- and overutilization are, for a given access system, inversely related, requiring that decision makers make tradeoffs among them. That is, unless the prevailing access system is dramatically changed, a reduction in overutilization would probably result in an *increase* in underutilization and vice versa.

While we may generally identify who bears the costs associated with the two access errors, their true magnitude is unknown. Disregarding the compelling argument that access to public services by those entitled to them is a right and not a decision to be made on a crude benefit-cost calculus, we can nonetheless assume (given the statistics cited at the beginning of this chapter and given that underutilization costs are but abstractions) both policy makers and the public probably see the costs associated with overutilization as higher than those of underutilization. Given prevailing attitudes regarding the monetary costs of social programs—costs that would dramatically increase were errors in program underutilization rectified—the creation of access systems systematically biased in favor of reducing overutilization appears to be the way in which the enterprise is forced to resolve the likely tradeoffs between the costs of utilization, underutilization, overutilization, and administering the access system.

SOURCES OF ACCESS ERRORS

In general, the lack of perfect congruence between the need and user populations may be attributed to one of two principal causes. First, if social institutions are seen as responsive to the changing preferences and needs of citizens, and if they are seen to derive from individualistic precepts such as those underlying the definition and behavior of "economic man," then a lack of congruence *must* be attributed to an improper specification of needs by professional and other societal groups acting on behalf of the individual. Within this view, people are seen to consume or utilize only what they want and not what they are said by others to need, and the definition of need and the need population must be made consistent with these individual wants if perfect congruence is to be achieved.

If, on the other hand, one views the lack of congruence from a collective perspective, one in which it is legitimate for some authority—professional, governmental, or otherwise—to determine both the purpose and pattern of individual consumption in the interests of the collective, then a lack of perfect congruence must be attributed to incorrect consumer behavior. For whatever reasons—fear, ignorance, physical immobility, insufficient income, or simply the disinclination to consume what they are said by others to need—people are not consuming the goods and services that others think they should consume. Strategies must be developed to alter this behavior; access to goods and services must be improved.

The middle ground between these two polar extremes derives from the United Nations' "mutual adjustment" model of social welfare. Within this view some synthesis of institutional responsiveness to human desires and control over those desires can be effected through the interplay of political and economic forces. For example, with respect to professionally defined health care needs, William Shonick conceives of this mutual adjustment process as follows:

> Wants are to be considered equal to needs in the long run. Either the consumer is to be educated to utilize the professionally determined needs or the professional will have to take into account consumer wants that were overlooked in the formulation of the needs standard.[7]

the process
of service utilization

The most important question that arises from the preceding discussion is, "Why?"—why do some individuals utilize a particular service or benefit and why do others fail to utilize certain services even when in need? While empirical research has provided us with few clear-cut answers to this question,[8] significant insight can be gained by adopting a view that help-seeking behavior, whether directed toward universally or selectively provided services, is a *process* comprised of a series of barriers to be overcome if the individual is to utilize a needed service.[9] Ideally, such barriers should function in such a way that service utilization by individuals not in need is retarded or eliminated while not preventing utilization by those possessing legitimate needs. Were this the case, our elusive goal of perfect target efficiency or perfect congruence between the need and user populations would be achieved.

John McKinlay has noted that service utilization behavior has been analyzed from at least six different perspectives in an attempt to isolate specific factors that might explain variations in utilization from individual to individual and from group to group.[10] These six perspectives emphasize economic variables, sociodemographic characteristics, geographical variables, social psychological variables, sociocultural variations, and the characteristics of the organized social service delivery system. What is clear from McKinlay's research is that no single perspective, no single set of variables, can fully explain why certain people utilize and others don't utilize social services. Rather the utilization process is affected at some point or another by factors emanating from all of these (and doubtless many other) dimensions of a person's life. With the exception of organizational variables, which will be discussed in greater detail shortly, McKinlay's six perspectives have been combined and reorganized somewhat to generate the comprehensive model of the service utilization process shown in Figure 5.2.

As is shown in Figure 5.2, the process of service utilization may be

FIGURE 5.2:
the service utilization process

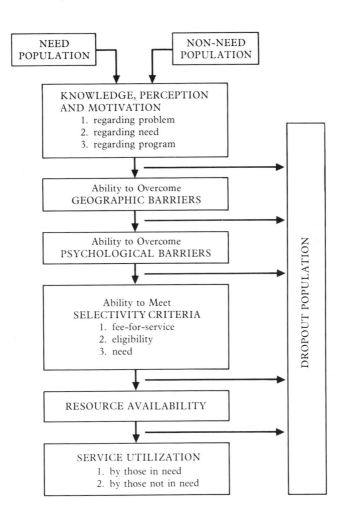

viewed much like the progression through the grades at school. Due to the existence of a variety of barriers (quizzes, papers, final examinations, grades, etc.) not all students who matriculate will graduate; some will drop out at various grades along the way. Similarly, not all individuals possessing a need or desiring to consume will ultimately utilize a service, and although the factors by which the utilization process may be described are highly complex, Figure 5.2 suggests five pertinent barriers to service utilization: (1) knowledge, perception, and motivation; (2) geographic barriers; (3) psychological barriers; (4) barriers created by the existence of various selectivity criteria; and (5) the availability of resources. While the sequence of barriers encountered cannot be considered necessarily the same for all individuals (i.e., psychological barriers may be confronted before geographical barriers), the model is a useful device both for understanding the myriad and complex factors that underlie the service utilization process and for providing a framework within which to better understand the alternative administrative strategies that might be invoked to alter and to control that process.

KNOWLEDGE, MOTIVATION, AND PERCEPTION

Possibly the most significant yet poorly understood of the barriers to service utilization is labeled here "knowledge, perception, and motivation." Its significance is twofold. First is the obvious fact that to utilize a service, any service, the individual must be motivated to do so, and a principal factor in this motivation is the perception that the individual possesses a problem that he or she cannot solve without outside assistance. Second is the problem of selection; once the decision to seek assistance has been made, where should one turn to obtain it?

Fundamental to the discipline of social psychology is the idea that motivation—the desire to adopt purposive behavior—predetermines the way we perceive our surroundings. If a person is motivated in the achievement, of, say, good health for him and his family, he is likely to perceive a wide variety of conditions as health-related—the job he holds, the food he eats, where he lives, his patterns of exercise, and his general attentiveness to mind and body. Another individual, differently motivated toward, say, the accumulation of wealth and material possessions, will most likely view these and other aspects of his lifestyle in a quite different context. In essence, as has been found in a variety of field and laboratory studies, motivation leads to selective perception of oneself and one's surrounding environment; one filters out nonessential information in pursuit of purposive behavior.[11]

Recall from Figure 4.3 in the preceding chapter that "conditions," "problems," and "needs" are not synonymous terms, nor is there a neat, deterministic relationship among them. The importance of the conceptual and analytical dynamic existing among these three terms cannot be over-emphasized, for it provides us with a major reason for the finding that, "different groups may utilize similar services for entirely different reasons, or given the same need, may turn to different services."[12] Following Robert Perlman's comment that while problems are subjective and "lie in the eye of the beholder,"[13] whether that beholder is service user or provider, conditions in contrast are presumably objectively identifiable, e.g., a "pregnancy," a "family of six," or a "family income of $6,218." Conditions, however, become problems only when either the individual or some external authority determines that they are undesirable and should be altered.

> [W]hether someone has a "problem" with a child, a job or a landlord is a matter of judgment. Problems do not have an objective, unambiguous meaning. How people and agencies define them therefore has important implications. On one side the consumers' definitions will influence when and where they go for assistance—indeed whether they go at all—what their expectations will be and how much time and effort they want to invest in getting help.
>
> On the other side, the policies of social agencies rest on their definitions of problems and this is reflected in the kind of services they offer, to whom they offer them, and what methods they employ. In other words, the agency's concept of the consumer's problem shapes what the agency believes the latter needs.[14]

A consistent theme adopted by many investigators of the utilization process holds that the initial decision to seek institutional assistance for one's problems is affected not only by such cognitive factors as the individual's perceived severity of the problem, the perceived benefits to be derived from assistance, or the barriers to be encountered in pursuit of that assistance, but also by the existence of some "trigger," some episode, that serves to translate motivation, perception, and knowledge into action. More often than not, this cue to action derives from what Irving Zola has called "the presence of sanctioning," emotional support provided by the individual's friends, relatives, and significant others with whom he has contact.[15]

In American middle-class culture it is traditional for individuals with problems they cannot handle themselves to seek the assistance of friends, relatives, and significant others *prior* to seeking institutional assistance.[16] Only when these attempts have been exhausted and have not remedied the condition will institutionalized assistance be sought. This raises the importance of what Elliot Friedson has called the "lay referral structure" in the individual's decision to utilize services. Although Friedson's analysis focuses upon the utilization of medical services, it seems germane to a wide variety of nonmedical services as well. Friedson argues that:

> the whole process of seeking help involves a network of potential consultants, from the intimate and informal confines of the nuclear family through successively more select, distant, and authoritative laymen, until the "professional" is reached. This network of consultants, which is part of the structure of the local lay community, and which imposes form on the seeking of help, might be called the "lay referral structure." Taken together with the cultural understandings involved in the process, we may speak of it as the "lay referral system."[17]

It is through an awareness of how this lay referral structure provides a bridge between service and user that we can better understand the second important decision in the process of seeking care—where to go for assistance. Friedson contends that the degree of "congruence" or similarity between the cultural milieux of the potential user along with his lay referral structure and the culture of the formal helping agency will largely affect the specific channels through which assistance is initially sought.[18] A primary indicator of cultural congruence, moreover, is the consistency with which a potential provider's definition of the problem requiring assistance *matches* the definition held by the potential service user. Not surprisingly, since many service users are poor and of ethnic minorities while many providers are of white middle-class origins, agreement on problem definitions may be remarkably low. For example, one study of a multiservice agency in the Bronx reported that agreement on problem definition existed between the user and the provider in only 58 percent of the cases analyzed.[19]

GEOGRAPHICAL BARRIERS

A substantial number of studies have shown that service utilization is inversely related to the distance between the potential user's place of residence and the service facility.[20] The relative decline in service utilization by persons living farther away arises because of what has been called the "friction of space."[21] Every potential service user will be required to overcome the "friction" generated by the time and costs of travel as measured in a variety of ways: actual travel distance; linear distance "as the crow flies"; travel time; total elapsed time including trip preparation and service time; and travel costs, including actual expenditures, and the psychological costs of traveling to an unfamiliar and perhaps threatening neighborhood. So important are these costs that for many policy makers and planners the ability to overcome geographical barriers has achieved equal status along with income as virtually synonymous with the more general problem of service access.

Seldom are the theories, concepts, and models of the physical sciences of much value in solving social problems; as a result, such reductionist approaches to theory building and explanation are generally spurned by social science scholars. A notable exception, however, is the *gravity model* commonly used in regional analysis, transportation studies, and increasingly in the analysis of service utilization. In physics it is known that the gravitational attraction between two physical bodies is dependent upon two principal factors: the mass of each body and the distance separating them. The force attracting the two bodies will increase as their combined masses increase and/or the distance separating them is reduced.[22]

As applied to problems of service utilization or any other situation involving the flow of people between two geographically separated points, the gravity model predicts that this flow will decrease as (1) distance between the facility and the population centers of its potential users increases, or (2) the size of those population centers decreases. If for simplicity we consider a single community and a single service facility, as shown in Figure 5.3, we can see the very dramatic decline in service utilization as distance from the facility increases. Fully 50 percent of the users of this hyothetical but realistic service facility reside within one-half mile of the facility; 30 percent between one-half mile and a mile; 15 percent between

FIGURE 5.3:
a gravity model of service utilization

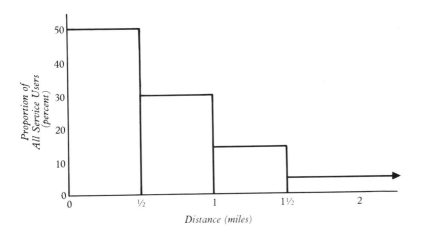

Distance (miles)

one and one and one-half miles; and only 10 percent of all service users reside at distances of greater than one and one-half miles away.

Of course, the rapidity of the decline in utilization will vary from facility to facility depending upon a number of factors not explicit in the simplified gravity model described above: the number of alternative facilities providing the same or a similar service at different locations throughout the region; the effectiveness, frequency, and route structure of public transit systems; transportation costs; and even the service facility's relative proximity to other complementary facilities (e.g., a nursery located next door to a child care center) are examples. The result is that the shape of the gravity model function will likely be different for each facility. Gravity models are quite easily constructed by using zip codes obtained from user intake records and assuming that the travel distance is equal to the linear distance from the center of the zip code area to the facility. Of course, other indicators of the friction of space may be more appropriate and can be incorporated into the gravity model, but they may require data not so easily obtained as those derived from user addresses.

The gravity model is useful in predicting the effects of geographical barriers on service utilization because it is conceptually simple and relatively easy to construct. A note of caution is in order, however, because this simple model is insufficient to explain all of the variation in utilization behavior, even among individuals living in the same zip code area; other barriers may easily predominate. Indeed, it has been noted that "certain groups will still underutilize, even when a facility is only a 'stone's throw' away."[23] Moreover, there can be little doubt that the handicapped individual in a wheelchair faces as substantial a "geographic" barrier from a six-foot flight of stairs as does the individual who must commute from miles away.

PSYCHOLOGICAL BARRIERS

If an individual possesses the knowledge and motivation to seek assistance and has been able to overcome geographical barriers to service utilization, he or she must still confront potential psychological barriers that will cause him or her to drop out of the assistance-seeking process. Psychological barriers are much like those that must be overcome in the decision to seek assistance. The initial fears of appearing inept, of divulging personal problems to friends and strangers alike, of possible social stigma attached to utilization, even of physical harm, do not magically disappear once the decision to seek assistance and the initial contact have been made. Indeed, and this is why psychological barriers have been included as a separate element in the utilization process, the service delivery system may actually *reinforce* those fears to such a point that the search for assistance is abruptly abandoned.

SELECTIVITY CRITERIA

Whether distributed by charitable organizations, through public agencies, or in the marketplace, the utilization of all social welfare services is governed by some set of implicit or explicit selectivity criteria. The two most frequently invoked are fee-for-service in the case of some public services and those provided in the marketplace, and formal program eligibility criteria, including the diagnostic determination of need, or some combination of the two.

Social services provided in the private sector, like much health care, nursing home care, child care, and counseling services, are governed by the ability to pay the required fee for service; hence the ability to overcome this barrier is largely dependent upon personal income. This raises the familiar notion of the existence of a "financial barrier" to many services. Especially in the field of health care where, in the United States at least, financial access to services is largely dependent upon third party insurance companies, utilization is dependent upon such factors as the ability to pay for the insurance (if not a part of employee benefits), the specific medical procedures that are part of coverage, and ancillary costs such as drugs that may not be covered.

The utilization of publicly provided services and benefits is as we have seen, with the exception of education, primarily restricted to individuals meeting formal eligibility requirements. Because the information required of users is frequently difficult to obtain with any accuracy, need standards often vary from political jurisdiction to jurisdiction, and because they are frequently quite complicated, ambiguity pervades the administration of many social welfare eligibility guidelines. While accountability demands that eligibility criteria be objective and administered equitably, and that they be applied in such a way that overutilization is retarded, the difficulty in obtaining the required information with sufficient speed and accuracy means that eligibility is often dependent upon the subjective impressions of intake workers. Income is frequently uncertain, as is family and employment status. The level of investigation required to ascertain such information is expensive and time-consuming, not to mention potentially degrading to the service user. Significantly, many of the administrative devices used to determine eligibility in the interests of retarding overutilization may also serve to retard utilization by those with legitimate needs. Thus, despite attempts to achieve program accountability through the enforcement of objective eligibility criteria, program eligibility and utilization often hinge upon the attitudes of the intake or case worker toward the potential user and knowledge of the "system" by the potential user.

In addition to the barriers created by formal eligibility criteria are those associated with the *process* of eligibility determination, which are often complicated, time-consuming, and demeaning. Consider the following description of the procedure which must be endured by an AFDC applicant in Oakland, California. It is not atypical of our approach to public assistance.

> When an Oakland mother with three children wants to apply for AFDC, she comes to one of the seven welfare offices in the county. After being given a number, she must wait in a rather unpleasant room until her number is called. She is then given a package of application forms, which she is told to take home and complete to the best of her ability. She is also told to return the next day for a group eligibility meeting, and to bring some positive identification for every member of the family, i.e., a birth certificate or a driver's license.
>
> The AFDC application form is 12 pages long and requires detailed information concerning the composition of the family, the assets of the family, including automobiles, real estate, and other personal property valued in excess of $100 per item. If the woman has a job, she will also be asked to provide information about her work and transportation expenses, deductions for social security, and so on. In addition, she must fill out a five-page application for food stamps, which requires similar information.
>
> The next day, in the group meeting, an eligibility worker (not a social worker) will help her finish any questions that she could not understand or answer. The worker will explain the regulations of the system, the right to appeal administrative decisions through a fair hearing, the responsibility to report immediately any change in earnings or family composition, and so on. After the meeting, the completed forms will be assigned to an "intake" worker, who will check them during the next seven days for missing information, and will phone the applicant if more information is required. Finally, an eligibility worker will visit the applicant at home to inspect living conditions, the welfare of the children, and so on.
>
> This whole process usually takes about 15 days. In emergency situations the time can be reduced substantially, or aid can be provided through other channels. Eligibility will be determined according to whether the woman's income (net of work expenses and certain other deductions) is below the needs standard of the county . . . and whether the total value of her assets (cars, furniture and other household goods, and real-estate equity) is less than the specified limits for each category. . . . If she qualifies for welfare and has no other income, she will receive a biweekly check for $174. If she has other income, her check will be reduced accordingly. Unearned income (like child support from

an absent father) will reduce the amount of the benefit check dollar for dollar. Earned income will reduce benefits according to the "$30 and one-third" rule. She will also receive authorization to buy a maximum of $166 of food stamps per month, at a cost of $95. She will be given a Medicaid card entitling her family to free medical care and reduced prices on prescriptions.

Each month on welfare, the woman will be required to fill out a two-page WR-7 form to report any changes in family income or family composition. Failure to submit this form on time will first bring a warning letter, and eventually benefits will be suspended.

If all of her children are at least six years old, she will be required by the Talmadge amendments to register at the local state-employ-ment-service office for job training and job placement under the WIN program. This registration is arranged automatically by the welfare department. Over time, a WIN service worker will encourage her to enter training, or to undertake a search for a job if she has none.[24]

In some service organizations a diagnostic determination of need may serve as the principal, if not the only, selectivity criterion. Diagnostic criteria are of increasing importance in the health care field, where the incidence of third party providers and prepaid medical care plans create a serious potential problem of overutilization of services. Evidence indicates that the elimination of a fee-for-service barrier results in less discretion being exercised by the consumer; absent is a useful "filter" or "gate-keeping" function which separates those in need from those not in need. A case in point is the experience of Kaiser-Permanente, one of the first and largest of the health maintenance organizations.

The Kaiser Foundation Research Institute and Permanente Medical Group operates a large number of medical clinics on the West Coast. Access to these clinics (as is the case with all HMOS) is provided through a prepaid medical care plan, in which users (or their employers) pay an annual, fixed fee to cover most health care needs; there is no fee-for-service charge on a visit-by-visit basis.

In prepaid plans the potentially higher operating costs of health care systems having relatively unrestricted access are in theory offset by two factors. First, relatively unrestricted access is conducive to a greater em-phasis upon prevention; early detection of relatively minor illnesses pre-vents more serious illness and more costly care later on. Second, since the organization reaps no financial reward for a medical procedure, there is an incentive to perform fewer unnecessary and costly operations and procedures.

In 1970, a study of one of the Kaiser-Permanente centers, an ambula-tory medical care center in Oakland, California, which had some 150,000 members enrolled, was initiated in an attempt to resolve an apparent

paradox in the relatively unrestricted access system. For in all of the Kaiser-Permanente centers and in many other prepaid medical care plans as
well, it had become apparent that

> the elimination of fee-for-service practice is not a simple solution to
> improved medical care for the sick. Anticipated benefits have been
> largely negated by a frustrating paradox: the elimination of personal
> fees have *impaired* rather than improved access and have seriously
> *inflated* rather than contained costs.[25]

Higher than anticipated utilization had created a familiar access dilemma
(one especially common in many universally available services). Waiting
times and appointment lead times had increased, thereby reducing easy
access to services. Simultaneously, it had forced the addition of new staff,
and had increased the operating costs of the centers.

The study was based upon the hypothesis that the dilemma derived
from a conceptual mismatch between the traditional delivery system (fee-
for-service and oriented to the sick) and the new system, which both
eliminated fees and was oriented toward prevention. The result of this
mismatch in this case was a substantial increase in what is called the
"uncertainty demand" for care, comprising three groups of service users:
the well; the "worried-well"; and the "asymptotic sick," "patients who
had no medical complaints but were found to have clinically important
abnormalities."[26] In a sample of more than 4,000 users during the period
of a year, it was found that 56 percent of the users were well; 11.6 percent,
worried-well; 3.9 percent, asymptotic sick; and only 27.7 percent, sick.[27]
That is, the *uncertainty demand for care exceeded 70 percent.* As a result of the
study's findings, a diagnostic screening process, using less expensive
paramedical personnel, was established, which both substantially reduced
user waiting times and appointment lead times and reduced center costs
by almost $33 per user.[28]

The theoretical premise underlying any HMO—that the provider is
obligated to administer to members' health problems—presumably guards
against a capricious and arbitrary use of the diagnostic process to deny
benefits to those in genuine need. And indeed, researchers discovered that
neither staff nor patients at the Kaiser-Permanente facility believed the
quality of care had declined because of the new screening process. But one
must question whether accountability to the client is thusly maintained in
the increasing number of public programs that also incorporate a diagnostic determination of need, but in which there is no similar contractual
obligation to maintain the client's present and future welfare. In such
cases, accountability to the client may be superceded—particularly in re-

sponse to inadequate program resources—by accountability to the organization.

RESOURCES

Despite the ability to overcome all previous barriers, the availability of resources *at the time of need* presents a critical barrier to service utilization. The emergency room that is understaffed to meet demand, the child care center that is filled to capacity, and the housing program that is short of cash are examples; in each case the access system may be used to *ration* scarce resources. One may identify two primary reasons that resources may not match potential levels of utilization: (1) the inflexible interaction of supply and demand in service organizations, and (2) the relative inflexibility of service budgets.

Especially in programs providing direct services rather than cash transfers, the fact that service organizations must possess the resources at the time of demand (i.e., services cannot be stored for future use) means that a balance must be struck between resource oversupply and undersupply. Since day-to-day demand for services is usually uncertain, it is common for service organizations of all kinds to adjust staffing patterns to meet some percentage of maximum expected demand during that time period; for example, 80 percent of maximum expected demand might by a typical level. If demand falls below this level, staff idle time will result in excessive costs to the organization; if demand is greater than staffing levels will allow, the cost burden is shifted to the user in the form of increased waiting time or even being refused service. This is what had happened in the Kaiser-Permanente center just discussed.

An area of research that has been the subject of intense and fruitful attention by management scientists is the study of waiting lines, often called *queuing theory.* The mathematical models developed as a result of this research are extremely useful for analyzing the relationship between service resource availability and the waiting times experienced by potential users. One interesting result of manipulating these models, a result that has been corroborated in actual experience, is that service organizations adopting the apparently sensible practice of setting staffing levels to accommodate average or expected demand during a particular time period will experience *infinitely* long waiting lines.[29]

Suppose, for example, that a counseling center has sufficient staff to accommodate an average of five service users per day, and that the average demand for services is also five per day; some days will experience less demand and some will experience more, but the *average* is five. Because the agency cannot recoup the idle time that occurs during days in which demand is less than five, yet cannot accommodate demand on days when it is greater, this apparently rational staffing level will, if users are persistent, eventually result in an infinite number of persons waiting an infinite number of days to utilize services. One solution, of course, would be to allow utilization by appointment only, which in turn creates an additional barrier to service access.

Programs that provide cash transfers as well as those charged with the delivery of in-kind services are frequently plagued by fixed, inflexible budgets, budgets that may inadequately reflect utilization. In many such programs, especially at the state and local level, the budget for the coming fiscal year may be at least partially influenced by forecasts of the number of program users, based upon simple forecasts of the appropriate population-at-risk. But because such forecasts are often unreliable and because —despite forecasts to the contrary—funding authorities grant only small, incremental budgetary increases, resource requirements may exceed those available. Even if other programs in the same agency are running behind in projected expenditures, limitations on interprogram transfers of funds create many situations in which even eligible individuals are denied benefits. Simultaneously, the program experiencing a projected budgetary surplus will more than likely have initiated efforts to increase utilization in order to expend its entire budget.

The interaction between resources and utilization in service organizations will be the subject of further discussion in subsequent chapters. The significant point to remember is this: if there is an imbalance between service capability and actual utilization, someone must bear the cost. The provider bears the cost of oversupply in the form of staff idle time, and the user bears the cost of undersupply in the form of increased waiting time or being denied service altogether.

administrative strategies
for facilitating access

In recent years it has become increasingly apparent that the legal specification of entitlements to specific groups alone is insufficient to ensure redistribution. It has been recognized that substantial variations in service utilization exist among different groups in the same need population. Even if goods and services are made available free of charge, it is apparent that there is still a problem of unequal access to services among different groups, which is in large part created by the organizational milieux in which services are delivered. To correct these apparent discrepancies it has become common to view the provision of access itself as a social service.[30]

The introduction of organizational factors into the utilization process forces a reorientation in the express purpose of access strategies. Rather than matching services to needs, the problem becomes one of matching human problems to the correct programmatic element, which in turn aids in matching services to needs. This problem is twofold. First, individuals with problems requiring assistance must make *contact* with the network of service organizations, somehow, somewhere. Second, if this initial bureaucratic match is incorrect—if the problem reflects a need that cannot be fulfilled by the program or agency—or if problems require contact with more than a single agency, then some set of techniques must be employed to *channel* individuals to the correct organization.

If the service network did not yet exist, but was still in the planning stages, two primary factors would determine its accessibility—convenience of location and congruence with the problems and needs as defined by potential service users. From the standpoint of ease of contact, it is clear that many dispersed neighborhood centers, culturally congruent with the neighborhood, are preferable to a large, centralized, monolithic welfare organization. This was the principal idea behind the Model Cities program, established in the sixties to deal with the physical and social problems of neighborhoods. The Model Cities program acted as a funnel through which federal dollars flowed directly to neighborhoods in some 150 cities across the nation. It was within the framework of the Model Cities program that the ideas of "storefront" multiservice centers, easily accessible to neighborhood residents, became a national trend. The watchword in the Model Cities planning stages—derived from the earlier experiences of the Office of Equal Opportunity's Community Action Agencies—was citizen participation. In large part, the idea behind citizen participation was not only to ensure that services conformed to neighborhood problems and needs, but also that the mode of delivery was consistent with the perceptions and expectations of neighborhood residents. In short, the Model Cities program was an attempt to minimize geographical and psychological barriers to utilization.

Nonetheless, even such efforts to tailor service programs to community perceptions of need do not guarantee success. Not all people participate in the planning process. Not all neighborhoods are sufficiently homogeneous to represent a single culture. Not all needed services can be provided by many small organizations located in every neighborhood. Not all people possess the necessary knowledge to ensure initial contact. And these realities give rise to two essential strategies for stimulating initial contact with the service network—outreach and information and referral services.

Outreach efforts are quite simply attempts undertaken by service agency and program personnel to recruit service users rather than waiting for the users to come to them. Most federal social programs are required by statute to provide some form of outreach services, but within this broad requirement variations on the outreach theme are endless, dependent upon program budgets, specific statutory requirements as interpreted by the courts, community attitudes, the level of unmet need within a community, and agency commitment to meeting those needs.

Some outreach efforts such as those conducted on behalf of the AFDC program, are simply informational, directed at groups or in the home on an individual basis. Others are combined with needs assessment activities. Still others (in the food stamp program, for example) may more actively promote utilization by individual clients—helping to motivate as well as inform; assisting in overcoming psychological barriers to utilization; providing transportation if necessary (or conversely, arranging for in-home visitation by service professionals); assisting in intake procedures; even performing follow-up to ensure that the user actually received needed services. In short, "the outreach worker . . . serves as an ambassador in the community, helping to bridge the gap between professional human services staff and the . . . people."[31]

It is important that this bridge built between the service organization and the community be biased in favor of the characteristics of potential users. That is, the outreach worker is more likely to be effective in helping to overcome the user-provider culture gap if he or she is a member of the target population. Senior citizens are more likely to respond favorably to an outreach worker who is also a senior than to a young person, for example. For this reason, outreach efforts performed by service-providing organizations are more likely to be effective if coordinated through organizations representing specific group interests; for example, senior outreach might effectively be coordinated through the local Gray Panthers or senior centers. Coordination with other organizations may also provide a means of achieving outreach objectives at relatively low cost. In one community, for example, the major electric utility operates a home visitation program designed to help those on fixed incomes reduce their consumption of electricity. The police run a similar program, primarily for seniors, designed to help safeguard homes from burglaries. In both cases it has been possible to take advantage of the personal contacts made on behalf of other programs by "piggy-backing" social service outreach efforts. As with most volunteers, their outreach function is primarily informational; although in many cases, initial contacts made by those not in social service agencies have led to more formal follow-up by professional outreach workers.

A second means of achieving a correct contact with the myriad organizational elements that comprise the social welfare enterprise is the provision of information and referral (I&R) services. In a community of any size these services are essential if the problems exemplified in the following are to be avoided.

Switchboard: City Hall, may I help you?
Caller: My daughter is handicapped and needs special transportation to her therapist. Who can I speak to in the city about this?
Switchboard (after a pause):   I think the Office of Aging handles things like that. Let me connect you.
Office of Aging: Good morning, Office of Aging, can you hold please? (Several minutes later.) Sorry to keep you waiting; can I help you?
Caller: My daughter is handicapped and needs special transportation to her therapist. Usually someone in the family helps out but it's not always . . .
Office of Aging: How old is your daughter?
Caller: She's only a teenager, but the switchboard . . .
Office of Aging: I'm sorry, but your daughter isn't eligible. Our program is only for senior citizens. Ask the switchboard to connect you to the Youth Bureau. I'll connect you back. (There are several clicks and the connection is lost. The caller dials the main city hall number again.)
Switchboard: City Hall, may I help you?
Caller: The Youth Bureau please.
Switchboard: Do you want the Delinquency Program or the Recreation Program?
Caller: I think it must be the Recreation Program. It's my daughter. I called earlier and was cut off, but I don't think I talked to you. I just wanted to . . .
Youth Bureau: Youth Bureau, Recreation, can I help you?
Caller: I hope so. My daughter is handicapped and needs special transportation to her therapist. I was wondering if you . . .
Youth Bureau: I'm sorry; we don't have information on that kind of program. You might try the Office of Aging . . .
Caller: But I . . .
Youth Bureau: . . . or the School Board. Their number is . . . [32]

Virtually every community possesses a service directory of some kind, ranging from simple pamphlets to sophisticated computerized catalogs of programs and services; many possess information and referral centers that serve as a general purpose entry point to the service network. Still others rely upon the I&R capability of individual service providers. The more effective I&R systems, for reasons that will soon be apparent, usually combine all three approaches.

In principle, the idea behind a general purpose I&R directory, center, or system is simple. As a practical matter, however, it is fraught with difficulty, and the structural complexity of the social welfare enterprise is a primary reason for this difficulty. Returning to the hypothetical telephone conversation presented above, what elements of information were conveyed in the initial contact? First was the problem: a person had to get to her therapist. Second were the characteristics of the potential user: a female, a teenager, and handicapped (no mention was made of family income). Third was the service required: special transportation.

Clearly, the needed service—special transportation—was available within the community. Clearly there were agencies—the Youth Bureau, the School Board—oriented to the target population of teenage females. More than likely, however, there was no specific program targeted at the population of "handicapped teenage females in need of special transportation." The job of an effective information and referral system is to *create* such a program by linking together available agencies, services, and existing programs.

Disregarding for the moment the subjective nature of conditions, problems, and needs, what is the essential information required to forge the necessary linkage? First, a list of specific services is required, in this case revealing the existence of special transportation. Next the list of agencies providing social services within the community—whether federal, state or

FIGURE 5.4:

an information and referral system model

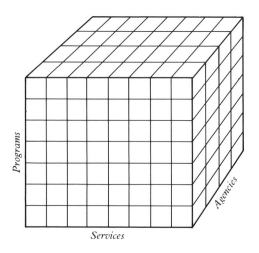

Services

local—must be compiled. And third, for each service and for each agency program characteristics must be delineated. In addition to the service provided under the program, one must include specific eligibility criteria, such as age, income, place of residence, race, handicap, employment status, marital status, and sex. To complicate matters many programs invoke multiple eligibility criteria; for example, a program may be aimed at persons who are elderly, poor, and living within the city limits of Danville. Ideally, all services and programs would be cross-referenced, yielding the three-dimensional I&R model shown in Figure 5.4.

Since the number of cells (a single linkage between program, service, and agency) in such a matrix can easily run into the thousands, the problem of linking problems to the appropriate program is one best solved by computer. With such a system, a series of key words—as in a library reference system—is used to sort through the possible combinations of agency, program, and service. In principle this is relatively simple; in practice, however, there are numerous difficulties. First, even the basic task of creating an inventory of community services, organizations, and programs is no mean feat, considering both the number of organizational elements involved and inevitable inconsistencies in program and service definition (although a system like UWASIS can help alleviate the latter problem).

A second problem, and perhaps the greatest technical barrier encountered in the construction of such a system, is created by the ephemeral nature of many service programs. Budgets change; agencies introduce new programs and discard the old in response to continuously changing attitudes and grant-in-aid incentives emanating from Washington; services are modified; agencies move to new locations; and eligibility requirements rise and fall with available resources. Even when such lists are stored and cross-referenced by computer, the necessary updating procedures are both time-consuming and expensive, and they generally fail to keep pace with significant changes in the service network.

A third problem is not readily apparent from the example of the handicapped teenager. In that case the individual's situation was such that both the problem and the need for service were apparent—a need for special transportation. In many cases—for example an elderly widow living alone, a person simply not "feeling well," or a teenager who continually argues with his parents—the translation from condition to problem to need to program is not so simple. The necessity for a preliminary "diagnosis" of need, not by a computer but by I&R staff, introduces the possibility of referral error—referrals made on a basis other than need.

In some cases referral errors result from the limited knowledge of referral agents; referrals are made to agencies and programs with which they are familiar. In other cases, a significant proportion of referrals will be made based on the affinity with program staff; "good" cases are referred to programs with whose staff the specialist is friendly, "bad" cases to those with whom the specialist is not. In other cases, the potential for I&R error results from the "different strokes for different folks" nature of need; oftentimes solutions are biased in favor of the referral specialist's perspectives and values rather than those of the potential user. To counter these problems, Alfred Kahn has suggested that community social service networks possess a general purpose entry point, a "professionally unbiased doorway" that does not persistently favor any particular perspective, any particular solution to an individual's problems. The implication of this approach is that the

> information-advice-referral service becomes an operationally autonomous, unbiased case channeling device, prepared for a case advocacy stance if needed, and aware of its redistributive mission for the most disadvantaged.[33]

To be geographically accessible such entry points would ideally be scattered in convenient locations throughout the community, "storefront" style. Preferably these would be staffed by individuals possessing cultural backgrounds similar to those of their primary users, and with sufficient training to have overcome their own cultural, personal, and service biases. In comparison to the semiprofessionals and volunteers who provide intake services and who currently staff many existing information and referral centers, highly trained professionals dispersed in locations throughout the community would represent a significant increase in cost, drawing resources away from the more substantive social services. Despite the attractiveness of the professionally unbiased doorway concept—both as an element for improving accessibility and possibly in network-wide evaluation—many communities are reluctant to expand or experiment with costly devices to improve access. Thus, while workable I&R systems seem essential to effective access, the technical difficulties encountered in their construction, their cost, and general lack of political support present perplexing barriers to their implementation.

THE CHANNELING FUNCTION: ACCESS AND SERVICE INTEGRATION

Given the complexity of creating a general purpose information and referral system that would ensure correct initial contact with the network, and realizing that a large proportion of service users possess multiple problems and needs, it is necessary that service agencies maintain their own internal channeling procedures. As originally discussed in chapter 2,

FIGURE 5.5:

a model of administered service access and integration

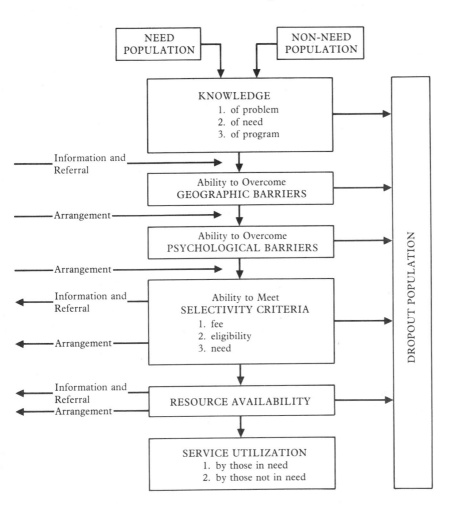

these intranetwork access strategies are a key component in the achievement of accessible, integrated, continuous service delivery. Some of the strategies employed and their intended effects on utilization barriers are shown in Figure 5.5, and of interest to any program are two sets of strategies—those which channel individuals *to* the program and those which channel them *away* to other programs.

From the standpoint of the service organization, it is obviously desirable that these intranetwork access techniques deliver service users possessing problems and needs that can be accommodated with program capabilities and guidelines. From the standpoint of the service user it is desirable that this channeling process first be correct, that one not receive the bureaucratic "runaround" from agency to agency. Second, the process should ensure continuity such that the many pieces of the service network puzzle fit together and that the user not vanish in the cracks between programs, services, and agencies. Third, the process should entail minimal time, cost, and aggravation on the part of the user.

The most passive of strategies used to channel individuals to the organization is the provision of information and referral services by another agency, presumably helping to overcome any knowledge barriers that might exist. A more activist strategy of channeling is here called an "arrangement" and is sometimes called "escort and advocacy" in social welfare agencies. The premise underlying the provision of various arrangements on behalf of service clientele is that simple information, or even arranging an appointment with another agency, is often insufficient to promote utilization of needed services. If geographical barriers are significant deterrents to utilization, then it may be desirable to arrange for transportation. If psychological barriers arising from fear or distrust are present, it may be desirable for a case or intake worker to provide personal escort and assistance through the intake phase of the new agency or program.

If problems of eligibility are encountered or likely to be encountered, then advocacy on behalf of the client or client group may assist in overcoming this barrier to utilization. Advocacy on behalf of a single client, or *case* advocacy, may be performed by information center staff or those from a substantive service agency, whichever has the "capacity and freedom for persistent follow-through."[34] Advocacy on behalf of a specific clientele group, or *class* advocacy, is sometimes invoked to redress persistent discrimination experienced by some client groups. Often combined with legal services, class advocacy may be directed at various elements of either policy or program, resulting in

> changes in laws, revised budgets, new procedures or adjustments in their application to the circumstances of some categories of individuals, reassignment of personnel, and so on.[35]

Increasingly, and with profound impact, the courts are being used as the primary vehicle through which class advocacy disputes are resolved. At issue in many of these disputes is the legality of "separate but equal" services, a doctrine first addressed and discarded by the U.S. Supreme Court in *Brown v. Board of Education* in 1954. While the Brown decision was directed at discrimination against racial minorities, the precedent set has been recently expanded to include a large number of disadvantaged groups. With respect to the handicapped, for example, Section 504 of the Rehabilitation Act of 1973 describes the mandate as follows:

> No otherwise qualified handicapped individual in the U.S. shall, solely by reason of his handicap, be excluded from the participation in, be denied the benefits of, or be subjected to discrimination under any program or activity receiving federal financial assistance.[36]

As many are aware, this law stands to have profound impact, not only in significantly improving accessibility to publicly funded activities by the handicapped, but in the basic structure and costs of social welfare programs as well; "mainstreaming" in the schools, the removal of architectural barriers from all public buildings, and fully "accessible" public transportation are only a few of its apparent implications.

BUREAUCRATIC PATHOLOGIES IN THE PROVISION OF ACCESS

Despite protection from the courts, citizen groups, and social service professionals, service users are still subject to the vagaries that accompany most large-scale bureaucratic efforts. Rather than ensuring that the service network be accountable to the needs of potential users, access strategies may also be invoked to further organizational, political, and professional ends. One of the most pervasive of these pathologies is "creaming" or adjusting the access mechanism to "select the more amenable, promising clients and turn away those who are 'difficult,' 'uncooperative,' or 'unappealing.'"[37] All professionals take satisfaction in the successful application of their knowledge and skills. It is therefore natural that they would prefer cases in which intervention has a high likelihood of success.

This raises a particular problem in some private social service agencies, where acceptance or rejection of a potential client is often discretionary. In such agencies it is not uncommon to shift the burden of these "undesirables" to the public sector. According to Richard Cloward:

> Thus private residential treatment institutions for juvenile delinquents, having made errors in intake, "pass on" their difficult cases to the public training schools; settlements and community agencies arrange to have the more difficult juvenile gangs worked with by public detached street workers; family agencies abandon so-called multiproblem families to departments of public welfare; private hospitals shrug off the chronically ill patient to the back wards of publicly supported custodial hospitals.[38]

This should not be interpreted to mean that only private agencies engage in creaming; nor should it be seen as simply a matter of professional preference. If an agency (public or private) is confronted with a higher level of utilization than can be accommodated within its budget, it will have to turn some people away. What "better" strategy to turn away those who promise to be high-cost users or those with a low chance of successful outcome? Creaming both increases the organization's apparent "success rate" and lowers the unit cost of services provided—both valuable assets in future quests for continued program funding.

In addition to creaming, the service organization may erect barriers that arbitarily reduce utilization in the face of excess demand for services, regardless of individual need. They can close down facilities, refuse to accept new applicants, eliminate outreach, reduce the hours of operation, or require that appointments be made well in advance of service provision. Oftentimes, organizations may play a game of "diversionary referral"— shunting people from organization to organization in an attempt to avoid serving them.

A somewhat different problem is encountered if it appears that utilization will fall short of the estimates upon which the budget was based. Since the ability to expend the entire budget is generally considered a prerequisite for increasing or maintaining the existing level of funding, the organization faces some pressure to increase—again, arbitrarily—utilization levels. Not only do such pathologies result in the failure to match resources to those in greatest need, but they may unfairly raise the expectations of service users and violate their individual freedoms as well.[39]

Managed access to services, then, is a two-edged sword. Certainly the administrative techniques for improving access can and are used to ensure that services are provided quickly and with a minimum of aggravation to those in need. But—largely because the concept of need *fails* to provide an objective and indisputable basis for allocating resources in short supply and because we lack the basic information necessary for evaluating accessibility—these techniques can also be (and are) useful devices for furthering organizational, political, and professional ends, often at the expense of the client.

notes

1. U.S. Department of Health, Education and Welfare, Social Security Administration *Social Security Bulletin,* 39, no. 1 (January 1976), 11.

2. Judith Barmack, "The Case of In-Kind Transfers: The Food Stamp Program," *Policy Analysis* (Fall 1977), 3, no. 4, 521.

3. U.S. Senate Committee on Government Operations, Subcommittee on Federal Spending Practices, Efficiency and Open Government, *Report of the Findings on Food Stamp*

Efficiency, 94th Congress, 2nd Session, September 1957, pp. 11. Note that foodstamp program rules have since been changed; one no longer pays for the stamps.

4. Ibid., p. 3.

5. Cited in John Bishop, "The Welfare Brief," *The Public Interest,* no. 53 (Fall 1978), 171.

6. See for example Ivan Illich, *Medical Nemesis* (Westminster: Pantheon, 1976).

7. William Shonick, *Elements of Planning for Area-Wide Personal Health Services* (St. Louis: C. V. Mosby, 1976), p. 9n.

8. John B. McKinlay, "Some Approaches and Problems in the Study of the Use of Services—an Overview," *Journal of Health and Social Behavior,* 13 (June 1971), 115.

9. Ibid.

10. Ibid., pp. 119–38.

11. Irwin Rosenstock, "Why People Use Health Services," *Milbank Memorial Fund Quarterly* (July 1966), 98.

12. McKinlay, "Some Approaches and Problems," 120.

13. Robert Perlman, *Consumers and Social Services* (New York: John Wiley, 1975), p. 13.

14. Ibid.

15. Cited in John B. McKinlay, "The Help-Seeking Behavior of the Poor," in *Poverty and Health,* eds. John Kosa and Irving K. Zola (Cambridge: Harvard University Press, 1975), p. 241.

16. Perlman, *Consumers and Social Services,* p. 5n.

17. Eliot Friedson, "Client Control and Medical Practice," *American Journal of Sociology,* 65 (1959–60), 377.

18. Ibid.

19. Perlman, *Consumers and Social Services,* p. 19.

20. See O. P. Williams, *Metropolitian Political Analysis* (New York: Free Press, 1971); or H. Rose, *The Black Ghetto: A Spatial Perspective* (New York: McGraw-Hill, 1972).

21. Avedis Donabedian, *Aspects of Medical Care Administration* (Cambridge: Harvard University Press, 1973), p. 425.

22. See Shonick, *Elements of Planning for Area-Wide Personal Health Services,* pp. 77–78 and Walter Isard, *Introduction to Regional Schemes* (Englewood Cliffs, N.J.: Prentice-Hall, 1975), pp. 39–45.

23. McKinlay, "Some Approaches and Problems," p. 122.

24. Frederick Doolittle, Frank Levy, and Michael Wiseman, "The Mirage of Welfare Reform," *The Public Interest,* no. 47 (Spring 1977), 78–80. Reprinted with permission from *The Public Interest.* © 1977 by National Affairs, Inc.

25. Sidney Garfield and others, "Evaluation of an Ambulatory Medical-Care Delivery System," *New England Journal of Medicine,* 294, no. 8 (February 19, 1976), 426, emphasis added.

26. Ibid., p. 427.

27. Ibid.

28. Ibid., p. 428.

29. See among others Elwood Buffa, *Operations Management: The Management of Productive Systems* (New York: John Wiley, 1976), pp. 309–23.

30. Alfred J. Kahn, "Perspectives on Access to Social Services," *Social Work,* 15, no. 2 (April 1970), 95–101.

31. Michael J. Murphy, "Organizational Approaches for Human Services Programs," in *Managing Human Services,* eds. Wayne F. Anderson, Bernard J. Frieden, and Michael J. Murphy (Washington, D.C.: International City Management Association, 1977), p. 216.

32. Ibid., p. 193.

33. Kahn, "Perspectives on Access to Social Services," p. 100.

34. Alfred J. Kahn, *Social Policy and Social Services* (New York: Random House, 1973), p. 168.

35. Ibid., p. 169.

36. Rehabilitation Act of 1973, Section 504.

37. Perlman, *Consumers and Social Services,* p. 72.

38. Richard Cloward, "Social Problems, Social Definitions and Social Opportunities," a paper prepared for the Regional Institute on Juvenile Delinquency and Social Forces, April 1963, p. 34. Cited in Martin Rein, *Social Policy* (New York: Random House, 1970), p. 54.

39. Marie R. Haug and Marvin B. Sussman, "Professional Autonomy and the Revolt of the Client," *Social Problems,* 17 (Fall 1969), 156.

Management control concerns the processes and techniques adopted to ensure the accountable, effective, and efficient pursuit of organizational objectives. Originally devised to harness the production potential wrought by industrialization, many of these techniques derive from values and depend upon information common to market-oriented production organizations. Consequently, it is within this context that the information essential to management control—the production function, the cost function, and the profit function—is initially discussed.

In the not-for-profit or public service-providing organizations of the social welfare enterprise, many of these conceptual and informational prerequisites to management control are found to be in short supply. Many of the difficulties can be traced to the absence of an adequate means for creating consistent definitions of the problems, needs, services, and programs which are the object of managerial attention.

Lacking these, a principal instrument for exercising management control and for ensuring accountability is the budget. The quest for funds which constitutes the initial stages of budgetary process is largely determined by what attributes of organizational performance—accountability and control, effectiveness, efficiency, planning—are to be emphasized by alternative funding authorities. Once funds are appropriated, the function of the budget shifts to one of ensuring that resources are used in accordance with limitations established by providers of funds.

management control

6

Regardless of organizational setting, management control is most generally seen as "the process by which managers assure that resources are obtained and used effectively in the accomplishment of an organization's objectives."[1] Fundamental to management control is the knowledge base which (1) enables the organization to seek, obtain, and maintain a continued level of resources, and (2) provides both administrators and external sources of accountability with the basis for assessing the effectiveness and efficiency of alternative organizational decisions. The elements of this knowledge base—what information is seen as important and why—provide the central focus of this chapter.

foundations
of management control

There can be little question that the development of techniques of management control has been a prime contributor to the material prosperity enjoyed by modern industrialized society. The substitution of capital for labor in the form of machine technology—the essence of the Industrial Revolution—necessitated the creation of organizational forms, processes, and techniques that could effectively harness that potential. The systematic melding of people and machines to achieve the efficient production of wanted goods was (and still is) the dominant focus of management control efforts. These efforts converge upon three concepts that are central to modern organization, whether public or private, production or service-providing—the maintenance of accountability, and the achievement of efficiency and of effectiveness. So pervasive is the market-oriented production view of contemporary organization, moreover, that it seems the logical place to begin our discussion of management control. For it is the unique conceptualizations of accountability, effectiveness, and efficiency as developed and used therein that provide a basis for management control techniques and expectations in the not-for-profit, service-providing organizations of the social welfare enterprise.

UNDERSTANDING EFFICIENCY AND EFFECTIVENESS
IN PRODUCTION ORGANIZATIONS

Efficiency and effectiveness in profit-oriented production organizations comprise a series of relationships over which management has some degree of control; by controlling (or partially controlling) these relationships, management indirectly influences efficiency and effectiveness. *Efficiency* is most generally defined as the ratio of goods produced per dollar cost;[2] if the same quantity of goods is produced at lower cost, or if more goods can be produced at the same cost, efficiency will be increased. Thus, management control over efficiency requires knowledge of and the ability to control both costs and the quantity of goods produced.

Effectiveness is most generally defined as the degree to which an organizational activity or decision contributes to the achievement of organizational goals.[3] Consequently, management control over effectiveness implies an understanding of organizational goals and the relationships between these goals and the possible activities that might be undertaken in pursuit of their achievement. While the goals of a profit-making organization may be only vaguely specified, for example, to promote "Better Living through Electricity," two useful *indicators* of its effectiveness are market share and profitability. Presumably, an organization which has increased either its market share or its profitability has also demonstrated increasing effectiveness.

Figure 6.1 shows how efficiency and effectiveness are normally perceived in profit-making production organizations. The physical transformation of inputs into finished outputs is called the production function; if costs are then attached to those inputs, through the relationship between costs and outputs, managers are able to establish measures of efficiency. Sales generate revenues, which in conjunction with costs, permit profitability to be established, a useful measure of effectiveness.

In profit-making production organizations, the relationships and measures embodied in the concepts of efficiency and effectiveness provide not only the basis for their assessment, but for their control as well. What can managers control? First, they can take steps to alter the production technology in an attempt to produce more at the same cost or the same amount of output at lower cost. If successful, efficiency is improved. Second, managers possess some degree of control over product quality, and

FIGURE 6.1:

efficiency and effectiveness in the production model

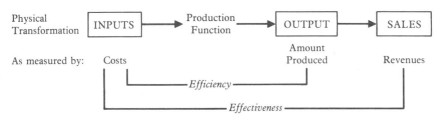

a great deal of control over how much is produced. And third, managers can control the mix of goods and services produced. When each of these variables is assessed in terms of its contribution to both revenues and costs, it is possible for managers to estimate the impact of alternative production decisions on organizational effectiveness. As Figure 6.1 shows, however, efficiency and effectiveness cannot be assessed independently of one another, either in theory or in practice; an increase in efficiency, if it is achieved by lowering product quality, will not necessarily result in an increase in profits and continued effectiveness.

Many production organizations frequently split responsibilities between production and sales departments and because of the tradeoff between efficiency and effectiveness, an element of friction is usually found in the relationship between the two departments. Either sales contends that it cannot respond to consumer desires within the "unreasonable" cost and technological constraints imposed by production, or production claims that it cannot meet the "impossible" price, quality, and quantity standards required by sales. In essence, through structural departmentalization, large profit-making organizations institutionalize the split between the generation of costs and revenues, with the important result that the natural tradeoff (and conflict) between efficiency and effectiveness becomes a central focus of their internal decision-making processes. We shall see shortly that this is not often the case in the social welfare enterprise.

In addition to consumers or groups acting on their behalf, managers in profit-making organizations must be accountable to the owners of the enterprise—the shareholders. This is ensured, in part, by providing shareholders (and other interested parties such as potential shareholders, banks from which loans are to be sought, and stockbrokers) with detailed reports concerning the organization's operations and use of funds. Many of these reports, including various financial and income statements, are governed —in the information they include, the methods by which it is gathered and organized, and the format in which it is presented—by principles established within the accounting profession. Additionally, it is this profession that largely establishes the principles of the internal handling of funds. A major objective of these principles is to ensure that a consistent and objective information base is available from which non-consumer groups can assess organizational operations.

APPLYING THE PROFIT-ORIENTED PRODUCTION MODEL TO SOCIAL WELFARE PROGRAMS

Suppose you are the program administrator responsible for writing a contract and monitoring the performance of a not-for-profit youth care center. Your agency provides funds to the center, which in turn provides protective services to children from troubled homes. Two concepts you would need to understand are (1) the production function, and (2) the cost function. The *production function* is the relationship between input and output; it specifies the type and amount of resources required to generate any level of output. Suppose we define one unit of output as one Average Daily Population (ADP)—one person receiving the service for a day's duration. Given this, we would then identify the various resources required to produce one ADP of youth care services. Keeping it extremely simple, these resource requirements might be summarized as follows:

*three meals per day
*lodging and facilities for one day
*one hour of individual counseling per day
*administration and overhead

The production function would then be generated by determining the total amount of resources—how many meals, how many rooms, and so on—required for, say, 10, 20, or 30 ADPs during the coming year.

Now, if we further knew the costs of each of these inputs it would be possible to construct a *cost function,* which shows the way costs behave relative to quantity of output produced; in general, costs are said to behave in three ways. First, costs may increase in direct proportion to the quantity produced; these are called *variable costs* and are represented in this example by the costs of providing three meals per day. Second, costs may increase in steps as more is produced; these are called *semi-variable costs.* Suppose that your contract with the provider stipulates that each child in the program will receive one hour of individual counseling per day; assuming an eight-hour day and no part-time counselors, the maximum capacity for each counselor is eight program participants. Thus, for anywhere between one and eight children enrolled, one counselor will suffice; increase the enrollment to nine, however, and the costs jump because another full-time counselor must be added to ensure that performance is in compliance with contract specifications. The third and final category of costs—*fixed costs*—are those that are incurred regardless of the amount of output produced; they are the same for zero ADPs as they are for twenty-five. In this example, the costs of operating and maintaining the physical facility and those of administration and overhead are fixed costs. Rather than varying with the number of ADPs, fixed costs are normally time dependent—a month's rental, a month's utilities and maintenance, a year's insurance, an annual administrative salary, and so on.

FIGURE 6.2:

elements of a youth care center cost function

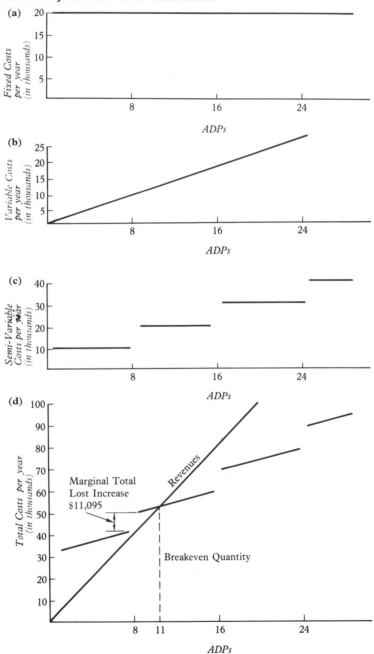

If we assume that fixed costs are $20,000 per year, that three meals per ADP is $3 per day or $1,095 per ADP per year, and that the annual salary of a counselor is $10,000, then the various elements of cost can be constructed as shown in Figure 6.2; the total of fixed, variable, and semivariable costs is shown in Figure 6.2(d). Since the total cost function expresses the relationship between units produced and the total cost to produce them, it provides administrators with an important tool for assessing efficiency as well as costs at various levels of output. In this example, it is easy to see that efficiency improves as the number of ADPs increases. If the total number of program participants is eight, then annual costs total $38,760 or about $4,850 per ADP; if total enrollment is sixteen, however, total cost is $57,520 or only about $3,600 per ADP. This demonstrates the characteristic known as *increasing economies of scale;* because fixed costs are spread out among more units of output, it is more efficient to produce greater amounts.

Although it is generally true that efficiency will improve as more is produced, this is not always the case in programs having a strong semivariable cost component; large increases in output may yield greater efficiency, but smaller increments may actually reduce it. The change in total cost as an additional unit of output is produced is called the *marginal total cost;* it is an especially useful piece of information in organizations that experience high levels of semivariable costs. For example, the marginal total cost of eight ADPs rather than seven is only the annual variable cost of meals or $1,095; but because a new counselor must be hired (assuming again no part-time personnel), the marginal total cost of increasing output from eight to nine ADPs is $11,095, the cost of an additional year's meals *plus* the cost of adding a new counselor to the staff. Once this cost is incurred, marginal total costs will revert to variable costs of $1,095 until the providing agency reaches a level of output that requires still another counselor.

Knowing how the different elements of cost behave in relation to quantity produced contributes to a final piece of managerial information. If the selling price of a unit of output is known (or the contract revenue per ADP in the case of publicly funded, private not-for-profit agency), it permits managers to determine the *breakeven* point, the quantity of output that must be produced and sold or otherwise funded such that revenues will exactly equal costs. In this example, assuming $5,000 revenue per ADP, the breakeven point is roughly eleven ADPs; a lower level of production will result in a loss, while anything greater will generate a revenue surplus.

On the surface, it would appear that the application of the production-oriented, profit-making model to social programs is relatively straightforward, and indeed, it does permit managers to generate information that is extremely useful for purposes of management control. Yet if this simple example illustrates the manner in which the model can and should be used, its simplicity masks many of the most fundamental dilemmas that plague management control in the social welfare enterprise. It is to these issues that we now turn our attention.

efficiency and effectiveness in the social welfare enterprise

From a management control standpoint, social welfare programs and agencies differ in two important respects from the "typical" production-oriented, profit-making model of organization. First, for the most part, they are not-for-profit entities (either private or governmental), and second, they are engaged in the provision of services rather than the production of goods. The combined effect of both differences makes social programs far less susceptible to traditional methods of understanding internal operations, much less achieving managment control over those operations.

THE NATURE OF NOT-FOR-PROFIT SERVICE-PROVIDING ORGANIZATIONS

If an organization is engaged in the generation of profits, it possesses a readily identifiable and measurable standard of evaluation. Whereas the output of profit-making organizations has a known value that is specified in the marketplace, the services provided by not-for-profit or governmental organizations are either subsidized or given away free; the value of the output—and hence the organization—is thus specified by the indirect workings of the political system. The net result is that efficiency and effectiveness considerations are often treated *independently*, the result of decisions made by a variety of actors that may be far removed from the interal operations of the social program. As a result, little formal consideration may be given to the inherent tradeoffs between program efficiency and effectiveness, nor is a means provided for reconciling these tradeoffs.

A number of characteristics distinguish service-producing organizations, whether their purpose is to promote well-being or otherwise, from those engaged in the production of goods. And while much has been made of the distinction between profit-making and not-for-profit organizations, that distinction is possibly less significant than that between service and production organizations. Regardless of the importance of profits, "a company that manufactures goods has certain advantages, from a control standpoint, that a service organization does not have."[4]

A primary characteristic of any service organization is the need to accommodate the inseparability of production and consumption. Consumption is not an "act" as it is commonly conceptualized in organizations producing goods, but is rather a *process* in which a variety of organizational resources may be consumed over a period of time. The inseparability of production and consumption means that service organizations are more susceptible to environmental uncertainty and instability than are industrial organizations. A primary management objective of the latter is to *insulate* production from consumption, enabling relatively stable and efficient production processes to operate independently of fluctuations in resource availability and price as well as those of consumer demand. Raw materials and goods can be stockpiled and warehoused until demand warrants their use at a specific place and time for a specific price; one cannot, however, stockpile services. As a result, service organizations must build into their structure and resource base a measure of flexibility substantially greater than those engaged in the production of goods, flexibility that may substantially increase the cost of providing services. Unavailable resources to meet demand is a denial of access, and unused service facilities and resources must be considered as perishable products.[5] To each contingency must be attached a cost.

Through variable pricing policies, many service organizations are able to modify, to smooth out, demand so that it will conform to available resources. To increase demand during normally slow periods, baseball teams hold "bat days" and resorts have off-season rates. Certainly, among the service organizations most successful at matching the level of demand with fixed supply is the Bell Telephone company, with its variable pricing policy (and substantial advertising thereof) designed to stimulate service utilization during the late night and early morning hours. However, since social welfare organizations are designed to respond to human needs that may demand immediate satisfaction, such fundamental strategies of relating supply to demand must obviously be viewed with caution.

A second important distinction is that services are less tangible entities than products, and therefore objective evaluation of the processes used to produce them is more difficult to perform. Services cannot be pulled off the assembly line, inspected by quality control experts using a predetermined set of criteria and sophisticated measuring devices, rejected if unsatisfactory, and the production machinery repaired. With the exception of monitoring the adherence of service procedures to standards of quality established by administrators or service professionals, the evaluation of services is highly subjective. The fact that service delivery is an interactive process between provider and consumer means that *every service encounter is different from any other;* this encounter cannot be completely standardized and subjected to formal external evaluation. Indeed, evaluation by the user many frequently invoke criteria that may be considered substantively irrelevant by providers: waiting time even though not considered crucial to the effectiveness of the service; the personal demeanor and appearance of the provider; even the physical appearance of the service facility. While such factors may *seem* unimportant, it is difficult to conclude out of hand that they are insignificant in determining the value of the service provided.

The lack of a profitability component and the service-oriented nature of most social welfare activities clouds both the meaning of efficiency and effectiveness as they are traditionally understood and, hence, the values to be pursued through management control efforts. Indeed, in most public sector and not-for-profit endeavors, it is becoming increasingly common to substitute the term *productivity* for efficiency. And while the *traditional* definition of productivity is usually expressed as the ratio of output to the hours of labor required in its production, the *emerging* meaning of productivity is the efficiency with which a service of *specified quality* is provided.[6] Efficiency is a relative notion; one cannot simply speak of efficient or inefficient organizations. Rather it requires a basis of comparison, and the value of the concept lies in the fact that it allows decision makers to *compare* the efficiency of one organization or one organizational process with another. To avoid comparing apples and oranges in evaluating efficiency, decision makers must first ensure that a consistent definition of output or unit of service is used. And second, they must ensure that each unit of service being compared is of equivalent quality.

EFFICIENCY AND THE UNIT OF SERVICE

Ideally, for a given level of quality, the assessment of efficiency in the service-providing organization would proceed along lines identical to the youth care example previously discussed. Create a production function that identifies the quantities of all inputs required to produce a unit of output; examine the behavior of each of these costs as output increases; and create a cost function. This will provide managers, funding bodies, and other interested groups with the tools necessary to assess changes in productivity over time or to compare productivity measures with different agencies providing the same service. A prerequisite to this approach is obviously the ability to identify the outputs and inputs that will enable comparison, to identify a *unit of service* and the various inputs required in its provision. Unfortunately, as the following will illustrate, each of these rather basic and simple measures has proven extremely difficult to define in practice.

In many communities the majority of social services are provided on a contract basis by relatively small, not-for-profit organizations. Each year, either in response to requests from state, county, or local units of government, or as part of the allocation process of charitable organizations such as the United Way of America, these not-for-profit service organizations submit proposals or budgetary requests to operate programs for the coming fiscal year. Included in the proposals are two items of crucial interest to funding bodies—estimates of program cost and of program output. Typically, these estimates become the major basis for selecting among providers competing to supply the same service, or if there is no competition, for determining the amount of dollars to be allocated to the program. Put yourself in the position of one member of a panel charged with reviewing a variety of such proposals. Based upon your understanding of cost functions and productivity, what questions would you ask?

Two proposals are received from two different providers to supply 5,000 meals for needy individuals over the course of a year. One proposal for $10,000 works out to $2 per meal; the other for $7,500 will cost $1.50 per meal. Why the difference? Is one program more efficient, or does the cost difference result from differences in quality? If you're like most people you'll ask what inputs go into preparing and serving the meals—how much food, how prepared, of what quality and nutritional value. You'll also probably want to know how much of the proposed budget represents fixed costs like administration and overhead.

Another agency intends to provide outreach services to senior citizens—one thousand contacts per year at a cost of $6,000. But what is a contact, you ask. How much time, how much travel is involved? How well trained is the outreach worker? How many of the one thousand individuals contacted will be placed in available programs as a direct result of the outreach service? What are the fixed costs of administration and overhead? Might it be more efficient to contract for two thousand outreach contacts?

Two crisis counseling centers submit identical proposals to provide two hundred counseling sessions designed to alleviate family crisis. The cost of each program would be $4,000. But are the two proposed programs really identical; are they of equal quality? How much input goes into each? Are the "sessions" of equal duration? Are they group or individual sessions? Are they staffed by professionals? Although crisis programs, are appointments still required?

A day care center submits a proposal to provide supervised care to children of migrant workers during the harvesting season. The $5,000 program will employ two persons and provide services to fifteen children, eight hours a day, for a total of fifty days. "How much service is provided?" one panel member asks. Two persons for fifty days at eight hours per day is eight hundred hours of service provided. "But how much is *received?*" another panel member wants to know. Fifteen children for fifty days at eight hours per day yields six thousand hours of service received. But which is the more appropriate unit of service, the panel heatedly debates—units provided or units received?

There is no single, universally accepted unit of output for social programs. Rather, the above illustrate that there are four common methods for defining and measuring service outputs: (1) a "contact" and a "counseling session" represent *activity* units; (2) a "child care day" either provided or received and an ADP are *time* units; (3) a "meal" represents a *material* unit; and (4) a "placement" such as might result from an outreach contact or a referral activity is an *outcome* unit.[7] The above further illustrate the difficulty one encounters in attempting to create succinct, consistent, and meaningful service unit definitions to be used in the assessment of productivity. In most social welfare programs the distinction between inputs and outputs is blurred because with the exception of material units such as a meal, there is no physical transformation of raw materials into finished goods and production and consumption occur simultaneously.

Rather than centering upon the physical transformation of raw materials into finished goods, the service-providing process reflects an *organizational* transformation in which a variety of knowledge and skills possessed by people are brought to bear on a problem or need. We may "input" a doctor, a nurse, or a counselor, and we still have a doctor, nurse, and counselor after the service has been provided; only their time has been consumed. In some cases, however, provider skills plus the incorporation of capital and supplies will result in the performance of a frequently performed and readily definable task or activity—a contact, a referral, or a commonly performed medical procedure such as an appendectomy. Moreover, with sufficient analysis it may be possible to attach a cost to capital, supplies and the time spent by persons possessing different knowledge and skill levels in the performance of the activity. This is a management activity that has come to be known as *human resource accounting.*

The idea behind the human resource accounting approach is to identify all of the skills, capital equipment, facilities, and supplies required to perform a common service activity. Consider, for example, a medical care organization. If one could identify all of the inputs—patient bed days, operating room time including preparation and cleanup, surgeon, anesthesiologist, and nurse time, drugs, linens, X-rays, and so on—for a standard procedure, say an appendectomy, one would have created a production function identical to that discussed in the preceding section. Further, were it possible to calculate the costs of each of the separate inputs involved, it would then be possible to generate a cost function, useful not only in determining the fees to be charged, but for evaluating and perhaps improving productivity.

Instead of performing this analysis for each and every possible medical activity, all other procedures might be expressed in terms of the input required to perform an appendectomy; in essence, the appendectomy becomes a common denominator for comparing dissimilar medical activities. For example, a heart transplant could be expressed in terms of the various resources required to perform a single appendectomy; perhaps 14.2 appendectomies are equal to one heart transplant. Much as a builder is able to estimate the costs of a house once the square footage is known—despite the many and varied inputs required in its construction—administrators in the field of medical care would have a standard basis, or *relative value system,* with which to assess costs, outputs, and relative efficiency.[8]

For some services, however, there may be no neatly definable or concrete activity that results from the input of specialized labor, capital, and supplies. In these cases, it is common to measure service output in terms of time—an hour of nursing care, a day of child care, ten minutes of consultation. Here too, however, the distinction between inputs and outputs may be blurred, but for a second reason. Since production and consumption occur simultaneously, it is often not clear whether output measures should focus upon services provided or services received. Clearly, a focus upon services provided—an hour of consultation by a trained specialist—is the more valuable for determining costs and relative efficiency. But one would suspect that the nature of services received (for example, whether counseling was performed on an individual basis or in a large group) is an important determinant of funds received and perhaps of effectiveness. It is here that the comparison of services of similar quality is important. If, for example, we can assume that quality and effectiveness are dependent upon whether individual or group consultation was provided, then we would not want to compare the relative productivity of individual versus group sessions.

Of the four, the ideal unit of output would seem to be service outcome, or the direct *result* of the service activity performed—an outreach contact or a referral results in a placement; a class action suit results in a change in program eligibility requirements; a medical procedure yields a cure; a day of child care permits a mother to work or earn a degree; an hour of counseling resolves a family crisis. The problems in defining and measuring service outcomes, as we shall see in the next chapter, are numerous and difficult to overcome. Lacking clearly established goals, it is often unclear which of many possible service outcomes are important. And when we do know what to look for, the ability to relate results to services performed is frequently beyond the technical capacity of current information systems and may raise serious questions regarding personal privacy as well.

Much effort has gone into the attempt to define (and refine alternative definitions of) service output as a basis for comparing and perhaps improving the efficiency with which alternative programs are carried out. In general, these efforts have tended to incorporate all four types of service unit, rather than attempting, for example, to express every service in terms of its principal activity. Typical of these studies is one recently performed by the Booz-Allen Public Administration Services in conjunction with the accounting firm of Touche-Ross & Company.[9] Symptomatic of the complexities involved, the study produced forty-nine different possible service units for only eighteen different services. Some examples of the service units developed are as follows: family planning, one medical contraceptive supply or device; transportation, one one-way trip; homemaker service, one hour of homemaker service; foster care for adults, one placement in a foster care home.

At present, there is no one best way of defining and measuring service output and, hence, no best way of measuring the efficiency with which alternative services are provided. Faced with this reality, social program administrators are well-advised to: (1) adopt like measures and maintain consistent data for services likely to be compared; (2) recognize that regardless of the sophistication of the measure selected, it will consistently capture only a fraction of the many factors affecting "true" service productivity; and (3) be aware that such measures will influence the behavior of those persons whose activities are being monitored and because the measures are crude they may actually promote behavior that brings about a decline in "true" productivity.

PROGRAM EFFECTIVENESS AND SERVICE QUALITY

Effectiveness is traditionally defined as the degree to which an organization achieves its objectives, and it is in dogged pursuit of those objectives that the organization is assumed to conduct and direct its various activities. While all social programs possess official objectives of varying specificity, we have seen they are probably lesser determinants of program activities than the various constraints imposed by groups and individuals to which the program will be held accountable and to which program administration must respond. Within an open systems perspective, then, it is not surprising that *flexibility* or the ability of the program to respond to various constraints is an important indicator of program effectiveness.[10]

Flexibility, however, is only an indicator of effectiveness. It is in an organizational characteristic whose only ultimate value may be the promotion of survivability. If, in contrast, the program is viewed as an instrument for correctly matching services to needs, our attention is drawn not to survival but to the manner in which effectiveness is perceived by groups and interests having control over program operations. We are interested in those aspects of program performance that are monitored and controlled in the interests of achieving effectiveness and to which limited administrative attention is inevitably drawn. One such indicator—and a key element in the definition and measurement of productivity as well—is the important idea of service quality.

Quality. You can see it, hear it, feel it, sleep on it, taste it, and you, indeed, pay for it. But it cannot be easily defined or measured. Although the precise nature of a "quality product" has no specific definition, we nonetheless possess certain *indicators* of quality for finished goods—long life, a good paint job, close tolerances for parts that fit together, reliability, quiet operation, and so on. Moreover, finished goods can be inspected and closely scrutinized by quality control or value engineering experts to ensure that certain defined and measurable standards—established by the producing organization—are maintained. And finally, the idea of product quality contributes to the effectiveness of the organization through the operation of the market; of two goods that are similarly priced, it can be assumed that consumers will demand that which is of higher quality.

If the idea of product quality is vague and imprecise, the quality of service is even more so. Consider the quality of your educational experience. How would you assess it? Most of you would include such *process* criteria as: the enthusiasm, accessibility, and "relevance" of the instructors; the quality of your friendships; even the quality of the football team. After the fact, you might assess its quality in terms of *outcome* criteria, such as your ability to get a rewarding job. And how is quality ensured by an accrediting board? By adopting *structural* criteria and standards: the proportion of the faculty possessing PhDs, the student-teacher ratio, the course content of the curriculum, average class sizes, characteristics of the physical facilities, and so on. This example illustrates the three most common means of defining and measuring service quality. Process criteria and measures are concerned with the actual nature of the *work* performed. Structural criteria and measures are concerned with the potential or the *capacity* of an organization to perform the work. And outcome criteria and measures concentrate upon the *results* achieved through organizational activities.[11] Because the outcome criterion has become the most specialized and technically complex it will not be discussed in detail here, but will be the subject of the following chapter.

Process criteria and measures of service quality are usually defined in reference to the activities performed on behalf of the individual user. And while the assessment of this notion of quality may entail direct observation of actual service activities by peers, supervisors, or external evaluators, the most important data are obtained from service records. Given such data, one would likely ask the following questions: What was the problem experienced by the service user? What services were provided? Were the services appropriate to the need? Was a referral provided and was it correct and timely, resulting in the provision of a service by another program? Process measures, moreover, may be aggregated to provide rough quantitative measures, sometimes useful in performing crude productivity comparisons between different organizations engaged in the provision of similar services. Common measures include the number of cases processed by intake workers, the average caseload, the number of clients visited by caseworkers, the number of referrals provided, and the average number of contact hours with service users.[12] Of course, each of these methods of measuring process quality requires successively more abstract interpretation, from direct observation, to written records, to aggregate data—interpretation that may distort and obscure the true "quality" of the service actually provided.

Structural criteria and measures are centered upon gross organizational characteristics, those related to the organization's capacity to perform work rather than upon the relationship of actual work activities to service users. Such factors might be the availability of various types of services, the adequacy and accessibility of facilities, the qualifications of staff as measured by educational achievement and professional certification, and the adequacy of certain support structures, such as data and information systems, accounting systems, and reporting procedures. Structural measures are those that often provide the basis for accreditation reviews of educational institutions, assessment of service contractors by agents of government charged with letting contracts, and licensing proceedings for various types of social service providers.

The evaluation of service quality by whatever method requires not only a variety of measures, but a set of *standards* that define acceptable program performance. In the absence of valid and reliable outcome measures, and yet amidst substantial impressionistic evidence that a social welfare program or organization may not be performing effectively, process and structural standards may become the lever through which external actors will attempt to alter organizational performance. Traditionally the responsibility of professional societies and federal, state, and local regulatory bodies, the establishment of many such standards clearly do protect the user. Indeed, a number of studies have shown that many process measures—courtesy, promptness, and the sensitivity of the provider to the unique problems and needs of the user—are of high value to the user.[13] Nonetheless, the heavy-handed nature with which service standards are established and imposed (and frequently reestablished and reimposed) is often a serious and costly matter for providing organizations; occasionally, however, the results are not without humor.

One such example concerns a recent attempt by the state of Washington to improve the quality of nursing home care. In this case the state imposed the requirement (one does not know how they were to test for compliance) that all persons in state-supported nursing homes would be required to wear underwear. Exemptions to this requirement would be allowed only with written permission from the individual's physician. An irate doctor, confronted with just such a request, writes in the letters column of the Washington *Daily Olympian:*

Today I was called from a local nursing home . . . to exempt a little old lady, 100 years old, who, if she is like many of the women of her generation now in nursing homes may never have worn a brassiere in her life. So, now in her 101st year, should she start?[14]

The inability of politicians, professionals, and administrators to formulate and enforce service standards that would ensure quality care for all individuals has largely been responsible for the growing influence of the courts over professional and administrative practice in social welfare organizations.[15] Clearly, the most publicized of the courts' activities have been in the area of malpractice in medicine, legal services, and in education, but such cases are generally argued on the basis of an alleged unsatisfactory service outcome. Another area of lesser known court involvement, but one of increasing significance, has been with respect to standards of performance—not merely in ensuring compliance with existing standards, but in the more important policy-making role of judging the appropriateness of the standards themselves.

In Alabama, a federal district court judge intervened and revised existing standards of care in that state's mental health institutions, resulting in a fourfold increase in the cost of care.[16] In Chicago, one federal district court ruling included detailed provision for the kinds of housing units to be provided under a public housing program, as well as for their location, and even their design. In Washington, D.C., the court established, on grounds of equality, the guidelines for an internal distribution of school department funds. In Massachusetts, the state was required by a federal district court judge to hire a specified number of additional social workers to implement the state's programs.[17]

The substantive reasoning behind the court's intervention in the details of policy implementation has its origins in the antipoverty and civil rights movements of the fifties and sixties, a time when it was widely believed that many administrators and politicians, especially in the South, were consciously hindering the implementation of these rights. Spurred on by a then liberal U. S. Supreme Court, an increasing number of judges came to believe that these failures reflected a sufficient "dereliction of duty as to require judicial intervention."[18] What was originally a constitutional guarantee of equal rights has become an issue of how these rights are to be implemented—the right to equal access to services, the right to equal access to services of equal quality, the right to humane services (in penal or public mental health institutions), the right to effective services, or the right to equal service outcomes. The question is: Other than the courts, who is to determine specifically which of these right is to be pursued?

Analytically and politically, issues of productivity and effectiveness in the social welfare enterprise are complex, involving the interplay of many forces largely beyond the administrator's control. The problems surrounding the definition and attainment of productivity and effectiveness have occupied the efforts of scholars and practitioners for years and promise much continued effort in the future. Yet there is a time when the theoretical, the problematic, and the abstract must be translated into action. And this occurs primarily through the budgetary process.

budgeting

In organizations lacking readily definable measures of productivity and effectiveness, the budget is of paramount importance in virtually all aspects of administrative decision making. Indeed, in most public and not-for-profit organizations one finds that the budget is the culmination of virtually all administrative knowledge and organizational aspirations. In the budget can be embodied a plan, a statement of program, an ordering of priorities, a means of ensuring accountability to a wide variety of interests, a method of control, as well as an instrument for improving organizational efficiency and effectiveness.

It is common to distinguish between the budgetary *instrument* and the budgetary *process,* both, in Aaron Wildavsky's words, ultimately "concerned with the translation of financial resources into human purposes."[19] It cannot be overemphasized that the budgetary process, which constitutes the search for and allocation of funds, is fundamentally a political process dealing quite clearly with the question of who is to get what, when, and how. Viewed from a federal perspective, the process may be seen to embrace four principal activities: the legislative adoption of law, which will include an *appropriation* of funds; the *allocation* of funds to the federal implementing agency, which will in turn allocate funds to appropriate state and local agencies; the *expenditure* of funds; and the *postaudit* of those expenditures. At the federal level, the elapsed time for the first three of these activities—from the initial spring preview of the executive budget by the Office of Management and Budget, to completion of the executive budget in January of the following year, to congressional action in the summer and fall, to eventual expenditure in the following winter and spring—will span nearly two years. "This is not control," Wildavsky quips, "but remote control."[20]

A substantial portion of social program funds, however, bypass much of the traditional budgetary process; these are the funds expended in support of various *entitlements.* Tax credits and deductions for housing, medical care, child care and other governmentally determined necessities bypass the budgetary process because the tax revenues that would otherwise have been collected were these entitlements not in force never enter the federal treasury. Other entitlements—social security benefits; public assistance benefits under SSI and AFDC; food stamps; and, until the federal ceiling was imposed, Title XX grants for the states for social services —are funded through *open-ended* appropriations. As long as the applicant, be it an individual or an agency, satisfies the statutory and administrative eligibility criteria, funds will be allocated. With the exception of legal and administrative determinations of who is eligible and who is not, little control can be exerted over program costs once the open-ended appropriation has been made—unless Congress adopts new limiting legislation. And with respect to the former source of control, if government desires to increase utilization by all those who are eligible, overutilization is likely to increase as well, thereby increasing costs. Cost can be decreased by "tightening up" on eligibility determination, but at the expense of underutilization by those who are eligible.[21]

For funds that are governed by the traditional budgetary process, it is useful to conceive of the initial stages in that process as creating a bridge between the goals and expectations—however vaguely expressed—of the funding organization, be it a governmental or nongovernmental entity, and the expressed intentions and capabilities of the potential recipient of funds. Initially, this process encompasses three principal activities: budget preparation, budget review, and budget approval. The instrument that provides the focal point of these three activities is what is often called the *legislative budget.* At a minimum the legislative budget submitted to funding organizations for approval will include: a summary of programs and their objectives; some definition of the service or services to be provided; an estimate of the need population and the expected level of utilization for the funding period; and a statement of anticipated program costs and requested funds.

The legislative budget is the document through which funding bodies will evaluate and weigh alternative requests for funds, requests that will almost surely exceed total funds available. Beyond the basic minimum, then, additional information required as part of the legislative budget will depend upon the basis of evaluation selected by the funding organization. This is reflected in one of a variety of possible budgetary formats adopted by the funding body, formats which specify the information required of all organizations seeking funds. As we shall see shortly, different formats will emphasize accountability to certain values and the importance of certain information differently—some will emphasize control over expenditures, others efficiency, and still others effectiveness. Like any instrument used to understand, evaluate, and improve organizational performance, each format is selective in the information deemed essential for sound, rational administration.

Once appropriations have been made, the budget takes on a new role; called the *executive* budget, it becomes the instrument through which control over expenditures is exercised and accountability to the funding organization is ensured. Regardless of the format of the legislative budget, seldom will it be sufficiently detailed to have fully answered all of the questions pertaining to budgetary implementation. Thus budget execution becomes a task of attempting to reconcile the general (and often ambiguously specified) legislative mandate with the legal restrictions that frequently accompany the appropriation of funds.

THE LEGISLATIVE BUDGET

The format specified for preparation of the legislative budget will generally be one or a combination of three major types: line item, performance, and program budgets, reflecting the values of control, efficiency, and effectiveness respectively. In recent years a number of hybrid budgetary formats have been developed, each seeking to improve the budget as a tool for rational decision making and control. These include the planning programming budgeting system (PPBS), zero-based budgeting (ZBB), and program performance budgets. In general, each of these attempts to combine in various ways and with varying emphasis the values of control, efficiency, and effectiveness promoted by the three basic formats.

The *line item budget* focuses upon the costs of basic *inputs* such as employee salaries and benefits, travel, utilities, and supplies required in the performance of an organization's activities; these "objects of expenditure" are generally compiled and listed by organizational department. The standard for evaluating funding requests within the line item format is incrementally based, occurring via comparison with the prior year's budget. Although the information contained in a line item budget is essential for maintaining control over inputs, its weakness as a legislative budgetary instrument is that it provides decision makers with little information as to why the money should be expended; it says nothing about outputs, or the objectives of the expenditure. The following statement by a voluntary trustee of a mental health organization typifies the weaknesses of the line item budget for much more than a basic tool of cost control, one of balancing revenues with expenditures.

> Customarily, about once a year the financial or accounting staff looked at the institution's expenses for heat, light, telephone, professional dues, and so on, and guessed how much these might increase next year. . . . I wonder how many of the trustees have shared my experience of masking feelings of impotence and ignorance as I solemnly

reviewed the lists of figures. . . . As soon as the budget was in balance, I approved it, without any real reason for knowing that the year should or could come out that way.[22]

A budgetary format that addresses one of the major weaknesses of the line item budget—a lack of information about outputs—is the *perfor-mance* budget. Whereas the line item budget focuses upon the costs of various inputs like personnel or supplies, the performance budget empha-sizes the costs of various *outputs*—the cost of a meal served, an appendec-tomy performed, or one ADP in a youth care center. Unlike the line item format, which promotes the use of a historical standard for evaluating requests, budgetary review within the performance format may be based upon standards of *efficiency.* However, since a prerequisite of the perfor-mance format is the ability to establish relationships between input costs and service outputs, it suffers from many of the problems associated with the production and cost functions previously discussed in this chapter.

Originally developed in the thirties and revived by the first Hoover Commission in the late forties, the concept of performance budgeting gained increased attention in the social welfare enterprise with the publi-cation in 1974 of the American Certified Public Accountants' Industry Audit Guide, *Audits of Voluntary Health and Welfare Organizations.* [23] The major contributions of this guide were two. First, it established that the development and use of performance measures were to be considered essential to the achievement of acceptable accounting principles within social welfare organizations. (One cannot underestimate the power of this professional organization when it comes to defining such principles of sound administrative practice; its role is central in determining, from the viewpoint of the accounting profession, what constitutes accountable financial practices.) And it was this manual that was largely responsible for initiating the tremendous effort that has recently gone into the definition of measurable units of service.

As a second contribution, the guide provided a widely applicable, if very general, scheme for a functional classification of expenditures, mak-ing it possible to transcend the original line item format and to include some crude measures of service output and organizational efficiency. Rec-ognizing that specific outputs will vary widely among different organiza-tions, the guide suggests only very general functional classifications and very general recommendations pertaining to their implementation. Basi-cally, the guide identifies two types of services. *Program* services are those that relate to the organization's social service activities. Included in this category are various measures of service units previously discussed—one child care day, one counseling session, one referral, and so on. The second category, *supporting* services, is broken down into two further categories:

administrative services and expenditures and fund-raising services and expenditures.[24]

Other than providing direction, the guide's contribution to the construction of workable performance budgets are, unfortunately, few. The development of the necessary production and cost functions continues to depend upon the ability to define adequate measures of service output. The format also requires, as we shall see shortly, substantial financial management expertise in correctly allocating costs among functions that are shared by various organizational departments and programs.

Program budgeting reorients the focus of evaluation away from the internal cost and efficiency concerns of line item and performance budgets, and concentrates instead upon the *purposes* of organizational activities and the *effectiveness* with which they are carried out. Consistent with this shift in budgetary purpose is a shift in structural orientation as well, from the organization or the department as the focus of budgetary efforts to the *program*, regardless of the number and variety of organizations, departments, or levels of government that might be involved with its planning, funding, and implementation. Rather than being prepared independently of or in response to previously established goals and objectives, the program budgeting format encourages an organizational synthesis which focuses upon the relationships between stated program objectives and the costs required (or proposed) to achieve them.

Despite the fact that program budgeting suffers from a number of drawbacks—a fragmented and decentralized organizational and planning environment upon which programs must often be superimposed, a weakness in its emphasis upon efficiency, a general lack of agreement upon goals and standards, and a shortage of useful and inexpensive methods of planning and evaluation—the program budgeting format spawned an even more ambitious format in the 1960s called the Planning Programming Budgeting System (PPBS). PPBS, developed by the RAND Corporation for adoption in the Department of Defense, and required of all federal agencies for a short time in the Johnson Administration, promotes a systems view of problem solving, combining long-range planning, programming, budgeting, and evaluation into a single comprehensive process. In particular, it expands upon the program budgeting format by requiring that the *benefits* to be derived from the achievement of specified objectives be determined and expressed in monetary terms. By adopting the essential elements of both program and performance budgeting to create quantifiable estimates of program costs and benefits, PPBS institutionalized benefit-cost analysis—the ultimate aid in rational administrative problem solving.

Books have been written on both the procedural and substantive pros and cons of this budgetary format,[25] and, for the time being at least, the cons appear to have won out. Among the most pervasive criticisms of the approach are the following: the analysis required to determine the economic benefits and costs of all decision alternatives is extremely difficult and expensive to perform, drawing resources away from the actual provision of needed services; it is ends-oriented, while American political debate frequently focuses upon the means; it biases results in favor of those objectives and strategies that lend themselves to easy quantification; and it is best performed for activities administered by centralized, comprehensive, and highly coordinated decision-making centers. While many of the difficulties with the approach were technical in nature, the abandonment of PPBS in its pure form was hastened on political grounds, because it was seen as the symbol of political forces opposed to incremental, decentralized, pluralist planning and decision making.

Since the advent and decline of PPBS, a number of additional budgetary formats have appeared, two of which deserve brief mention here. Both reflect the goal-oriented, rationalistic spirit of PPBS, but both represent a significant retreat from its global rationalistic optimism. The first of these is zero-based budgeting (ZBB), a technique originally developed in private enterprise and now being implemented in many federal, state, and local governmental agencies.

ZBB is a budgetary format specifically designed to combat a common problem of all large-scale organizations, public, and private alike—the year to year funding momentum that develops within existing agencies, in which each year's budget becomes but an incremental increase (or decrease) over its previous allocation. To counter this trend, agencies and departments are required to submit a number of alternative budgetary requests that are, say 80 percent, 90 percent, 100 percent and 110 percent of the previous year's levels (despite its label, "zero" is never used in ZBB). The format promotes the achievement of efficiency, since it focuses upon marginal increases in activities performed or outputs provided—say the number of ADPs—and the marginal costs required; it thus permits budgetary decision makers to evaluate the gains (or losses) expected to result from a 10 or 20 percent change from the previous year's request. The strategy is implemented by requiring all prospective recipients of funds to create alternative "decision packages" for alternative levels of funding, which reflect internal priorities for existing activities. Funding bodies then select the set of decision packages, say the 90 percent budget from one agency, the 100 percent budget from another, and so on, up to their maximum level of funds.[26]

Like PPBS, zero-based budgeting is committed to rational planning and priority setting; unlike PPBS, however, plans and priorities do not emerge from the results of a global benefit-cost calculus, but are rather initiated in the decision package rankings supplied by decentralized decision-making units. Additionally, ZBB planning cycles are of much shorter range—normally one year—than are those of PPBS, creating a better match between the planning and budgetary periods. At present, the verdict on ZBB is inconclusive, with some critics suggesting that for many of the same reasons it will suffer the same fate of its predecessor, and with others claiming that its practice is little different from incremental budgeting.[27] However, as long as it is supported in Washington and pressures to reduce governmental expenditures continue to mount, zero-based budgeting or a variation on the theme may continue the object of experimentation for some time.

A final format, called *program performance budgeting,*[28] combines the principles of performance and program budgeting; the result is a *dual emphasis upon efficiency and effectiveness.* Although similar, program performance budgeting retreats from PPBS in a number of significant ways: it is amenable to far greater degrees of decentralization; it does not include multiyear fiscal plans; and, most important, it does not attempt to enumerate the dollar costs and benefits of alternative program outcomes.

Implicit in the discussion of budgetary formats thus far is the important idea that, in addition to emphasizing alternative conceptions of administrative accountability, each budgetary format tends to mirror the structural parameters of the organization in which it is implemented. The line item and performance budgets tend to reflect hierarchically centralized organizations factored by function; the program budget and PPBS centralized organizations factored along program lines; and ZBB, decentralized organizations usually factored by program or "profit centers." Each of these formats reflects a singular basis of performance, information flows, and control. Because of its dual emphasis upon efficiency and effectiveness, the program performance budgetary format is amenable to an organizational structure that emphasizes *both* functional and program conceptions of performance, information flows, and control. Such a structure is called a *matrix* organization.[29] And although they may not be represented as such in the ubiquitous organization chart, many social welfare agencies charged with the implementation of multiple programs can easily be visualized in the matrix format, comprising two intersecting lines of authority that facilitate *lateral relationships* between different functions and different programs.

It is important to note at this point that the dual emphasis upon function and program is not the only way to conceive of or to construct a matrix organization. Rather any two (and sometimes more) means of factoring social welfare agencies may be combined. One might, for example, combine programmatic and geographical dimensions. Or—as would be the case in agencies where a caseworker is used to facilitate lateral relations among different programs on behalf of one or a group of clients—a matrix emphasizing client and program dimensions might be appropriate. In principle, the design should reflect the dimensions within which the need for lateral relations among organizational units is greatest. If, however, the functional classifications developed by the American Institute of Certified Public Accountants is used to represent a common function division of activities,[30] the function-program matrix shown in Figure 6.3 results.

The essential feature of this matrix organization is that it purposefully separates control over the process of converting resources into necessary functions from the process of transforming functions into tangible program outputs and outcomes. That is, the heads of functional departments are responsible for the "production" process of converting input resources into functional outputs. Program managers are responsible for organizing these outputs into goal-related programs; many—like fund raising, intake, referral, and other functions—will be shared among a variety of programs within the same agency. In effect, because the program is the conduit through which resources flow to the organization, program managers "purchase" their varied functional needs from the heads of departments. Inevitably, however, there will be conflicts created by these two lines of authority;[31] functional departments may not be able to provide the needed functions, at either a sufficient level of quality or quantity, at a price the program manager can justify within the budget. But much as the conflict existing between production and sales in profit-making organizations tends to focus upon the inevitable tradeoff between efficiency and effectiveness, the application of matrix principles brings such conflict to the surface and purposefully creates a forum in which it can be debated, assessed, and controlled.

Because of its requirement that dual lines of authority be maintained —a requirement that may initially increase agency costs—the matrix structure is considered by many experts to be among the most complex of organizational structures.[32] Nonetheless, and paralleling the advantages of the program performance budgetary format with which it is conceptually consistent, the matrix organization is one of the few structures that permits centralization and decentralization to coexist. It thus allows the organization to adapt to an uncertain and dynamic environment, one in

FIGURE 6.3:
a matrix organization

	Programs		
Functions	*Program A*	*Program B*	*Program C*
Program services			
Support services			

which an agency's programs and funding levels may quickly change in response to external forces, but where the common functions performed remain relatively constant. Most important, neither requires radical change, only evolutionary development in current budgetary and organizational practices.[33]

Whatever the theoretical emphasis of the prevailing budgetary format—better planning, greater effectiveness, improved efficiency, better control—it will almost certainly change. Indeed, in most governmental and not-for-profit organizations merely keeping pace with new developments in the budgetary process is a major task. In the social welfare enterprise this task is made dramatically more complex and time-consuming because it is likely that funds—many to be applied to the operation of the same program —will be sought from a number of different sources. Each source of potential funds will very likely implement the budgetary process on a different schedule, have adopted a different budgetary format, possess different reporting requirements, promote the attainment of different objectives, and even operate under a different funding cycle and a different fiscal year. The lack of budgetary standardization is a characteristic feature of a decentralized, pluralist society; it helps guarantee a balance among the three prime thrusts of administrative accountability: efficiency, effectiveness, and cost control. That new formats come into vogue and rapidly recede, but that the line item is always there as a backup is indicative of which of these thrusts reigns perpetually supreme.

Yet from the viewpoint of the service provider who must rely upon a variety of funding sources, each of which may allocate only a fraction of total program or agency costs, this fragmentation of funding creates a number of serious difficulties. First, the nearly full-time preoccupation with a variety of different budgetary processes may frequently divert attention away from the very improvement in program each process is attempting to stimulate; fund seeking becomes a full-time job. A second problem is the uncertainty caused by the failure of even a single source of funds to materialize which may result in the need to drastically modify program plans or to eliminate a program altogether. "To obtain its budget," writes Peter Drucker, the agency "needs the approval, or at least acquiescence, of practically everybody who remotely could be considered a 'constituent.'" Concerning the impact of budgetary pluralism on the ability of the organization to plan and to establish priorities, Drucker continues:

> Where a market share of 22 per cent might be perfectly satisfactory to a business, a "rejection" by 78% of its "constituency"—or even a smaller proportion—would be fatal to a budget-based institution. And this means that the service institution finds it difficult to set priorities; it must instead try to placate everyone by doing a little bit of everything—which, in effect, means achieving nothing.[34]

Once funds have been applied for and allocations received, the function of the budget shifts from a device for seeking funds to one through which control over organizational performance is exercised. Until this point, the budget has represented, in effect, a plan of action; now that plan must be implemented. But the complexity created by multiple programs designed to achieve multiple objectives receiving funds from many different sources does not diminish during budgetary execution; indeed, a primary function of the executive budget is to ensure that accountability is maintained by preserving the various distinctions among programs and budgets.

BUDGET EXECUTION

The fundamental idea behind budget execution is that funds be expended in a manner accountable to the legislative mandate which is either explicitly or implicitly attached to the appropriation of funds. The basic building block of a governmental or not-for-profit executive budget is the *fund,* a specific allocation of dollar and other resources which is earmarked "for the purpose of carrying on specific activities or attaining certain objectives in accordance with special regulations, restrictions, or limitations."[35] Unlike a private business enterprise in which all revenues go into a single pot and from which disbursals are made in pursuit of organizational objectives, most public and not-for-profit organizations will exercise control over a number of distinct funds, each of which must be treated as a unique financial entity. The central importance of the fund concept, in which the receiving organization is considered a "steward" for the funds and is held legally accountable for ensuring that they are expended in accordance with the restrictions attached to them,[36] is twofold. First, as self-balancing financial entities, expenditures are clearly limited to the amount appropriated; one cannot overexpend the budget without formal approval. Second, the existence of various funds—even if applied to the same program or service—means that it is necessary to keep track of the amount and purpose of expenditures from each fund.

For example, a local not-for-profit aging program may receive funds from a variety of sources to provide a variety of in-home care services to the elderly within the community. As shown in Figure 6.4, it may receive, among others, funds from the Department of Health, Education and Welfare, which flow through a state Department of Elderly Affairs, and which are provided to the program under a purchase-of-services contractual agreement. It may have applied for and received a project grant directly from HEW. Furthermore, if the recipient of services resides in a designated neighborhood, the program may have received Community Development Block Grant funds from the Department of Housing and Urban Development, which flow through and—as would be the case were it also receiving

FIGURE 6.4:

a typical funding arrangement for a local social welfare program

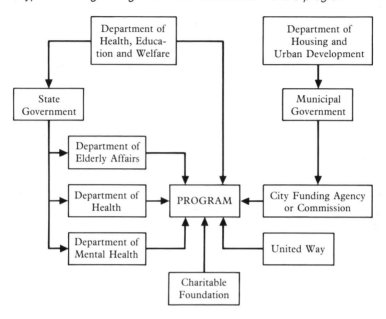

Source: Adapted from Comptroller General of the United States, Information and Referral for People Needing Human Services—A Complex System That Should Be Improved *(Washington, D.C.: General Accounting Office, March 20, 1978), p. 19.*

general revenue-sharing funds—are allocated contractually by a general purpose municipal government. The program may also be under different contracts from the state departments of mental health, and health, which —in consideration of the appropriate match from state general revenues, usually requiring state legislative action—have received funds from HEW. The program may have applied for and received a prepayment project grant from a charitable foundation. And finally (and this does not exhaust the the possibilities) the program may receive funds in the case of a budgetary shortfall, under the deficit financing arrangements used by the local United Way.

Typically, each funding organization will administer its allocation as if it were the sole source of funds provided to the program. This entails different reporting requirements for each source of funds, and even different planning and expenditure periods. For example, the federal government operates on a fiscal year that has recently changed from October to October; most state and local governments are still on the previous federal fiscal year, which runs from June to June; and the United Way will use a fiscal year that matches the calendar year. Statistical reporting requirements may easily differ for each funding source and for the Area Agency on Aging which in this case has coordination responsibilities. The charitable foundation may only require information stating the total number of persons served, while restrictions on the Community Development Block Grant funds require that their place of residence be ascertained and reported. Required supportive activities may also differ; some funding bodies may require outreach and referral efforts, while others will not.

Among the most common of restrictions attached to the use of social welfare funds concerns what is called their *fungibility*—the freedom with which administrators can interchange or replace them with other funds.[37] Frequently, the restrictions that accompany the receipt of funds provide for limited or nonexistent fungibility. The Community Development Block Grant funds just discussed provide an excellent case in point; they cannot be used to support programs that were funded by other sources in prior years. If a child care program were funded out of city general revenues in one year and it were desired to free those revenues for other purposes this year, the void cannot be filled by transferring Community Development Block Grant funds to that program.

If a measure of organizational effectiveness is its flexibility—its ability to respond to unforeseen changes in an uncertain environment—then restrictions in the transferability and interchangeability of funds is a serious barrier to the achievement of effectiveness in the social welfare enterprise. Consider two programs designed to provide care for the elderly. One program with its independent fund is intended to subsidize the cost of nursing home care at an average cost of $10,000 per user per year. The other program, also with its designated fund, is designed to provide the necessary support for seniors desiring to live at home. Cost of noninstitutionalized care: $2,000 per user per year. Mid-fiscal year it becomes apparent that the agency responsible for administering both programs has seriously underestimated the need for home care, while it appears that the nursing home program will be underutilized. Since both programs deal with the same user population and since both are presumably aimed at similar objectives, it would seem both legitimate and desirable to transfer funds from the nursing home program to the home care program; a large number of seniors appear to want the program and it is a cheaper mode of care to provide, the desirable attribute of promoting personal independence notwithstanding. In many cases, however, restrictions on fungibility would make this apparently rational action all but impossible.

As previously discussed in this chapter, costs of production—variable, semivariable, and fixed costs—are generally classified by their behavior in relation to the level of production. Organizations engaged in the administration of more than a single program will doubtless perform many activities in support of all programs including administration, outreach, the provision of referrals, and so on. Since many costs are *shared*, it is necessary to develop categories of cost related not to the quantity of services produced, but rather categories which show how they are to be *allocated* among different responsibility centers, be they programs, departments, agencies, or levels of government. For cost allocation purposes it is common first to distinguish between *direct* and *indirect* costs. Direct costs are those that are directly incurred in the operation of a program; in a meals program, for example, direct costs are those incurred in the preparation and serving of food, or any publicity that might accompany the program. Indirect costs are incurred by activities that are only partially or indirectly related to the program; general administration and overhead or the use of the agency's general purpose meeting hall are examples.

In organizations possessing relatively simple or well-defined production processes, direct and indirect costs are rather easily determined. But few organizations that need to be concerned about cost allocation procedures are simple; as a result, it has become increasingly common to speak not of direct and indirect costs, but rather of the way in which managers *choose* to treat them. If there is a reasonable way for managers to determine "the right or proper amounts of costs that should be incurred"[38] by a responsibility center in the performance of its activities, then these are referred to as *engineered* costs. Most variable costs of production are readily engineered. Conversely, if "there is no rational way . . . or no rational basis that management is willing to rely on"[39] for allocating costs, then these are termed *discretionary* costs. Many semivariable and virtually all fixed costs are treated as discretionary costs.

To illustrate the differences, consider the out-of-home youth care program discussed at the beginning of this chapter. It is conceivable that the not-for-profit provider might have received funds from two separate sources—one interested in promoting the welfare of children under the age of eighteen, and one for youth between the ages of eighteen and twenty-one. Typically, the costs incurred on behalf of each age group would have to be recorded and reported separately. The costs *could* be engineered by recording the amount of effort expended on behalf of each age group and hence the costs that should be applied against each separate fund. Subsequent analysis might reveal, for example, that the older age group eats more but requires less supervision than the younger children; if so it would be reflected in the cost allocation. Or administrators might choose a discretionary method of allocating costs between the funds; a typical method would be to allocate total costs in proportion to the number of ADPs within each age group.

This example severely understates both the importance and difficulty of allocating costs in social programs, where there are few variable costs which can readily be engineered. In labor intensive service organizations, many costs are semivariable costs. Since the level of service provided may not be proportionately related to the cost incurred, the establishment of principles for engineering these costs is difficult. Furthermore, a very large proportion of costs are the administrative and other overhead expenses that comprise fixed costs, many of which are shared among a variety of responsibility centers. It is extremely difficult to devise a reasonable means for engineering such costs.

Among the most difficult costs to allocate correctly in social welfare organizations are administrative costs, since these are frequently shared by a number of different programs. The crucial question becomes one of how much of shared administrative and overhead costs should be allocated to program A, to program B, and so on. A recent experience within the Social Security Administration provides an excellent example of the problems encountered in answering this question.[40]

When the Supplemental Security Income program (SSI) was initiated in 1973, administrative responsibility for that program was given to the Social Security Administration, which thus became responsible for administering programs financed from two distinct funds. SSI was to be funded out of general tax revenues, while the agency's original responsibility, the Old Age Survivors and Disability Insurance program(OASDI), continued to be financed from a special trust fund to which most employees and employers contribute in the form of the social security tax. The Secretary of the Department of Health, Education, and Welfare is required under provisions of the Social Security Act to determine the proper proportion of the total administrative costs—$2.3 billion in 1976—to be charged against SSI and OASDI and thus to be borne by the general revenue and trust fund accounts respectively.

This requirement is fulfilled in part by engineering those administrative costs that can be directly related to each program's work loads. Using classical work sampling and measurement techniques—the work load of each employee in each of the Social Security Administration's more than 1300 field offices is sampled once a week—auditors are able to determine the average amount of time and the average cost incurred in performing each of fifty-three defined tasks carried out in the field offices, for example the time and cost of updating an SSI beneficiary's address. Knowing for a given year how many times an SSI address was updated nationwide, the auditors know the total cost incurred for that particular task. The identical procedure is followed to engineer the total administrative costs of each of the fifty-two remaining categories of work for each program. Indirect costs, such as those for training and supervision, are not engineered but rather are charged against each program in proportion to the man-years' direct effort as computed above. A similar process is used to allocate fixed and semivariable costs—like data processing, rent, and supplies—at the Social Security Administration's headquarters.

If an individual applies for benefits under *both* the SSI and the OASDI programs, at least two administrative tasks will be common to each application, because the OASDI and SSI programs have two common eligibility criteria. First, persons who are disabled may be eligible for benefits under both programs; this will occur in the case of a disabled individual who has a sufficient work history to qualify for benefits under the disability provisions of OASDI, yet whose benefits and assets are sufficiently low to quality for disability benefits under SSI as well. Second, a person whose OASDI retirement benefits, income from other sources, and assets are sufficiently low, will qualify for benefits under both programs. Two tasks then— determining proof of age and disability determination—are performed but once, although they are required for both programs. The cost of performing these activities for joint applicants—$87 million in 1976—is not engineered, but rather is allocated to each program in proportion to the benefits disbursed. Since persons eligible for both programs received an average of 28 percent of benefits from SSI and 62 percent from OASDI, 28 percent of these administrative costs are charged against the SSI general revenue fund.

Many costs which are treated as discretionary by administrators can, with sufficient time and expense, be converted into engineered costs. It is possible in many cases to break down each of the organization's many activities into a set of discrete tasks, record the time spent by various personnel on each, and come up with an average cost of, say, providing a referral. Knowing how many of each of these tasks are performed on behalf of a particular program during the course of a year, one can then allocate costs to various funds on the basis of work actually performed, rather than by incorporating discretionary methods. One can see, however, that such an approach requires the establishment of consistent and nonoverlapping definitions of service functions, activities, inputs, and outputs, and it can be time-consuming and expensive to perform. Lacking a useful classification scheme for these and lacking the motivation for their establishment—such as might be provided by the marketplace in the case of profit-making organizations with well-structured processes of production, or as might possibly result from an audit—most social welfare organizations are willing to continue allocating many costs via discretionary methods.

No one likes to be audited, either in the capacity of private citizen by the Internal Revenue Service or in the capacity of an administrator by the General Accounting Office or by another federal, state, or local auditing agency. Yet, the possibility of an audit is a fact of life in any organization, public or private and, with respect to social welfare programs and agencies, promises to become even more important in the future.

In general there are two types of audits: the financial or compliance audit and the so-called operational audit.[41] The purpose of the *compliance audit* is to ensure that an agency's financial operations are conducted according to proper accounting procedure, that its financial and other reporting requirements are properly adhered to and presented fairly, and that the agency has complied with applicable rules and regulations governing its conduct.[42] While what constitutes "proper accounting procedure" is gradually being standardized in the social welfare enterprise, as we have seen in the previous section, the nature of the information that must be collected, organized, and maintained, as well as the specific rules and regulations to which the agency must adhere, will vary from funding source to funding source. Normally, these requirements will be stipulated in the funding and implementing guidelines, but like all guidelines, are subject to continuous evolution during the implementing process.

Like the traditional line item budget whose general emphasis it parallels, the compliance audit initially grew out of the need to ensure that funds were spent honestly; initially the compliance audit "was about private avarice."[43] As public purposes, policies, and their instruments have grown more complex, however, so has the need for an expanded conception of the auditing function, one that would help ensure that agency and program practices are consistent with more lofty values. Is the program being implemented in a manner consistent with legislative intent, and is it being administered economically and efficiently? In part, the compliance audit helps fulfill this role, because it monitors the degree to which specific implementing rules and procedures have been adhered to. But this assumes that rules and guidelines accurately steer agency practices in a direction that is consistent with these values; as we have seen in an earlier chapter, this is not always the case.

While the principal device for maintaining agency and program accountability remains the compliance audit, in recent years a second auditing format—the *operational audit*—has come into prominence. And, like the compliance audit, the two principal thrusts of operational auditing—helping to ensure economy and efficiency and the achievement of desired program results—also have their budgetary correlates, mirroring the espoused purposes of performance and program budgeting formats respectively. From the General Accounting Office's influential *Standards for Audit of Governmental Organizations, Programs, Activities and Functions*, the two emphases of operational auditing are defined as follows:

> *Economy and Efficiency*—determines whether the entity is managing or utilizing its resources (personnel, property, space, and so forth) in an economical and efficient manner and the causes of any inefficiencies or uneconomical practices, including inadequacies in management information systems, administrative procedures, or organizational structure.
>
> *Program Results*—determines whether the desired results or benefits are being achieved, whether the objectives established by the legislature or other authorizing body are being met, and whether the agency has considered alternatives which might yield desired results at a lower cost.[44]

Clearly, operational auditing will require a broader knowledge base and a different set of skills than those required in the performance of a compliance audit. It is obviously one thing to monitor the "books" and to ascertain compliance with accepted accounting procedure and quite another, for example, to define and to ascertain the *causes* of program inefficiencies. Especially in large agencies or programs, operational audits are often conducted by large accounting firms, like Touche-Ross or Arthur Anderson, which possess operational expertise surpassing that of most members of the accounting profession. Nonetheless, they are cautioned to tread lightly, for "when accountants imply they know how to run a school, a hospital, or any other organization better than the professions who have spent their careers managing such organizations, their work is resented and, if possible, disregarded."[45] The fact of the matter is that, like judicial review of operations, it is becoming increasingly *impossible* to disregard the findings of an operational audit, especially if conducted by one of the more prestigious accounting firms.

Thus far, our discussion of operational auditing has concentrated upon the achievement of economy and efficiency. What about program results? If desired program results are unknown or unclear, the result of vague policy, then an audit clearly requires that they be clarified before changes in program and agency activities can be assessed and, if necessary, carried out. Frequently, this will occur as part of a *legislative review* (at the state level) or *congressional oversight* (at the federal level), which is defined as "behavior by legislators and their staffs . . . which results in an impact, intended or not, on bureaucratic begavior."[46] Normally initiated and conducted by the committee or subcommittee responsible for program legislation and appropriations, oversight is seldom an automatic matter; some programs will be the object of oversight proceedings and others will not.

It is useful for program administrators to be aware of some of the factors that might precipitate legislative review or congressional oversight proceedings. With respect to the latter (although they would be equally applicable to legislative review), Morris Ogul contends that the frequency and intensity of oversight proceedings stems from both the *opportunity* for individual congressmen to oversee agency operations and the perceived *political rewards* arising from that activity. Opportunities, he argues, are dependent upon a number of factors, including a given committee or subcommittee's legal authority to act; the staff resources available; the complexity of the subject matter involved; the structure of the congressional committee, in which the greater its decentralization the greater the opportunity for individual initiative, and the greater the possibility of oversight; and an individual's status on a committee, the higher status member being more likely to initiate oversight proceedings.[47]

Behaviorally, it is convincingly argued that, faced with constraints upon their time, legislators will act in response to apparent political payoffs and losses and that, "in such a calculus, oversight has fewer potential payoffs than other activities."[48] This finding is noteworthy because it suggests that the creation of new laws is of higher legislative priority than the scrutiny of compliance with and the results achieved by existing laws. Given the opportunity, Ogul does identify factors that might create a worthwhile payoff for becoming involved in oversight proceedings: the lower the level of confidence in key administrative personnel, the greater the possibility for oversight; party affiliation, in which a congressman who is a member of the party not in control of the White House is more likely to perceive a payoff from oversight; and finally, the less an individual legislator agrees with the thrust of the program being implemented, the greater the rewards from oversight.[49] In short, the rationality that underlies the initiation and conduct of congressional oversight is not one that is premised only upon the achievement of desired program results, but is as well the rationality of legislative politics.

to manage is not to control

For those of you who maintain that the professed goal of any social program should be correctly matching services to needs, it is perhaps paradoxical that many of the day-to-day activities of social program administrators are concerned with the achievement of management control. And since, as Phillip Selznick has observed, "these activities come to consume an increasing proportion of the time and thoughts of participants, they are—from the point of view of actual behavior—substituted for the professed goals."[50] The resulting problem—commonly known as goal displacement—arises largely because policy makers and their constituents place a higher value upon the control (symbolic or real) of program activities than the achievement of program results. In short, they control problems that should be managed.

Controlling a problem that should be managed—by occupying administrative attention with oversight proceedings, reporting requirements, and making budgetary formats—results in the generation of errors that, because attention is otherwise occupied, go unrecognized and, hence, uncorrected. "Control technologies," it has been noted, "must be developed on a categorical basis, in terms of classes of problems, and their degree of success is directly proportional to the level of knowledge available."[51] The information that is available, however, is not always what is required. If our general goal for social programs is acceptable, information about how they generate outcomes and might better do so in the future is required. Such information is the subject of the following chapter.

notes

1. Robert Anthony and Regina Herzlinger, *Management Control in Nonprofit Organizations* (Homewood, Ill.: Richard D. Irwin, 1975), p. 16.

2. Ibid., p. 19.

3. Ibid.

4. Anthony and Herzlinger, *Management Control in Nonprofit Organizations,* p. 44.

5. John Rathmell, *Marketing in the Service Sector* (Cambridge, Mass.: Winthrop, 1974), p. 7.

6. Nancy S. Hayward, "The Productivity Challenge," *Public Administration Review,* 36, no. 5 (September/October 1976), 544.

7. Gary E. Bowers and Margaret R. Bowers, "The Elusive Unit of Service," *Human Services Monograph Series,* no. 1 (September 1976), p. 9.

8. Among the best known and most widely used is the *California Relative Value System.* Significantly, however, a recent Federal Trade Commission ruling would prohibit—on the grounds that it creates a form of price fixing—its adoption in other states.

9. Bowers and Bowers, "The Elusive Unit of Service," pp. 30–35.

10. W. Richard Scott, "Effectiveness of Organizational Effectiveness Studies," in *New Perspectives on Organizational Effectiveness,* eds. Paul S. Goodman, Johannes M. Pennings, and associates (San Francisco: Jossey-Bass, 1977), p. 74.

11. Ibid., pp. 75–89.

12. Ibid., p. 83.

13. Ibid., p. 88.

14. Edmund V. Olson, M.D., letter to the editor (Washington) *Daily Olympian*, February 21, 1978.

15. Donald W. Horowitz, *The Courts and Social Policy* (Washington, D.C.: Brookings Institution, 1977).

16. Ibid., p. 6.

17. Nathan Glazer, "Should Judges Administer Social Services?" *The Public Interest*, no. 50 (Winter 1978), 65–66.

18. Frank M. Johnson, "Observation: The Constitution and the Federal District Judge," *Texas Law Review*, 54, no. 5 (June 1976), 906.

19. Aaron Wildavsky, *The Politics of the Budgetary Process* (Boston: Little, Brown, 1964), p. 1.

20. Aaron Wildavsky, "A Budget for All Seasons? Why the Traditional Budget Lasts," *Public Administration Review*, 38, no. 6 (November/December 1978), 507.

21. Ibid.

22. Roderick K. MacLeod, "Program Budgeting Works in Non-Profit Institutions," *Harvard Business Review*, 49 (September/October 1971), 49.

23. *Audits of Voluntary Health and Welfare Organizations* (New York: American Institute of Certified Public Accountants, 1974).

24. Ibid., p. 24.

25. See among others Ida R. Hoos, *Systems Analysis in Public Policy: A Critique* (Berkeley: University of California Press, 1972); and Charles J. Hitch and Roland McKean, *The Economics of Defense in the Nuclear Age* (Cambridge: Harvard University Press, 1961).

26. Included in this expanding list are Peter A. Phyrr, *Zero-Based Budgeting: A Practical Management Tool for Evaluating Expenses* (New York: John Wiley, 1973); and Logan M. Check, *Zero-Base Budgeting Comes of Age* (New York: AMACOM, 1977).

27. Wildavsky, "A Budget for All Seasons?," p. 506.

28. John Gundersdorf, "Management and Financial Controls," in *Managing Human Services*, eds. Wayne F. Anderson, Bernard J. Frieden, and Michael J. Murphy (Washington, D.C.: International City Management Association, 1977), p. 276.

29. See Stanley M. Davis and Paul L. Lawrence, "Problems of Matrix Organizations," *Harvard Business Review*, 56, no. 3 (May–June 1978), 131–42.

30. *Audits of Voluntary Health and Welfare Organizations*, p. 24.

31. Leonard R. Sayles, "Matrix Management: The Structure with a Future," *Organizational Dynamics* (Autumn 1976), 16.

31. Davis and Lawrence, "Problems of Matrix Organizations," 134.

32. Jerry Dermer, *Management Running and Control Systems* (Homewood, Ill.: Richard D. Irwin, 1977), p. 126.

33. Bill Henderson and Randy Young, *Program Performance Budgeting: An Effective Public Management System for Evaluating Municipal Services*, Special Bulletin no. 1976A (Chicago: Municipal Finance Officers Association, 1976), p. 10.

34. Peter F. Drucker, "On Managing the Public Service Institution," *The Public Interest*, no. 33 (Fall 1973), 52.

35. Walter B. Meigs, A. H. Mosich, and E. John Larsen, *Modern Advanced Accounting* (New York: McGraw-Hill, 1975), p. 66.

36. Malvern J. Gross, Jr., "Nonprofit Accounting: The Continuing Revolution," *The Journal of Accountancy* (June 1977), p. 66.

37. Deil S. Wright, *Understanding Intergovernmental Relations* (North Scituate, Mass: Duxbury Press, 1978), p. 90.

38. Anthony and Herzlinger, *Management Control in Nonprofit Organizations,* p. 26.

39. Ibid.

40. Report of the Comptroller General of the United States, "Social Security Administration's Procedures for Allocating Administrative Costs to the Supplemental Security Income Program," Report no. HRD–78–12 (Washington, D.C.: General Accounting Office, November 17, 1977).

41. Anthony and Herzlinger, *Management Control in Nonprofit Organizations,* pp. 309–12.

42. Comptroller General of the United States, *Standards for Audit of Governmental Organizations, Programs, Activities and Functions* (Washington, D.C.: U.S. Government Printing Office, 1973), p. 2.

43. Wildavsky, "A Budget for All Seasons?," p. 509.

44. Comptroller General of the United States, *Standards for Audit,* p. 2.

45. Anthony and Herzlinger, *Management Control in Nonprofit Organizations,* p. 311.

46. Morris S. Ogul, *Congress Oversees the Bureaucracy* (Pittsburgh: University of Pittsburgh Press, 1976), p. 11.

47. Ibid., pp. 11–16

48. Ibid., p. 20.

49. Ibid., p. 17–22.

50. Cited in David I. Sills, *The Volunteer* (New York: Free Press, 1957), p. 64.

51. Martin Landau and Russell Stout, Jr., "To Manage Is Not to Control: Or the Folly of Type II Errors," *Public Administration Review,* 39, no. 2 (March/April 1979), 153.

Program evaluation is a formal analytical process that entails the comparison of measurable program outcomes with defined standards of performance. Its purpose is to provide both policy and program decision makers with information useful for program improvement. Evaluation is bounded by a theoretical perspective which holds that the social welfare program is, above all, an instrument of change; both outcome measures and the standards against which they are judged are thus change-related.

Of prime importance is to determine whether measured change was caused by the program or by some set of forces unrelated to program activities. The process of sorting out various causal hypotheses is governed by the principles of research design. The advantages, disadvantages, and examples of three broad classes of designs—experimental, quasi-experimental, and comparative—are discussed.

Using evaluative findings is central to the maintenance of accountability, but the failure to implement the results of evaluations plagues most public programs, particularly those of the social welfare enterprise. The existing theory-practice gap may be closed by adopting evaluative strategies that foster a meeting of the minds among those in command of evaluative techniques, those responsible for making and carrying out program decisions, and the many publics that surround the program.

evaluating
social programs

7

Evaluation can be many things to many people, and the range of perspectives and activities that fall within its domain is virtually boundless. Indeed, many of the topics discussed thus far in this volume are evaluative in nature, because evaluation entails a judgment as to what is desirable. Any decision requires judgments concerning desirable futures and the best strategies for achieving them; decision making entails evaluation before the fact. Needs assessments are used to judge the scope and magnitude of human problems existing within a community, and in the process implicitly to evaluate the performance of the organizations that comprise the social welfare enterprise. The establishment of access mechanisms involves a judgment as to the appropriate pattern of service utilization. Management control activities presuppose a judgment regarding what constitutes effective, efficient and accountable organizational performance and the best ways to achieve it. And policy itself presumably results from an evaluation of public attitudes and action alternatives that might serve to promote individual well-being and the public interest.

Evaluation is the comparison of what *is,* relative to what *was* desired or expected when an activity was proposed and implemented; unlike planning, it occurs either during or after the fact. In recent years, paralleling and strongly associated with demands for increased accountability, a body of knowledge has evolved that seeks to formalize the evaluative process. Since the program represents the action arm, the instrument of social policy, it is not surprising that the development of evaluative theories, activities, and methodologies has tended to focus upon the program. The broad framework within which the evaluative ideal would be used to guide program choice and program change is sometimes called cost-utility analysis.

cost-utility analysis

Cost-utility analysis is a process designed to establish relationships and tradeoffs among various components of value, the possible strategies and decisions that might be used to achieve them, and the monetary costs associated with each alternative. If performed before the fact, cost-utility analysis can provide a source of information for program planning and budgeting; if conducted during or after implementation, it can be used to guide evaluation. While cost-utility analysis can be performed in reference to anything of value, two of its most important applications are concerned with the dollar benefits arising from organized action and the degree to which various decision alternatives contribute to the achievement of stated goals. These techniques are called, respectively, benefit-cost analysis and cost-effectiveness analysis.

BENEFIT-COST ANALYSIS

Within the benefit-cost framework,[1] social programs are seen as investments, and like any investment in business, alternative program possibilities are judged against the criterion of "profitability." A program's impacts are assumed to generate a stream of future benefits and costs. All benefits that occur over the life of the program are converted to dollar values, and are adjusted to their value in the present; the same is done for the stream of program costs. The present value of costs is subtracted from the present value of benefits to yield a dollar measure of program profitability. After each alternative program possibility has been analyzed in this way, the one that appears the most profitable is selected for implementation; this is the theoretical basis of choice in PPBS discussed in the preceding chapter.

Because the benefits of many programs will occur at some point in the future, but program costs are generally grouped about the present, it is necessary to adjust the dollar flows of costs and benefits to a single point in time; this adjustment leads to what is called the *present value* of costs and benefits. The present value of a future benefit or cost of specified dollar value is the amount of money which, had it been invested or borrowed today at a fixed interest or discount rate, would yield the future value. Thus, if $100 were invested today at an annual interest rate of 10 percent, it would be worth $110 one year hence. Present value analysis works this investment theme backwards; at a 10 percent interest rate, a $110 benefit or cost experienced a year from now has a value in the present of $100. Similarly, were the $100 invested for two years at 10 percent, it would yield (1.10 X 1.10 X $100) or $121. Thus, the present value of a $121 cost or benefit occurring *two* years in the future is also $100. The general formula for computing the present value of either costs or benefits is given by:

$$\text{Present value} = \frac{\text{dollar amount of future cost or benefit}}{(1 + i)^t}$$

Where: t is the number of years in the future
  i is the annual percentage interest or discount rate divided by 100

It is important to note that present value analysis is *not* an attempt to accommodate inflationary trends. Correction for inflation (that a dollar in 1990 will probably be worth less than a dollar in 1980) may require a separate adjustment using the Consumer Price Index or some similar price deflator.

The value of the discount rate selected for use in present value analysis will greatly affect the measured profitability of a program. The discount rate represents the organization's *opportunity cost of capital*—the rate of return it *expects* to receive on its investments. Any expenditure made for one purpose is clearly unavailable for other investment opportunities, and the discount rate is a reflection of the value of these lost opportunities. If you can safely invest your money in a bank at, say, 10 percent, then this is probably your appropriate discount rate. But if you select a lower rate, say 5 percent, you are undervaluing your opportunity cost of capital. Suppose, for example, that you have an investment opportunity that will yield $108 a year from now on an initial investment of $100. You select a discount rate of 5 percent and compute an *apparent* present value profit of $2.86 as shown in the first part of Table 7.1. But suppose that you could invest the same $100 in a bank at 10 percent annual interest, yielding $110 a year from now. Clearly the $8 return on the first investment is inferior to the bank investment. As the second part of Table 7.1 demonstrates, applying the 10 percent discount rate (the real opportunity cost) reveals that *with respect to other investment opportunities,* the $8 return results in a net *loss.*

Although the determination of the appropriate discount rate is a significant issue, it is minor in comparison to the dilemmas encountered in

TABLE 7.1:
the discount rate and the opportunity cost of capital

Discount rate = 5%: Present value of cost = $100

Present value of benefits = $\dfrac{\$108}{1.05}$ = $102.86

Profit = $102.86 − 100 = $2.86

Discount rate = 10%: Present value of costs = $100

Present value of benefits = $\dfrac{\$108}{1.10}$ = $98.18

Profit = $98.18 − $100 = ($1.82 loss)

---

attempting to establish the dollar benefits of public programs. In general, the dollar benefits of social weflare programs are of two principal types: (1) those accruing to the individuals to whom the program is directed, and (2) the benefits that accrue to nonparticipants in the form of reduced negative externalities. Two of the most common methods for computing the dollar value of individual benefits are subjective valuation and human capital investment analysis.[2]

In the human capital investment approach, individual benefits are those associated with the value of a productive human life, and the social program is seen as a vehicle for increasing human productivity, either through physical rehabilitation or intellectual and vocational development. The increase in productivity is enumerated by computing the expected increase in earnings over the person's lifetime that is attributable to the program, and then discounting the earnings stream to the present value.

Although widely used in health care and educational analyses, among the most widely publicized applications of human capital investment analysis concerns a National Highway Traffic Safety Administration (U.S. Department of Transportation) study of the benefits arising from traffic safety programs. For the average person—of average age and average earnings—the 1972 societal cost components of an average automobile fatality are as shown in Table 7.2; thus, traffic safety program benefits are computed as reductions in these costs. Inflation has since pushed the figure to better than $350,000; the net benefits of programs aimed at reducing traffic fatalities would then be the total number of fatalities prevented multiplied by the $350,000+ figure.

Apart from its dispassionate, calculated instrumentalism (who is to place a value on human pain and suffering?), the human capital investment approach contains a number of interesting anomalies. First, the more productive the individual, the greater lost earnings, and the greater the benefits of saving or prolonging a life. Programs aimed at the wealthy are thus more profitable than those aimed at the poor. Second, the approach assumes that the worth, the quality of one's life, is solely dependent upon one's earnings. Third and finally, programs aimed at the young, those whose productive lifetime is still ahead of them, are more profitable than those for the elderly who have few earning-productive years remaining.

A second approach to valuing the benefits of alternative public programs, one that avoids many of these anomalies, is *subjective valuation.* Subjective valuation addresses one's *willingness to pay* to receive program benefits. The approach might be used, for example, as a means of setting priorities among different community needs. Suppose that a local Area Agency on Aging (AAA) wanted to consider the relative priorities of meeting the need for a senior center facility and a meals-on-wheels pro-

TABLE 7.2:
societal cost components for fatalities

Component	1971 Costs
Future productivity losses	
Direct	$132,000
Indirect	41,300
Medical costs	
Hospital	700
Other	425
Property damage	1,500
Insurance administration	4,700
Legal and court	3,000
Employer losses	1,000
Victim's pain and suffering	10,000
Funeral	900
Assets (lost consumption)	5,000
Miscellaneous accident cost	200
Total Cost per Fatality	$200,725

Source: Mark Dowie, "Pinto Madness," Mother Jones, 2, no. 8 (September/October 1977), 28.

gram (two needs, incidentally, that would probably *not* be compared in practice because they are funded through different grant-in-aid programs). While no fee would be charged for use of either program, the Area Agency on Aging could conduct a survey to learn how much potential users would be willing to pay to receive the benefits of either program, say on a per meal basis or a day's use of the center. The AAA analysts would then estimate the total number of meals to be served and the total number of senior center user-days over the programs' lifetimes, multiply each of these by the average of all individual subjective valuations, discount to the present value, and arrive at a dollar value of benefits arising from each of the two programs. Knowing the costs of each, it would theoretically be possible to determine which of the two programs would be the most "profitable."

One of the problems with subjective valuation is that the value of benefits is often overstated; persons often say that they would be willing to pay more than they actually would. But a second and perhaps more serious problem arises because the goals of public programs are frequently redistributive, generating benefits, financed from middle- and upper-income individuals, that accrue to the poor. As in many needs assessments, the crucial question thus becomes: whose subjective valuation is more appropriate, those who receive the benefits or those who are to pay for the program?[3] If altruistic motives are disregarded, the dollar benefits accruing to those who finance programs which they themselves do not use are often valued as reductions in *negative externalities.* That is, a person who helps finance, but who does not directly use a program, may nonetheless benefit in very tangible ways from those who do. A common example is found in public health programs, which may prevent the spread of contagious diseases, thereby reducing the negative externalities (a positive benefit) that would otherwise accrue to nonusers.

Benefit-cost analysis has enjoyed varying degrees of popularity since its development as a decision-making tool within the Department of Defense following World War II. In the 1960s it achieved some notoriety as the central methodological element in the Planning Programming Budgeting System (PPBS), sporadically adopted and then quickly abandoned within a wide variety of state and federal agencies. The decision-making value of benefit-cost analysis—and a major thrust of PPBS—is that it allows policy and program planners to establish tradeoffs between activities with widely disparate goals. It does this simply by reducing the benefits and costs of each activity to a common denominator—money. Once accomplished, "apples and oranges" comparisons become possible; for example, policy planners would be able to evaluate the relative merits of a parks program, a health care program, and a new highway. Each is judged in terms of a single criterion—its ultimate profitability.

Within certain program areas—for example, those concerning the development of physical entities like dams, in which the investment orientation may have some intrinsic validity—it is possible that benefit-cost analysis can contribute to better policy and planning decisions. But in social policy and program—where the benefits and costs are largely unknown and intangible, where the goals are consciously redistributive and where the programs are highly interdependent—benefit-cost analysis is of little practical consequence. If performed at all, it provides merely one of myriad political statements on the relative desirability of alternative public decisions.

COST-EFFECTIVENESS ANALYSIS

While the terms are often used interchangeably, cost-effectiveness analysis differs in one important respect from benefit-cost analysis, which greatly increases its value as an aid to rational decision making. In cost-effectiveness analysis no attempt is made to place a dollar value on program benefits. The goals of a program are assumed given and beneficial, and planning focuses on the most cost-effective or efficient means of attaining them. Consider, for example, an outreach program, with the goal of increasing service utilization by those in need. A number of alternative strategies may be adopted in pursuit of this goal: advertising in the various media; home visits by professionals; home visits by volunteers; or a series of public meetings. Each alternative has the same broad objective of ensuring that persons who need or who are otherwise entitled to benefits actually receive them. Since outreach services represent only one of many factors affecting program utilization by the target population, it would be logical to express the program objective as an increase over current levels of utilization; say the goal is to achieve a 25 percent increase in utilization among members of the target population. Each alternative is then evaluated in terms of its probable effectiveness in achieving this goal as well as its cost. In the ideal situation, the program planner or evaluator would determine the level of expenditure required for each program to achieve the preestablished objective and then simply select the least expensive for implementation. In many cases, however, this is not possible; there may be constraints imposed by availability of professionals or volunteers, meeting halls, or media saturation factors that no dollar amount can overcome. The more likely situation is shown in Figure 7.1.

Note that each outreach program strategy has a different level of effectiveness (only one achieves the stated goal) and different costs. If the objective is considered absolute, only one strategy—professional home visits—is acceptable because it alone achieves the stated objective; but it is also the most expensive. Oftentimes, cost-effectiveness analysis enables planners to identify possible tradeoffs among goal achievement and program costs. In this example, the media strategy can be eliminated outright as a possible candidate, because it is less effective than the less costly strategy of volunteer home visits. Further analysis is more difficult, however, because each increase in effectiveness can be attained only with an accompanying increase in program cost. Lacking a basis for evaluating the

FIGURE 7.1:

the cost-effectiveness of four alternative outreach strategies

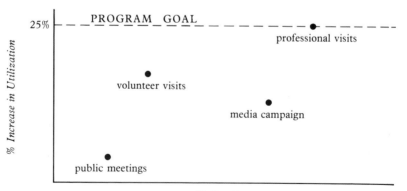

tradeoff between costs and effectiveness (such as would be possible were the dollar benefits of increased utilization enumerated in dollar terms), the decision as to which constitutes the "best" of the remaining programs is often aided by the technique of *marginal analysis.*

Marginal analysis concentrates upon the *change* in both cost and effectiveness from the least to the most expensive alternative. The media strategy was eliminated on the basis of marginal analysis, because in comparison with volunteer visits, its marginal effectiveness was negative; any program with negative marginal effectiveness can easily be eliminated. But what about those whose marginal effectiveness is positive? In this case, a volunteer home visitation program yields a substantial improvement in effectiveness for a small increase in cost over the public meeting strategy. Similarly, evaluating the change between volunteer and professional home visits, one can see that a relatively small increase in effectiveness is achieved, but at substantially increased costs. Which is the most cost-effective alternative is still a matter of judgment, but marginal analysis would appear to favor the slightly less effective but far less costly strategy of volunteer home visitation.

While certainly less global than benefit-cost analysis, cost-effectiveness analysis has become an indispensable tool of the program planner and the administrator. Nonetheless, while it is true that benefits need not be assigned dollar amounts, program goals—and outcome measures that allow analysts to determine their attainment—must be known and expressible in quantitative terms. In "real" organizational systems, as we shall shortly see, this constraint is often difficult to satisfy.

outcomes: the theoretical basis for assessing program effectiveness

Programs, we have seen, are instruments for changing the undesirable or for maintaining the desirable; they are thus based upon some theory or set of theories as to how this is to be accomplished. The role of the theory is to generate predictions regarding the consequences of organizational action in comparison with organizational goals. By far the most significant facet of organizational decision-making occurs when these predictions are compared to what actually occurred and the results of the comparison used to alter, to correct organizational action. This is the learning process most commonly known as *program evaluation.*

It is a paradox that this organizational learning cycle is frequently broken, that theories are generated, programs designed around them, funds appropriated, and action initiated, but that—despite requirements frequently imposed by funding bodies—useful evaluation of the results so seldom occurs. It is a paradox because the preponderance of social welfare programs are the result of a pervasive American ethic which holds that: (1) the efforts of man, in conjunction with organizational instruments, can significantly alter his social environment; (2) that such change is desirable and worth pursuing; and (2) that the results of such actions are tangible and can be measured.[4]

A major factor that should (but often doesn't) guide evaluative practice is the use to which the evaluative exercise is to be put. Michael Scriven has proposed, and his typology has been widely adopted, that evaluation activities be considered as one of two major types.[5] One, called *summative* evaluation, is considered to occur following termination of the program; the program is evaluated for the purpose of providing information of use in planning and implementing future programs. A second type, called *formative* evaluation, is performed for the purpose of correcting and improving ongoing program activities. Summative evaluation, then, is of greatest use in evaluating experimental programs of the kind that were widely promoted and implemented during the sixties. The experimental thrust seems much less prevalent today, at least with respect to major programs implemented nationwide; as a result, the focus has shifted to the development of methods of evaluating ongoing programs (explaining why they are not working as expected), and just as important, to the development of an organizational capability to use their results.

CHANGE AND PROGRAM EVALUATION

What we know as formal evaluation—evaluation that is focused upon program outcomes—is most often applied to programs and services designed to solve individual and societal problems that arise from individual "abnormalities." Seldom, then, are the techniques of formal evaluation used to assess changes in individual well-being possibly generated by the personal social utilities, for the beneficial outcomes arising from these services are most fruitfully ascertained and judged—as is the case with goods and services provided in the marketplace—by the individual service user. Our understanding of the remainder of social welfare programs is conditioned by a relatively simple model of purposeful intervention and resultant individual and social change, and it is this model that largely determines the design and conduct of formal program evaluation. First, through either negotiation and compromise among competing interests, or through the more formalized process of needs assessments, certain problems or conditions demanding rectification are discovered among various groups of individuals. Second, a search of available theories will identify the probable reasons or causal processes underlying the undesirable condition; or if need be, a new theory or set of theories will be generated. Third, an intervention, hypothesized to alter the undesirable condition, is specified. Fourth and finally, a program—the vehicle through which the intervention is administered—is designed and implemented.

Within this model of change, Carol Weiss has identified two primary sets of variables that intervene between the program and the desired outcomes,[6] as Figure 7.2 demonstrates. The first set of variables, called *bridging* variables, are those that stand between the specific intervention administered through the program and the program outcomes; bridging variables "represent the theory of the program."[7] The second set, called *program operation* variables, are those that define the causal processes linking the program as an organizational entity to the activities and processes that comprise the service intervention.

For example, it may be hypothesized by program and policy planners that "job counseling services" will alter work attitudes and will thus create employment among the user population; "job counseling services" is the program output or intervention, "work attitudes" the bridging variable, and "employment" the desired outcome. "Impact," to be discussed shortly, is an aggregate measure of outcome. In addition, there are many possible ways in which job counseling services can be provided: in groups or individually; on a one-shot basis or over a period of time; in a threatening or a supportive manner; without or in conjunction with job referral; to the hard-core unemployed or to the easily employable; and so on. These and other factors that affect the *specific* nature of the intervention as it is *actually* carried out are the program operation variables.

The distinction between bridging variables (those comprising the theory of the program) and program operation variables (those affecting

FIGURE 7.2:
evaluation and the program model of change

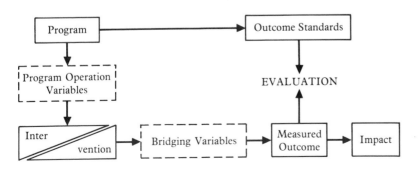

its actual practice) permits a distinction between theoretical and implementation error. Theoretical error, attributable to improper specification or a failure to understand the interaction among myriad bridging variables, is found to occur when the program delivers the "correct" intervention, which in turn has the expected effect upon the bridging variable(s), but desired program outcomes fail to materialize. For example, as predicted a job counseling program may have indeed changed the employment attitudes of its participants, but lacking necessary skills, program participants were unable to find employment; or work attitudes may have only a minor effect on employment. Implementation error, in contrast, occurs when a breakdown or improper specification of program activities leads to a failure to achieve desired changes in the bridging variable, which had they occurred would have generated the desired outcome. For example, a job counseling program that administers but a series of veiled threats and exhortations to work will likely produce little beneficial change in the work attitudes of participants, and thus little or no change in participant employment.

The distinction between theoretical and implementation error is simple in principle, but difficult to ascertain in practice. In practice, when the chains of causation linking interventions to desired outcomes are usually distended, complex, and possibly complicated further by interventions emanating from other programs, and where the exact nature of the desired service intervention is usually difficult to specify, seldom is it possible to apply the model directly. The latter reason is of special significance, because it is so often overlooked by evaluators and administrators alike. The theoretical service intervention may bear little or no resemblance to the intervention as it actually occurs in *practice.*

FORMAL EVALUATION: MEASURES AND STANDARDS

While any evaluative endeavor will entail a comparison of what is against some normative standard of what should be, formal program evaluation is unique in two important respects. First, formal program evaluation relies upon quantitative measures of outcome and quantitative normative standards as the basis of comparison. Thus, the ability to define valid and reliable quantitative measures of program outcomes and, equally important, to establish the instrumentation—the methods for generating and maintaining a data base—that will permit empirical documentation of those outcomes are necessary prerequisites to the conduct of formal program evaluation. Second, since social programs are premised upon either implicit or explicit theories of individual, service network, or societal change, the outcome measures, the standards and the data base must be change-related.

Two of the most important measurement questions that must be addressed by the program evaluator are, first, what to measure and how, and, second, over what period should measurement activities be carried out? General answers to these questions are elusive because of the diversity of program types and approaches to formal evaluation. What is measured and how will depend, however, at a minimum upon the specificity of the program's theoretical underpinnings (as indicated by the number of variables included in the social program model of change (Figure 7.2)) and how the results of the program evaluation are to be used. In general a summative evaluation will require a greater range of more complex measures—including those pertaining to alternative possible bridging and program operation variables as well as interventions and outcomes—than will be required (or possible) in a formative evaluation. Other factors affecting the selection of evaluative measures include the specific evaluation design selected; the type of program, whether emergency, preventative, remedial, or maintenance; and finally, the specific objectives the program is intended to achieve and, thus, the outcomes it is expected to generate. Ideally, each of these factors will have been specified or will be apparent in the substantive program plan. In reality, however, program plans seldom provide the necessary guidance to program evaluators, usually requiring that these and other questions be resolved by assumption. We shall return to this important issue later in this chapter.

Social program outcomes are generally identified as one of two types of change: change in individual program users and change in the operation of the service network. Each of these, moreover, will require different measures and different instrumentation. At the level of the individual three outcome measures are commonly used. First, analysts may be interested in the degree to which the program provoked a change in the cognitive or affective status of program participants; a variety of intelligence and attitudinal instruments are available for measuring these attributes. Second, program outcomes may be defined as changes in individual behavior or health status, which may be measured by observation or a variety of diagnostic procedures. And third, the program may generate impacts or aggregate individual change within a community—the change in unemployment, mortality and morbidity, marital stability, and so on—which may be measured through the use of social indicators. For programs designed to improve the operation of the service network, evaluation requires measures—derived from observation, the records of service agencies, the subjective impressions of service users, and the results of needs assessments—that relate to accessibility, continuity, the lack of fragmentation, and accountability to the service user.

As well as the type of measurement, a fundamental decision concerns the interval of time during which measurements are to be taken. For programs designed to achieve only short-term change, measurements taken soon after the intervention are probably appropriate. But it is often long-term change that is a true measure of a program's success, for example that a person remained employed for a substantial length of time as the result of a job counseling program. The measurement of a long-term change, however, is confronted by a number of practical and conceptual difficulties. Probably the most important of the practical difficulties is the problem of locating program participants even a few months following their completion of the program, especially in our increasingly mobile society. If they can be located, they may be reluctant to be "measured" or, quite naturally, they may attempt to create a favorable but distorted impression on the evaluator. Finally, the conceptual difficulty with measuring long-term outcomes is that the purity of the relationship between program activities and outcomes will likely have been contaminated by intervening variables over which the evaluator has little or no control; the effects of the program tend to become "washed out" with the passage of time. This problem will receive greater attention later in this chapter.

Without normative standards there can be no formal evaluation, for it is the standard that provides a reference and gives meaning to the quantitative measures. In contrast to many measurement standards, for example, those that we use as references for measuring and comparing distances, velocity, time, or temperature, the standards imposed upon evaluative measures are consciously normative; evaluation entails comparison against a *normative* standard. And like the data from which the measures themselves are derived, evaluative standards may be: nominal, the program is either good or bad; ordinal, program A is better than program B; or cardinal, program A is three times better than program B.

The most common, the most discussed, the most criticized, and yet the most frequently used measurement standards for program evaluation are program goals. In this approach, evaluative measures are designed to reflect the degree to which program goals are achieved, and the level of evaluative sophistication that is possible largely depends upon the precision of the goals themselves, upon the extent to which the goal standard is (or can be) quantified. For example, a program with the goal of "providing job counseling" is virtually impossible to evaluate because the goal standard is so loosely defined and creates few concrete expectations as to results. Job counseling to whom, for what purposes, to how many individuals, over what period of time? As stated, the goal, "to provide job counseling," provides an insufficient yardstick against which to determine the program's success. Of course, we have seen that politicians and administrators may find it expedient to avoid precise goals; in their absence, however, formal evaluation is all but impossible.

The use of goals as evaluative standards has also been frequently criticized on the grounds that it will result in evaluations that are too narrowly focused, and that insufficient attention is paid to the unanticipated consequences of program activities. At the extreme, consider a program with the quantifiable goal of "totally eliminating crime in the United States by 1990." This is, in fact, accomplished by assigning a police officer to every citizen (including other police officers), under whose ever-vigilant eyes no crime could be conceived, much less committed. The desirability of the goal notwithstanding, the consequences related to the *action* but unrelated to the *goal*—personal freedom, for example—are obviously intolerable.

Unanticipated consequences are seldom as blatant as in the above example, but rather arise from a variety of more subtle reasons.[8] Program goals may generate expectations beyond those intended, which when unfulfilled may create undesirable consequences. Social programs are almost always based upon inadequate knowledge of the causal processes surrounding them. Worthy goals, rationally pursued, may trigger causal processes leading to consequences more costly than the benefits derived from the attainment of the goal. Programs may possess multiple goals that are in conflict or different programs may possess conflicting goals; the inability to assign priorities and to establish tradeoffs among them is a frequent cause of undesirable, unexpected consequences. Oftentimes, one organization's goals may infringe upon another organization's turf, and the resultant bureaucratic infighting may contribute to a decline in effectiveness of both programs.

A second evaluative standard, or more appropriately a set of standards, treats program effectiveness in a way similar to that of efficiency— as a relative idea. Rather than evaluating program performance in relationship to a fixed, absolute goal standard, the evaluator would adopt a more flexible standard of comparing performance with programs performing similar activities.[9] As political symbols (and devices useful for obtaining maximum resources from funding bodies), stated program goals are often unrealistically ambitious, not only unduly raising expectations, but also creating a standard that may be impossible to achieve. Suppose that the goals of a job training and placement program specify that 75 percent of its participants will be gainfully employed one year following the completion of training, but in fact only 40 percent are found to be employed one year later. Since the program did not even come close to achieving the goals espoused by its designers, it would most likely be judged a failure. But suppose also that other programs of similar size, with similar resources, using similar program strategies, having similar user populations, operating in similar economic climates, and so on, have an average success rate of only 25 percent. In comparison with the average and presumably the majority of similar programs, our "failure" can quite reasonably be judged a success.

The advantage of comparing program outcomes with those of similar programs, and not against absolute goal standards, is that it addresses the feasible rather than the utopian. As is frequently the case, by focusing upon what is, interprogram comparisons are better able to generate process and structural standards of performance that may result in undramatic but still significant improvements. While more humbling, perhaps, such comparisons do at least force decision makers and evaluators to confront the inevitable limitations of organizational technologies in achieving change. As we shall see shortly, however, it is an evaluative approach that may require more exacting methods of research than those incorporated in goal-oriented approaches.

Regardless of the level of outcome measurement or the standards that permit those measures to be used in judging program performance, a crucial question remains unaddressed. Did those outcomes occur *because* of program activities or did they simply occur as the result of unknown external forces? To answer this question requires that the causal processes linking program activities to the desired outcome be understood. This is the function of research design.

establishing causation: the role of experimental research design

The experimental research design is the tool through which evaluators attempt to establish an objective causal relationship between program interventions and the measure or measures selected as representative of program outcome. In virtually any real-world situation the causal variables and processes surrounding both program and outcome variables will be numerous and complex; some degree of measured change may be caused by the program; some changes generated by the program will go undetected; and the remainder of observed change is either uncaused (random) or caused by extraneous variables outside the control of program administrators. If the effectiveness of a job training program, for example, is to be measured as the number of participants employed one year after training, it is necessary to create a baseline, to isolate and to hold constant all factors unrelated to the program that might affect the outcome—the situation of the economy, support from family and friends, prior educational levels of participants, and countless others.

Controlled experimentation using the pre-test–post-test control group design is the classical means of evaluating theoretical propositions in the biological, behavioral, and social sciences. To implement the approach, a hypothesis postulating a single cause-effect relationship is identified for experimentation. Two groups are selected at random from the larger population of organisms or individuals for which the casual relationship is hypothesized to obtain; random selection helps to ensure that in the aggregate the two groups are initially identical. The outcome hypothesized to be affected by the causal agent or experimental variable is defined and measured for both groups prior to experimentation. One group (the experimental group) is randomly selected for exposure to the experimental variable, while the other (the control group) is not. With the sole exception of the experimental varible, great care is taken to ensure that both groups are exposed to otherwise identical stimuli during the course of the experiment. Finally, the characteristics of both groups are remeasured after experimentation. Since experimental controls are designed to ensure that the only difference in the two groups is their exposure to the experimental variable, and differences identified between the before-and-after measurements must be attributed to that variable. At this point, a number of standard statistical techniques may be applied to determine if post-measurements for the two groups are significantly different or simply the result of sampling errors or other statistical aberrations.

The goals of any experimental design are the achievement of high degrees of internal and external validity,[10] and the controlled experiment ranks high in both regards. Experiments characterized by a high degree of *internal validity* are those that permit researchers to isolate or otherwise account for the effects of causal factors other than the experimental variable. In the physical sciences, it is often possible to physically isolate— through the use of sterile laboratories, near-perfect vacuums, and other controlled environments—the effects of extraneous variables upon experimental outcomes; in such cases a high degree of internal validity can be achieved without the use of a control group. In the behavioral and social sciences, where isolation is virtually impossible and where participants are subjected to numerous extraneous variables whose importance and effects are unknown or uncertain, the control group baseline is essential to the achievement of internal validity.

External validity means that the experimental results obtained from a small sample are general representations of the larger population. And while this important attribute is dependent upon a number of experimental design characteristics, a major factor contributing to an experiment's external validity is its replicability. Seldom will the results of a simple experiment be sufficient to generate general conclusions regarding the entire population. The tight controls associated with the controlled experiment, however, make it rather easily replicated in many different settings and under many different conditions; if the results remain basically the same in each case, then experimental findings gradually assume the status of universal, scientific fact.

As applied to the evaluation of social programs, the experimental ideal is designed to determine the effects of alternative programs upon various aspects of participant behavior; thus the program is assumed to be the causal agent, and a change in participant behavior the effect or outcome. Because of the need for rigid selection procedures and tight controls —meaning that the program cannot be altered during the course of the experiment—the experimental ideal is best considered as a technique of summative evaluation, with results to be incorporated into the design of future programs. It is important to note at this point that controlled social program experimentation is different than the conduct of demonstration projects, the latter of which while the object of numerous evaluative efforts, are merely established to determine the operational feasibility of a given program. In contrast, while more elaborate and expensive, controlled experiments can yield a variety of information of value in planning future programs.

We have seen that the social program is a complex entity, and this complexity must be reflected in the design of a controlled social program experiment. Since its purpose is to guide the design of future programs, the experiment must ideally account for all causal relationships that exist among all possible combinations of program variables, like the nature of the allocation, and its method of delivery; all possible sociodemographic groups who might be eligible; and probably most difficult to identify, all significant program effects or outcomes. Clearly, the design of such experiments requires a complex set of theoretical propositions linking together each of these dimensions, and what appears on the surface to be a single experiment, will in many cases be a series of many experiments designed to evaluate a near endless set of possible cause and effect relationships. Some of the questions addressed by the Income Maintenance Experiments (in which recipients were to receive a guaranteed level of income) conducted during the seventies and early eighties are representative of this complexity.[11] What is the effect of different levels of guaranteed support, in combinations with different effective tax rates on earned income, upon a recipient's work patterns? What are the effects of different eligibility criteria? Are the effects consistent, or do they vary with different sociodemographic groups? Are the effects consistent nationwide, or are they subject to regional variations? Are there significant effects—such as divorce rates, for example—that are unrelated to work patterns?

Beyond the issues of theoretical and design complexity, evaluation researchers confront a number of additional dilemmas that threaten internal validity during the implementation of controlled program experiments.[12] One such problem, known as attrition bias, arises because not all individuals who start in an experimental program will participate to its completion; especially if the experiment is of long duration, it is quite possible, for example, that the experimental results will be biased in favor of geographically stable families. A related problem, the horizon effect, is dependent upon the duration of the experimental program; experience with the income maintenance experiments has demonstrated that program duration (three years versus twenty years, for example) has a significant impact upon a participant's work-related behavior, with short-term experiments thus generating conclusions that may be inappropriate for a permanent program. The well-known Hawthorn Effect—in which behavior is altered not because of program variables, but simply because participants are aware that they are under constant observation—poses a persistent barrier to internal validity in any social program experiment. Finally are issues of sample representativeness. While representative samples can be determined in principle (normally stratified sampling procedures are used to ensure that all important sociodemographic groups are included in both the experimental and control groups), the vagaries of screening procedures, noncontacts, and refusal by those selected for participation may raise serious questions regarding the experiment's validity.

Controlled social program experiments raise a number of ethical dilemmas as well, because any experiment inevitably involves the conscious manipulation of people's lifestyles and behaviors, particularly those who are members (usually voluntary, however) of experimental groups.[13] The program may, for example provoke behavior that is only beneficial to the individual as long as the experimental program is in operation, but that —as in the case of a family who uses the added income to purchase more expensive housing—may have detrimental effects upon completion. While essential for measuring outcomes, the information required of experimental program participants may be sought by other social agencies to ascertain eligibility to other program benefits. Finally, and with respect to members of the control group, experimental programs may unduly raise expectations and create the equally compelling moral dilemma that arises when valued goods and services are consciously withheld from individuals having genuine need of them.

Although it is highly valued by researchers, and with sufficient time and resources may provide the only practical solution to questions of future program design, the classical controlled experiment is in most cases best considered a standard—an ideal—for those engaged in the formative evaluation of real-world programs. Moreover, there are alternative designs that have the potential to achieve degrees of external and internal validity remarkably close to the experimental ideal. Known as *quasi-experimental* designs, they do not attempt to control extraneous variables, but incorporate a variety of statistical techniques to isolate, explain and to *accommodate* their influences on program outcomes. Less exact, but still potentially valuable—especially for evaluating the effects of program operation variables on outcomes—is a second body of research designs generally subsumed under the rubric of *comparative* evaluation.

QUASI-EXPERIMENTAL DESIGNS

Quasi-experimental designs are used to establish relationships between program interventions and outcomes when the creation of a control group that is statistically identical to the experimental group is infeasible. In the absence of a control group against which the changes in those receiving the intervention can be compared, some other baseline must be created. And among the most common of quasi-experimental designs are the nonequivalent control group, the interrupted time series, and the multiple time series designs.

The *nonequivalent control group* design differs from the classical experiment only because the control group has not been randomly selected from the population. Though this difference seems trivial, unless the control and experimental groups are selected by identical procedures, there is no theoretical reason to believe the groups are initially identical and thus the intervention is responsible for any differences in the two groups following experimentation. To illustrate, it is common practice, especially in social program experimentation, to construct a nonequivalent control group from program dropouts;[14] it is an expedient approach because presumably all participants will have undergone the same "before" measurements. The question that must be answered, of course, is whether dropouts or members of any other nonrandomly selected control group are the same as those who have remained. If the answer is no, the evaluator must seek to discover plausible and important differences in the two groups, make explicit those differences in the "before" measurement instrument, and attempt to estimate the effects of these differences on the differences in outcomes between the two groups. In effect, the researcher's prior theoretical knowledge is substituted for the controls that would be in force were the two groups initially identical and the experiment rigidly controlled.

For example, in a job training program, individual motivation may be a primary factor contributing to desirable program outcomes, but it is highly likely that the motivational levels of dropouts will be lower than those who have remained in the program. If so and if it is possible to administer a test for motivation prior to experimentation, it becomes possible using statistical techniques to "filter out" the effects of motivation upon the observed differences between the two groups. Only if this can be done for *all* factors that might create significant differences between the two groups will the internal validity of the nonequivalent control group design begin to approach that of the classical control group experiment.

Interrupted time series designs require a series of outcome measurements be taken before, during, and (if not an ongoing program) after implementation. If they are indeed discernible, program effects will be evident as abrupt changes in the historical pattern of outcome data during the time in which the program is in operation. In all time series designs, it is the historical pattern of outcome data that provides the baseline against which program results are compared. Suppose, for example, that a researcher desires to assess the effectiveness of a state-operated job training and referral program in reducing the welfare rolls. The program is to be implemented in April on an experimental basis and will last one year; the results of this summative evaluation are to be used in the design and conduct of future programs. Following completion of the program, the researcher determines that in the year prior to implementation eight thousand persons were on the rolls, while a year later the number had dramatically declined to four thousand. Can the researcher conclude that the decline was attributable to the program?

Were only these two outcome measurements taken—one before and one after measurement—the answer would be an emphatic no, because there is no way of determining whether the decline was a result of program activities or merely an extension of prevailing historical patterns of welfare enrollment. The observed decline might be attributable, for example, to a long-term decline that was already in progress when the program was established; or the rolls might actually fluctuate over time and the program just happened to have been implemented during a declining year. Because they lack a long-term historical baseline, studies based upon simple before and after measurements have little or no validity.

To improve validity, the researcher would seek to determine if the program appears to have disturbed the natural long-term pattern of the outcome data, which then serves as the baseline for assessing program effects. To do this, the researcher would look for historical consistencies in the behavior of the data during a number of years before and after program implementation, and usually the easiest to identify and most commonly analyzed consistencies is the trend—the general long-run increase or decrease in the value of the outcome measure over time. In Figure 7.3(a) the ideal situation exists for it is impossible to neatly fit a *single* trend line to the historical data; rather a good fit can only be achieved if two

FIGURE 7.3:
a time series analysis of the welfare rolls

(a) The "Text Book" Ideal

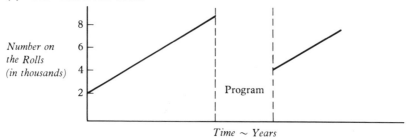

(b) The Real World Time Series

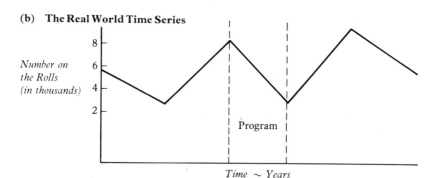

(c) The Decomposed Time Series

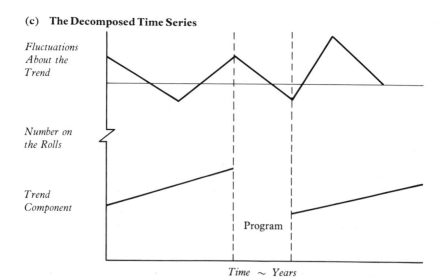

different lines are used—one representative of the trend before and one after program implementation. In this ideal case, the "before" trend line shows the size of the welfare rolls to be steadily increasing until program implementation; a dramatic drop in the rolls then occurs and again begins to rise—as indicated by the "after" trend line—following program termination. If the outcome data do look like this, there is compelling reason to believe the job training and referral program has, indeed, had a significant impact upon the size of the welfare rolls.

Unfortunately—and despite what the authors of many statistics texts would have you believe—the patterns in time series data are seldom this apparent, but rather usually look like that shown in Figure 7.3(b). Here, casual observation does not allow one to conclude that the program had any significant effect when compared to the trend, because a trend line fitted to the data might only "explain" 20 or 30 percent of the variation in the size of the rolls. It appears that they *may* be increasing over time, but this is clouded because the data are wildly fluctuating. Casual analysis of the fluctuations appears to show that every year in which there was an increase in the rolls was followed by a year in which the size of the rolls declined; it may simply have "happened" that the program was implemented during a year in which we might expect a decline to occur naturally. Were the researcher to conclude on the basis of casual observation or by fitting a trend line that the program was responsible for the decline, the conclusion would no doubt be open to challenge. At this point very little can be concluded.

Within the past several years, however, increasingly powerful computer hardware and software have created analytical possibilities not available to even the most sophisticated researchers a decade ago. Developed primarily for generating time series forecasts but useful for evaluation as well, these new tools allow the researcher to identify and explain a variety of consistent historical patterns in the data in addition to the simple trend. One such possibility is the method of *decomposition,* in which, step by step, an apparently randomly fluctuating time series can be broken down or decomposed into several discrete patterns which are then analyzed separately. Normally the method of decomposition permits one to sort out three components in any time series: trend, seasonality (variations within a single year, requiring monthly data), and cycles (longer term fluctuations). Since our data are yearly there is no seasonal component, and decomposition of the time series proceeds as follows. First, a least squares trend line is fitted through the data and the values explained by the trend subtracted from the original data, leaving what are commonly called *residuals*. Then the residuals are analyzed by fitting them to a consistent cyclical pattern about the trend. This process of fitting consistent patterns and analyzing residuals continues until the remaining residuals are ideally purely random fluctuations or "noise." As Figure 7.3(c) shows, the time series has been decomposed into trend and cyclical components; having explained and eliminated the cyclical components, and trend looks very much like that in the ideal or textbook case.

Despite such detailed analysis of a single time series, one can never be sure the program caused the abrupt change in outcomes, for the interrupted time series design implicitly assumes—with the sole exception of the program—the future or "after" pattern in the data is influenced by the identical forces that influenced the data pattern prior to implementation. But in many instances, this will not be the case. In the case just discussed, for example, a sharp improvement in economic conditions might have occurred during the time the program was in operation and continued throughout all those years for which "after" measurements were taken. Hence, the results may be invalidated by the intrusion of a new variable having a significant effect upon the measured outcome.

An improvement over the single time series design, and one that is closer to the experimental ideal, is called the *multiple time series* design. In essence, it is a time series design that uses another nonequivalent time series as the basis for comparison. In the present example, the researcher might select a number of states, ideally similar in socioeconomic makeup to the state being analyzed, but that did not introduce a program to reduce the welfare rolls; to accommodate differences in population size, outcome might be expressed as the number of persons on the welfare rolls per thousand population. Each of the resulting time series could be decomposed as before and a comparison of trends made, with the results possibly resembling those shown in Figure 7.4. If so, it presents even greater evidence that the program was indeed responsible for the observed decline in the welfare rolls.

FIGURE 7.4:

a multiple time series analysis of the welfare rolls

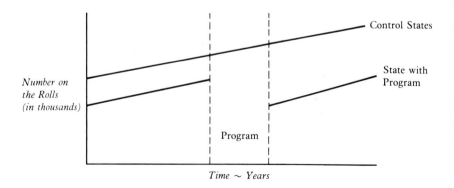

Quasi-experimental designs are not the ultimate answer to the problems with the experimental ideal, and they must be used with a great deal of caution. For example, when using a non-equivalent control group design it might not be impossible to identify, measure, analyze, and account for all of the extraneous variables that could conceivably explain outcome differences in the two groups; yet this is necessary if the effect of the program on outcomes is to be isolated and assessed. In either of the time series examples, it is impossible to isolate the effects of alternative causes that might have been occurring simultaneously. For example, a general tightening of welfare eligibility might have coincided with the establishment of the job training and placement program; neither of the time series methods would have allowed the analyst to apportion the observed decline in welfare enrollment between the two possible causes. Nonetheless, increasingly refined methodologies and the increasing capabilities to handle large quantities of data—provided that reliable data exist—permit greater explanation of the behavior of outcome variables than has been heretofore possible, explanation that is required if analysts are to approach the validity inherent in conclusions drawn from the experiment ideal.

comparative designs

Oftentimes a large number of programs built upon similar theories of intervention and change will be in operation at the same time. Such is the case, for example, when the federal government establishes project grants-in-aid to support a variety of demonstration programs operated at the state and local level. While similar in theory and having similar objectives—for example, all may be built upon the theoretical premise that job training services will improve employment among welfare recipients—many will differ in the specifics of implementation. When such differences in operational variables can be detected and codified, the comparative approach to evaluation may yield valuable information to program planners and administrators.

In truth, comparative designs must probably be considered as nonexperimental, for there is no attempt to create—either by design or through the application of various statistical methods—a control group baseline that approximates the "no program" situation. Instead, the baseline in comparative evaluation is comprised of the aggregate of other programs that are somehow similar in nature, for example, programs with similar goals or intervention strategies or those with similar outcomes. Indeed, comparative evaluation is the identical approach normally adopted when assessing the relative notion of productivity, and it suffers from many of the same problems as well.

Suppose, for example, that an evaluator wanted to compare the relative effectiveness of two programs designed to improve employment among members of a target population; one program adopts a strategy of neighborhood training and placement, while the other emphasizes on-the-job training. First we would have to agree upon a common outcome measure for each; let's say we agree that a reasonable measure is the percentage of participants placed and still working one year following completion of the programs. Then we would gather outcome data for each program and compare the results. If only two programs are compared, the results will be virtually meaningless because any variety of factors unrelated to differences in operational variables might have caused the differences in outcomes. However, were we to collect outcome data for a large number of each type of program (say fifty of each) and plot the results as shown in Figure 7.5, the subsequent comparison might be more enlightening.

In this case it is apparent that, on the average, on-the-job training is a more effective contributor to the desired outcome than is a strategy that emphasizes neighborhood training and placement; one could easily apply one of a variety of available statistical techniques—for example, a statistical comparison of means—to "prove" the obvious if so desired. But it may prove fruitful to probe further. Note, for example, that while the average performance of neighborhood training and placement centers is less than for on-the-job training, it is also less variable; its performance is more consistent. How might this be explained?

One method of analysis that is gaining increasing favor in the social

FIGURE 7.5:
a comparison of employment programs adopting two different service strategies

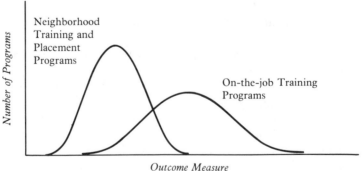

Outcome Measure
(percentage of participants placed and working one year later)

sciences involves close examination of the "outliers," or cases that deviate substantially from the mean.[15] Thus the evaluator might select for closer scrutiny the ten "best" and the ten "worst" of each type of program. Having done so, further analysis might lead the evaluator to conclude that much of the variability between the best and the worst within each program type is attributable to environmental differences over which program operators have little or no control—differences in gross economic conditions, differences in program resources, differences in participant sociodemographic characteristics and so on.

But it may be that some variations in outcome cannot be explained in terms of environmental forces alone; rather, differences in program operation variables may be responsible. Upon closer scrutiny it might be found, for example, that a number of the apparently "best" programs engage in the practice of creaming, of selecting only those applicants likely to succeed in the employment market; while a number of the "worst" consciously attempt to recruit the hard-core unemployed. It might be learned that some of the best on-the-job training programs were initiated by and have the full support of potential employers; in some of the worst, employers have little commitment to participant employment, wishing only to enhance their public image. In some of the best neighborhood training and placement centers, attendance is high, classes are small, and training is geared to imparting skills for which there are existing needs in the community; in some of the worst, training is but a ritualistic exercise.

In sum, the evaluator would methodically attempt to explain all sources of variablity between different and among similar programs, just as the evaluator attempts to identify all sources of historical variability in time series approaches to evaluation. Were the process sufficiently rigorous, it would be possible to define different subcategories of programs within each major type on the basis of major defining operational characteristics, and to use statistical techniques such as analysis of variance and regression analysis to relate these to different levels of program outcome. Thus, as shown in Figure 7.6, the evaluator might identify four major subcategories of on-the-job training programs and three subcategories of neighborhood training and placement centers, and use the common attributes of each program category to help explain the differences in program outcome.

Such continuous refinement and explanation within the comparative approach requires a theory or a set of theories of program performance; the researcher has to know what significant differences (and similarities) in strategy and program operation are important, and it is a theory that provides this insight. For example, although it has been neglected above, it might be true that the principal difference between successful and unsuccessful neighborhood training and placement centers was whether their

FIGURE 7.6:

further subcategorization of employment programs

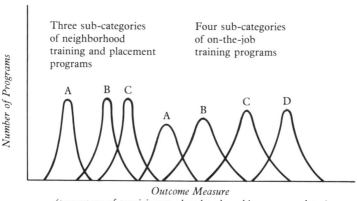

Outcome Measure
(percentage of participants placed and working one year later)

offices were located on the first floor of the building or the second. However, the evaluator would need some theory, some reason to suspect that this variable was worthy of attention. Among the program differences most difficult to detect are those pertaining to the intervention itself; variations that are subtle and not easily identified by cursory examination may be among the most important determinants of program success. This important barrier to sound comparative evaluation is further complicated as we have already seen because analysts and administrators lack a coherent, standardized scheme for categorizing and quantifying either the inputs or the outputs of service interventions. In sum:

> Few programs are designed with precise variations among them for the evaluator to use in analyzing the similarities and differences so necessary for comparative designs. Because of the state of theoretical knowledge about the processes of service programs, separating relevant differences between programs and measuring their impact on program effectiveness are difficult. Because many service programs have only small effects on a target population and programs contain numerous uncontrolled variations, the task becomes cumbersome and exploratory, requiring a great deal of statistical expertise, time and money. Few programs have the resources necessary for such evaluations.[16]

In addition, few operational programs remain static; goals change, environmental conditions change, operational variables change, personalities change, and commitment changes. Almost always, there will be a time lag between the measurement of program outcomes and the documentation of relevant program characteristics. What was *actually* happening when outcomes were generated, when personnel may have been different, may not be readily determined by the evaluator.

> Although the problem is not unique to comparative designs, programs tend to shift and change as a result of trying one approach, discarding it, and trying another. Program change almost always creates havoc for evaluators. When program change occurs during the data-gathering stage, comparisons become meaningless; when it occurs any time afterward, comparisons become anachronistic.[17]

COMPARATIVE ANALYSIS:
EVALUATING PROGRAM IMPLEMENTATION

Of particular significance to program administrators is the increasing use of formal evaluative procedures by organizations charged with allocating funds to and overseeing the operations of implementing agencies. Were the allocation of funds—especially in large federal grant-in-aid programs —wholly discretionary or only loosely directed by implementing guidelines, the funding agency would continuously face charges of capricious and arbitrary behavior, especially by jurisdictions whose funding levels fall short of expectations. And there would be little or no guarantee that limited resources would be used in the most efficient and effective manner possible. One way to solve the first problem has already been discussed in chapter 2: develop mathematical formulas that govern the amount of federal funds to be allocated to each jurisdiction. These formulas, as we have previously seen, are generally based upon surrogate indicators of need within the jurisdiction to which funds will flow—population size, median income, number of elderly or children, percentage of population below median income, the level of unemployment, and so on, depending upon the nature of the program.

Once allocated, however, the funding agency has little direct control over the effectiveness and the efficiency with which funds are spent and programs actually implemented within the jurisdiction; in general, actual program operation is only loosely governed by a series of process and structural standards—standards that may have little effect upon program outcome—imposed within the program guidelines. A variation on the traditional formula grant, in which formula developers attempt to account for possible variations in program efficiency and effectiveness, has recently come into prominence within a number of federally funded programs, including some administered by the U.S. Department of Housing and Urban Development (HUD) and the U.S. Department of Transportation.

The Performance Funding System, currently in operation within HUD, uses funding criteria developed on the basis of comparative evaluation and provides an especially instructive example.[18]

One of HUD's major responsibilities is to administer this nation's public housing grant-in-aid program, and prior to 1969, the majority of HUD housing grants to local governments were used to subsidize the construction of new housing units; the costs of operating the facilities were largely covered by tenant rental payments. However, with the passage in that year of the Brooke Amendments to the Housing and Community Development Act, which provided that public housing tenants would not have to pay more than 25 percent of their incomes on rent, it was clear that rental revenues would no longer be sufficient to cover operating costs. As a result, HUD was authorized to subsidize local housing authorities for operating expenses as well as the capital outlays for housing construction.

A number of complex issues surrounded HUD's implementation of the operating subsidy, but among the most important was the development of a set of rules for specifying the amount of subsidy for each local housing authority. Clearly, the simplest rule would provide that the subsidy would cover any difference between local operating expenses and revenues. But Congress was concerned that such an unrestricted approach would virtually eliminate any local incentives for efficiency and economy of operation; as long as any operating losses would be covered by the subsidy, Congress maintained, there would be few incentives for local housing authority administrators to maintain a watchful eye on costs. As a result, following an interim period in which subsidies were based upon the level of operating expenditure prior to the amendments, in the Housing and Community Development Act of 1974 Congress authorized HUD to:

> establish standards for costs of operation and reasonable projections of income, taking into account the character and location of the project and characteristics of the families served, or the costs of providing comparable services as determined in accordance with criteria or a formula representing the operations of a well-managed project.[19]

Thus fell to HUD—as it also falls to government organizations responsible for monitoring and regulating wages and prices in industry—the responsibility for developing a set of standards, taking into account environmental differences, which were to reflect how much it *should* cost to operate local housing projects. While Congress had specified that one of two alternative approaches might be used—either a set of criteria based upon judgment and a set of absolute standards, or one that was based upon an assessment of "comparable services"—it was the comparative approach that was adopted. The approach taken by HUD, with major support from the Urban

Institute, was a relatively straightforward comparative analysis, much like that described in Figure 7.6. First, out of a national sample of 199 housing authorities, those considered to be "well-managed" were identified. Second, a prototype equation, which established a relationship between operating costs and a number of environmental variables, was developed for the well-managed projects only. And third, this equation was used to determine a range of operating cost subsidies for all local housing authorities.

To classify housing authorities as either "well" or "poorly" managed, analysts focused upon public housing outcomes, bypassing any specification of output. To do this, a series of questionaires incorporating twenty-four separate outcome measures was administered to local housing commission members, commission staff, project staff, and housing tenants. The measures included such factors as: "residents' satisfaction with the project"; "residents' evaluation of how well the local authority is meeting its objectives"; "job satisfaction of authority employees"; "residents' perception of their present and future quality of life," and so on.[20] A variety of statistical procedures was then applied to the results and the sampled housing authorities separated into two groups, high and low performance, indicative of well and poorly managed authorities respectively. Significantly, those projects eventually classified as high performance had average operating costs substantially *lower* than those classified as low performance.

Having thus classified the sample of local housing authorities, regression analysis was performed on the high performance or well-managed projects in an effort to develop a prototype equation relating the effects of extraneous variables on operating costs. Eventually, it was determined that some 80 to 85 percent of the variation in operating expenses among high performance authorities could be explained by six prototype equation variables beyond the local administrator's control: a variable accounting for regional differences in operating costs, population of the area served by the project, the average number of bedrooms per housing unit, the average age of the buildings operated by the authority, an estimate of the fair market rent of the units, and the months of unit vacancy.[21] In effect, the prototype equation became the cost and funding standard for a high performance authority, operating within a specified set of conditions. Thus, the older the buildings operated by an authority, the larger the average number of bedrooms per unit, etc., the higher the allowable operating subsidy.

In cases where an "objective" standard, such as that yielded by the prototype equation, is used as a primary funding criterion, not surprisingly those who are hurt by the criteron will attack its integrity; the standard becomes the focus of political debate.[22] Those who were hurt in this case were the authorities who had or claimed to have had operating expenses in excess of the amount allowable under the prototype equation, *and* who argued that the higher costs did not stem from poor management but rather from factors beyond their control. Based upon our earlier discussion, critics might be expected to challenge the failure of the criterion to adequately account for differences in housing *output*, (only differences in outcome were measured), and indeed this has been the case. For example, it might be legitimately less expensive to operate a set of garden apartments than a high-rise; it may be more expensive to operate a project in which a range of social services and meals is offered, and so on; none of these variables was explicitly taken into account in the prototype cost equation.

But the most compelling arguments challenge the validity of the methods used to identify high performance or well-managed authorities. Critics claim that, in particular, the statistical relationship between high performance and low operating cost (and therefore lower operating subsidies) may be spurious; cost and performance may simply be responding to an unknown third variable or set of variables that are indeed uncontrollable. This claim is shown schematically in Figure 7.7.

In support of this argument, for example, it has been noted that the housing authorities classified as high performance are generally:

> located outside metropolitan areas, have projects that are located in better quality neighborhoods, have newer buildings, have lower density (units per acres), have fewer large apartments, have a lower incidence of tenants on welfare, have lower percent minority households, and have better original designs.[23]

In essence, what is being said is that the high performance projects also confront easier problems and, thus, are naturally less expensive to operate. Since it is these projects upon which the cost standard is based, the standard unfairly penalizes projects with more difficult problems (for example,

FIGURE 7.7:
the spurious relationship between performance and cost

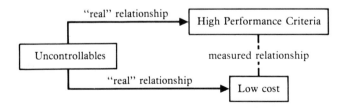

housing projects located in "undesirable" neighborhoods for the purpose of promoting racial integration), and that require as a consequence substantially higher expenditures than those allowable. Robert Shafer, a principal critic of the current allocation formula, puts the central question as follows:

> Is dissatisfaction with management the same as bad management or is it blaming management . . . for conditions over which management has no control?[24]

The Urban Institute HUD study, while fraught with numerous methodological difficulties not mentioned here, still represents a highly ambitious, sophisticated, and thoughtful piece of analysis, certainly representative of the state of the art in nonexperimental evaluative designs. Yet the critique demonstrates the vulnerability of such designs: without experimental controls and without substantial replication, regardless of the sophistication of statistical attempts to accommodate this shortcoming, they are always open to attacks on their validity. Unlike the experimental ideal, for example, analysts cannot isolate administrators, tenants, and others whose values and opinions determine housing project quality and performance measurements from the myriad external factors that may affect the desired outcome. It is extremely difficult to say that performance is "caused" by factors that can be manipulated by administrators. Nonetheless, there is a value to such analyses and standards because they stimulate discussion and debate of the meaning of important evaluative terms; evaluation thus comes out of the laboratory. And it is in this attempt to make concrete and public the standards of evaluation, and in the debate that such factors engender, that the real benefits of formal approaches to evaluation will be realized.

using evaluative findings

In discussing evaluation thus far it has been impossible to avoid nouns like "evaluator," "researcher," or "analyst" to describe the persons doing the evaluation. Implicit in this is the important idea that formal evaluation is generally performed by individuals and institutions that are not a part of the administrative superstructure. Yet in a very real sense, all persons are evaluators; all persons judge what is against what might be. Some individuals, moreover, act on the basis of these judgments, and this is called rational behavior. Others, however, for want of a plan of action, or lacking the resources, incentives, and control necessary to adopt those plans, are frequently unable to act with purpose.

The same is true of organizations with one important difference that further compounds the problem; evaluators are usually external judges, external agents of change whose conclusions often have little or no impact upon either policy or administrative decisions. There are two sides to every story and the saga of evaluative failures is no exception. From an administrative standpoint, evaluative efforts almost always contain at least one of the following major flaws: they are expensive to conduct, drawing resources away from more productive activities; they are packed with mysterious jargon, statistical tables, and equations whose meaning is unclear; they address the wrong problem or a problem beyond the administrator's control; they are insufficiently timely; they make ludicrous simplifying assumptions; and, above all, they are insufficiently conclusive to serve as the rational basis for program change.

Naturally the evaluator sees the problem differently. Administrators are loathe to support the conduct of evaluative studies because program flaws and administrative foulups will be exposed to groups upon which the survival of the program depends; administrators are reluctant to alter the comfortable status quo; they are unwilling to relinquish power to outside experts; and, above all, administrators are unable or unwilling to establish the sufficiently rigorous definition of program objectives and assumptions necessary to the conduct of formal evaluation.

Lacking a meeting of the minds, administrators are prone to conduct informal in-house evaluations using methods whose validity and reliability are gravely suspect. These efforts are often little more than symbolic responses to requirements imposed by funding bodies and other groups to which the program is to be held accountable, or symbolic responses to crises that dictate that something—anything—be done to restore confidence in the program and its administrators. In recent years, however, both theorists and practitioners have begun to address the gap between evaluation theory and practice, with an eye toward providing program decision makers with more timely, useful information with which to improve program performance. These approaches all require a measure of compromise: evaluators must withdraw somewhat from adhering to restrictions imposed by the hard, "scientific" model of evaluation, while planners and administrators must "harden up" their conception of program.

CLOSING THE THEORY-PRACTICE GAP

Three evaluative approaches, each of which addresses one or more of the issues creating the theory-practice gap, have been identified, implemented, and themselves evaluated by Joseph Wholey and his colleagues at the Urban Institute in Washington, D.C.[25] Each of the three—evaluability assessments, rapid feedback evaluations, and performance monitoring

—is relatively inexpensive and quickly completed. And, since they provide a test of management's general receptivity and ability to respond to outside evaluation, as well as a test of the evaluator's ability to meet administrative needs, they are ideally performed *prior* to any decision to adopt a more formal evaluation of program performance.

The conduct of formal evaluation studies is premised upon two often implicit assumptions: (1) that the program is conceived and designed in such a way that evaluation is possible, and (2) that program administrators are willing and able to use the results of the evaluation to alter current activities and to improve program performance. The *evaluability assessment* is a procedure designed to determine the validity of these two crucial assumptions. A program represents a set of activities oriented to the achievement of a goal or set of goals; ideally, both the goals and the means for their attainment are clearly specified in the initial stages of a well-designed program. Yet, even if well designed, we have seen that a program's evolution is frequently governed by the goals of external actors, which act as increasingly restrictive constraints upon program activities— resources must continuously be secured, constituent support mobilized and maintained, issues of turf reconciled, and a variety of process and structural standards accommodated. These constraints, together with the fact that internal rewards and sanctions are seldom sufficient to ensure that participant behavior is in compliance with stated program goals, often lead to a divergence between the real and stated goals and theories that govern program activities. In such cases, or if the program is poorly conceived initially, a fundamental question must be asked: is the program capable of being evaluated?

The evaluability assessment proceeds with the collection of information—derived from interviews of staff, program documentation, etc.— pertaining to program objectives, activities and underlying assumptions. From this information, what is called a *rhetorical program model* is developed. This model provides

> a description of the program that captures all program activities and objectives, *as defined by management and program documentation* (including the authorizing legislation), and that clearly describes the assumed causal relationships among program activities and objectives.[26]

The evaluator then analyzes the rhetorical model to determine if it is sufficiently unambiguous to permit a useful evaluation of performance. Two criteria are employed in performing this analysis. First, does documentation reveal or has management been able to agree upon a set of concrete, *measurable* objectives? And second, does the rhetorical model embody *testable* assumptions linking program activities to the achievement of these objectives?[27] Once the rhetorical model has been thus scrutinized, an evaluable program model emerges, which is a synthetic model of program embodying only those goals and assumptions that are important to administrators *and* are able to be measured and tested by the evaluator.

At this point, the results of the evaluability assessment are presented to program management, together with recommendations as to what information must be collected and measures taken in order to test program assumptions and to evaluate program performance. In many cases, the discrepancy between the rhetorical model (the one the administrator understands) and the evaluable model (the one the evaluator understands) will create the basis for valuable dialogue between evaluator and administrator. It may be, for example, that the evaluable model is sufficiently devoid of content to reveal to the administrator the need for more precise delineation of program goals, activities, and assumptions. If so, the evaluator can be a valuable resource in helping to ensure that any new program specifications adhere to the criterion of empirical evaluability. Or, the dialogue may reveal—to both the evaluator and the administrator—that the latter possesses neither the authority, the ability, the resources, nor the motivation either to create an evaluable program or to use the results of evaluation to alter program activities. If so, this is unpleasant but still valuable information. Additionally, the dialogue may reveal that while certain assumptions (the effects of various bridging variables, for example) are indeed capable of empirical verification, the administrator may have little or no use for such information. While a job training program may be built upon the assumption that attitudes will be changed, for example, the administrator may see no real need to validate this assumption with an attitude-measuring instrument, preferring instead to focus evaluative efforts on employment-related measures of outcome. Finally, administrators may decide to adopt the evaluable model and to pursue the collection of needed information required to test assumptions and measure performance. This decision can lead directly to a major evaluative undertaking or, if time is of the essence, an intermediate strategy may be pursued.

A prime determinant of both the time and monetary costs of evaluation is information, information that as we shall see shortly may not be readily available from agency records or other readily accessible sources; information is expensive. Indeed, most evaluators would agree that information collection is governed by a corollary to the well-known Murphy's Law, which states that if something can go wrong it will. The corollary or Murphy's Law of Information is: if you assume the needed information is readily available, it isn't. *Rapid feedback* represents a strategy consistent with this "law," one that is geared to providing the administrator with a careful assessment of what is currently known about the program and a set of options for future information purchases, if the current knowledge base is judged inadequate.[28]

With the evaluable model guiding efforts, readily available information on program activities, costs, and performance is collected, and this provides the basis for a preliminary evaluation of program assumptions and performance. In the course of conducting the preliminary evaluation, discrepancies between available information and that required to evaluate the program will be identified. If more detailed evaluation is desired, rapid feedback provides the basis for assessing the likely costs and the probable benefits of collecting this needed information. The decision to proceed, or not to proceed, to a higher level of evaluation can then be made rationally. If funding for evaluation studies is available from external funding sources and is discretionary, the rapid feedback assessment can provide an excellent case in support of requests for funding further evaluative studies.

Whereas rapid feedback is performed in the spirit if not the detail of the experimental or quasi-experimental models, the third readily implementable approach, *performance monitoring,* does not attempt to isolate measurable program outcomes from extraneous causal factors. It simply focuses upon measurable *indicators* of program performance. Using such devices as relatively inexpensive telephone surveys, crude comparative analyses, and site visits by expert observers, the performance monitoring approach is used to identify, establish, and maintain various sources of information that will enable managers to make rough comparisons of actual with expected program performance. Because it does not require elaborate statistical controls, nor does it pretend to corroborate program assumptions, the performance monitoring approach seems especially well suited to smaller local programs with limited evaluation budgets.

The disadvantage of performance monitoring is that, unlike more rigorous and sophisticated evaluative approaches, it does not incorporate formal methodologies to isolate the sources of program success or breakdown; it cannot explain why a program is or is not performing up to expectations. And yet few formal evaluative studies are conclusive in this regard anyway. Except in the most unusual circumstances, the responsibility for explaining program failure, and for developing and implementing strategies for improvement within identified constraints, ultimately rests with the program administrator.

IMPLEMENTATION, EVALUATION, AND ACCOUNTABILITY

While evaluation is more fruitfully viewed as an interactive process between persons with formal measurement and methodological skills and those with administrative capabilities (rather than simply the responsibility of a technically trained analyst), it does not guarantee that the social welfare organization will be accountable to some concept of the public interest. Despite agreement on the appropriate evaluative model and appropriate measures and standards, evaluation still does not ensure that the results will provoke desirable changes in the behavior of organizational participants. Nor does the dialogue between evaluator and administrator ensure that the imputed objectives are in fact appropriate to the program's true mission. It is thus the added responsibility of the administrator to ensure that both the internal and external accountability linkages are maintained.

Internally, the solution to the accountability dilemma becomes one of ensuring that evaluative results become a prime factor in determining the behavior of on-line organizational participants. In many cases, this may mean that administrators must search for ways to circumvent or at least minimize the behavioral effects of externally imposed standards that often tend to concretize the program, making desirable change all but impossible.[29] If evaluative findings are to become instruments of program change, it will require substantial participation in the design and conduct of the evaluative process by persons whose behavior is expected to be altered by the results, and the establishment of incentives that are directly tied to measures of program performance.

Here the administrator must be aware of and careful to avoid either satisfaction with or the promotion of performance indicators that are merely symbolic. A very real problem with measures and standards of program performance, whether these focus upon productivity, process, structure, or outcome, is that they often foster what might be called *criterion behavior*—the adoption of behaviors and the performance of activities that maximize the achievement of measurable criteria, but that may actually retard the achievement of "real" program effectiveness. Creaming is the result of criterion behavior, as is the practice of limiting access to ensure low caseloads and high yield professionally saturated services, as is the practice of timing before and after outcome measurements to create the appearance of success or the practice of setting unrealistically conservative and therefore readily attainable program goals.[30] In short, it is the prime responsibility of the administrator to continuously monitor the intended as well as the unintended effects of evaluative criteria and measures on participant behavior, to ensure that when program performance measures increase, an increase in well-being actually accrues to program users.[31]

The achievement of accountability to a program's myriad publics—professionals, users, funding bodies, and the public at large—demands that the evaluative process accommodate their different outcome expectations.

Merely focusing upon outcomes that are consistent with apparent program guidelines and that are measurable may therefore be insufficient. Rather, to achieve accountability the evaluative process must permit periodic reporting of how well the program is doing in terms that the various publics consider important and that they understand. That is, it must provide "the information that the intended users have defined as relevant to *their* values and needs."[32] The development of methods for ascertaining these values and needs—and of ensuring that they can be accommodated within the evaluative process—is seldom a simple task, requiring as it does an interactive process far less constrained than that confronting the evaluator and administrator. At the state and local level, at least, the needs assessment-type process seems an ideal framework within which the necessary forum can be conducted.

While there are risks associated with opening the evaluative process to the outside, it may yield two very tangible benefits to program administrators. Inevitably there will be conflicts among the many values, goals, and expectations identified by a program's publics, creating the necessity of identifying, reconciling, and establishing tradeoffs among those goals. And it may assist in identifying the standards, data, measures, and other information that is essential if social program evaluation is to contribute to improved efficiency and effectiveness. How the necessary information is generated and used are the subjects of the next chapter.

notes

1. For a detailed discussion see Roland N. McKean, *Efficiency in Government through Systems Analysis* (New York: John Wiley, 1958).

2. See Vincent Taylor, "How Much Is Good Health Worth?" *Policy Sciences,* 1, no. 1 (1970), 49–72.

3. Taylor, "How Much Is Good Health Worth?" pp. 67–68.

4. Edward A. Suchman, "Action for What? A Critique of Evaluative Research," in *Evaluating Action Programs,* ed. Carol H. Weiss (Boston: Allyn S. Bacon, 1972), p. 53.

5. Michael Scriven, "The Methodology of Evaluation," *Evaluating Action Programs,* pp. 123–36.

6. Carol H. Weiss, *Evaluation Research* (Englewood Cliffs, N.J.: Prentice-Hall, 1972), pp. 47–50.

7. Ibid., p. 49.

8. Weiss, *Evaluation Research,* pp. 32–34.

9. Amitai Etzioni, *Modern Organizations* (Englewood Cliffs, N.J.: Prentice-Hall, 1964), p. 17.

10. Donald T. Campbell and Julian C. Stanley, *Experimental and Quasi-Experimental Designs for Research* (Chicago; Rand McNally, 1963), p. 5.

250 evaluating social programs

11. Robert Ferber and Werner Z. Hirsch, "Social Experimentation and Economic Policy," *Journal of Economic Literature,* 16 (December 1978), 1379–1414.

12. Ibid., p. 1394.

13. Ibid., pp. 1395–96.

14. Thomas J. Kiresuk and Sander H. Lund, "Program Evaluation and the Management of Organizations," in *Managing Human Services,* eds. Wayne F. Anderson, Bernard J. Frieden, and Michael J. Murphy (Washington, D.C.: International City Management Association, 1977), pp. 300–301.

15. See for example N. R. Draper and H. Smith, *Applied Regression Analysis* (New York: John Wiley, 1966), pp. 109–10.

16. Jack L. Franklin and Jean H. Thrasher, *An Introduction to Program Evaluation* (New York: John Wiley, 1976), p. 65.

17. Ibid.

18. Robert Sadacca, Morton Isler, and John DeWitt, *The Development of a Prototype Equation for Public Housing Operating Expenses* (Washington, D.C.: Urban Institute, 1975).

19. *United States Code: Congressional and Administrative News* (October 15, 1974), p. 3,282.

20. Robert Sadacca and others, *The Development of a Prototype Equation,* pp. 91–96.

21. Robert Sadacca and Joan DeWitt, *Working Paper: Development of a Revised Prototype Equation for Public Housing Operating Expenses* (Washington, D.C.: Urban Institute), p. 14.

22. See Bruce L. Gates, "Knowledge Management in the Technological Society," *Public Administration Review,* 35, no. 6. (November/December 1975), 389–93.

23. Robert Shafer, "Public Housing Operating Costs, Management and Subsidies," in Citizen's Housing and Planning Association, *Operating Subsidies for Public Housing* (Boston: Metropolitan Boston, 1975), p. 22.

24. Ibid.

25. Joseph S. Wholey, Joe N. Nay, John W. Scanlon, and Richard E. Schmidt, "Evaluation: When Is It Really Needed?" *Evaluation,* 2, no. 2 (1975), 89–93; and Joseph S. Wholey, "The Role of Evaluation and the Evaluator in Improving Public Programs: The Bad News, the Good News, and a Bicentennial Challenge," *Public Administration Review,* 36, no. 6, (November/December 1976), pp. 679–83.

26. Joseph Wholey and others, "Evaluation: When Is It Really Needed?" p. 91, emphasis added.

27. Ibid.

28. Ibid., p. 92.

29. Robert A. Walker, "The Ninth Panacea: Program Evaluation," *Evaluation,* 1, no. 1 (Fall 1972), 47.

30. Ibid., p. 53.

31. Ibid.

32. Carol H. Weiss, "Alternative Models of Program Evaluation," *Social Work,* 19, no. 6 (November 1974), 80, emphasis added.

Information systems are formal structures used to gather, store, and translate a wide variety of data into useful information. Information systems development in the social welfare enterprise has proceeded along two separate paths: (1) the establishment of systems to improve the control of internal operations, particularly with respect to the use of financial resources; and (2) systems designed to generate information about program users. While much valued research and evaluation information could be obtained through a merger of the two often completely separate systems, political, organizational, and technical factors have hampered this synthesis.

Information systems design is concerned with matching information needs to the organization's data processing capability. This capability is dependent upon four primary system components: the availability of analytical models that determine how data are to be organized into useful information, the data processing technology that actually controls that organization, the structure of the data base, and the pattern of the data and information flows that define the overall structure of the information system.

Because they are often potent instruments of program and agency change, information systems are not self-implementing. Rather, their design, development, and implementation should ensure the participation of all organizational members who are expected to use the information generated by the system.

information systems

8

We have seen in previous chapters that the administrative role in social programs is one of responding selectively to myriad and often disparate external influences in an effort to integrate the essential programmatic activities required in correctly matching services to needs. Central to understanding and managing this process is information, which like the program's important environmental forces and critical activities, serves to focus the limited attention of program staff. In short, "that certain information is regularly collected focuses the organization's attention on it."[1]

Why do organizations collect certain elements of information and yet disregard others? Pfeffer and Salancik have outlined a number of reasons.[2] First, organizations tend to concentrate upon information that is simple to collect; they are more likely to collect readily available information—the names of service users, for example—than, say, information about service outcomes. Second, organizations are more likely to collect information that is easily coded, processed, and transmitted, usually quantitative information; thus, for example, social welfare programs are more likely to code a client's present situation by defined category—say "unemployed"—than in narrative form. Third, information may be collected by organizations or organizational subunits because it is believed to enhance their power and status; hence graduate schools in increasingly competitive markets for students often maintain records of the starting salaries of recent graduates. And fourth and finally, information may be collected because it is required—either to satisfy external reporting requirements or because it is essential to decision making. With regard to the latter, information becomes the theoretical "memory" of the organization, documenting decisions made in the past and, when compared to outcomes, permitting it to learn from past errors.

Largely stimulated by an increasing number of reporting requirements, the availability of project grant-in-aid funds to support the development of information systems, and the dramatic advances in data processing technologies, the social welfare enterprise has in the past decade or so undergone a profound change in both the quantity and quality of the information it is capable of generating. The focus of these developments is the formal information system, which has been defined as

> a systematic formal assemblage of components that performs data processing operations to (a) meet legal and transactional requirements, (b) provide information to management for support of planning, con-

trolling and decision-making, and (c) provide a variety of reports, as required, to external constituents.[3]

While it might have been possible for agency and program administrators to avoid this often complex and sometimes jargon-laden subject only a few years ago, its actual and potential impact upon virtually all aspects of program operation is such that this is no longer the case. Because they both delimit and focus attention, changes in the organization's information base and information processing capabilities will also generate changes in how programs are understood and in the decisions resulting from that understanding. As a consequence, it does not seem unreasonable to conclude that information system technology may be *the* most important source of change in social programs—change which, depending upon the degree to which the technology can be harnessed may afford a more rational programmatic response to human needs. This chapter provides a basic introduction to a rapidly changing and often complex field, covering the rudiments of information systems design and the constraints and opportunities these potent agents of change offer for improving the administration of social programs.

the two (and one-half)
dimensions of information

Three fundamental types of information—each (usually) supported by a separate information system—are of value to social welfare agencies and programs. The first, *client information systems,* are concerned with the generation, organization, and dissemination of information pertaining to the client and his or her interaction with the program (and in some cases a whole network of programs). The second, *organizational information systems,* are designed to support basic administrative functions like planning, budgeting, reporting, and cost control. And the third, called here *performance information systems,* are designed to support improved decision making and thus embrace information required for assessing various facets of program productivity and effectiveness. Clearly, the information generated within one system will overlap that required in the others, but this is especially true of performance information, which pertains to the relationship between program operations and program users and thus requires a synthesis of client and organizational information. We shall see shortly that the failure to achieve this necessary synthesis is a major barrier to evaluating many aspects of social program performance.

The structure of an information system, as we shall see in some detail shortly, is not unlike that of an organization; that is, information systems —like the organizational systems they are designed to support—are factored and sub-factored into increasingly specialized units. It is common, then, to speak of information systems as comprised of various subsystems, each of which supports one of many activities required to perform a major program function. Likewise, just as an organizational structure is superimposed upon activities in an effort to ensure they contribute to the performance of a function, an information system is constructed to ensure each of its subsystems are compatible with one another. Indeed, subsystem compatibility—that the information building blocks stored in different subsystems can be combined and recombined in different ways—is *the* defining characteristic of an information *system.*

The functional basis of any client information system centers upon the provision of allocations to program users and, as a result, it is convenient to view its important subsystems as reflecting activities normally undertaken during that process. While the specific activities will doubtless vary from program to program, a representative model of that process— a more detailed version of that previously presented in Figure 5.5—is shown in Figure 8.1.

Associated with each activity in the process, as Table 8.1 shows, is an information subsystem, into which basic client information is entered and stored for later use. Note from Table 8.1 that some of the information generated within each of the activities is cumulative. That is, information generated during performance of earlier activities is required in later activities; for example, problem information generated at intake is later com-

FIGURE 8.1:

activities common to the provision of services

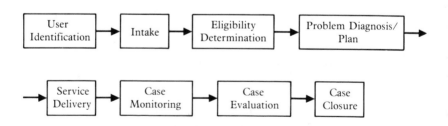

Source: Gary E. Bowers and Margaret R. Bowers, "Cultivating Client Information Systems," Human Services Monograph Series *(Washington, D.C.: U.S. Department of Health, Education, and Welfare, Project Share, 1977), p. 11.*

TABLE 8.1:

types and sources of client information

Activity	Data/Information Normally Obtained
User identification	Lists of persons actually or potentially eligible or in need of program services. Provided by referrals from other agencies, informal contacts, or through a variety of outreach activities.
Intake	Generates demographic and biographical data pertaining to an individual, or in the case or child welfare programs, a family or a case. Includes data pertaining to individual or family problems in need of resolution.
Eligibility determination	Although generally performed at the same time as intake, yields data specific and perhaps unique to a particular program's eligibility requirements. Determines who will pay for services: what program, what third party, what user fees, if any.
Problem diagnosis/plan	Provides information documenting the perceived relationship between problems, needs, and plans. Problem assessment is often in narrative form, while plans generally include personal or case goals that are rather specific.
Service delivery	Requires information about specific services provided when, and by whom—the agency, another agency as the result of a service arrangement, or through a purchase of service contract with another provider.
Case monitoring	Compares the plan with the actual services provided, and may generate *new* information only if there is a discrepancy between the two.
Case evaluation	Intended to generate information about service outcomes for each case or individual. May occur prior to or after case closure.
Case closure	Occurs when the individual or family is no longer the recipient of services. Information obtained generally includes the reason for case closure—voluntary termination, successful achievement of goals, unsuccessful achievement of goals, relocation of another area, and so on.

Source: Gary E. Bowers and Margaret R. Bowers, "Cultivating Client Information Systems," Human Series Monograph Series (Washington, D.C.: U.S. Department of Health, Education and Welfare, Project Share, 1977), pp. 10–13.

bined with that generated during the development of a case plan to provide the information required in performing a case evaluation. We shall return to this important idea of combining basic information building blocks shortly, but for the time it is important to note that both Figure 8.1 and Table 8.1 represent an idealized client information system. Even if they perform all of the outlined activities, only a very few social programs possess a coherent information system capable of monitoring and of integrating all of the information generated during the performance of service provision activities. Instead, most will have separate—and often incompatible—standardized systems to support client identification, intake and eligibility determination, service delivery, and so on.

ORGANIZATIONAL INFORMATION SYSTEMS

By necessity and by tradition, the design of organizational information systems has been dictated by budgetary, accounting, and reporting requirements, which are often imposed by external sources of funds. Typical functions supported by organizational information systems include: needs assessments, facilities and operational planning, budgeting, research, personnel and payroll, accounting and cost control, statistical reporting, and forecasting.[4] Note that some of the organizational functions require the same information as is generated by the client information system, but in a less detailed and more aggregated form than that required to support the actual provision of services.

The basic source of organizational information is the operating unit or service provider, significantly the same unit or individual responsible for generating and updating information about clients as well. But whereas client information is ultimately concerned with the questions of "who did what for whom, where, when, and to what extent"[5] the organizational system, regardless of its specific function, requires and processes information pertaining to the question of who spent how much from what fund for what purpose. Basic data are usually generated by object of expenditure—time and salary, rent, travel, training, supplies, diagnostic or treatment procedures, contract purchase-of-service invoices, and so on. Ideally, these expenditures are charged against the applicable fund at the time incurred; this may in fact occur at a later time—after assessing the fund balance.

This basic information is then sorted and aggregated in summary form for higher level organizational units, perhaps program administration as well as various functional departments. The way the information is aggregated and presented will largely depend upon the particular requirements of each of the agency's functional departments—for example, the information needs of a research department will differ from those required in budget preparation—and the reporting requirements imposed by external sources of funds. The latter constraint will often depend upon which of a variety of possible budgeting and accounting formats is currently in vogue. For example, a line item format will necessitate that information be aggregated and organized by object of expenditure, which was probably its original mode of collection and organization. A performance format will usually require that costs and other resource expenditures be organized in relation to specific services provided or received, while a program format may require that expenditures be related to the total number of persons receiving services intended to achieve certain goals. Note that the performance and program formats require a synthesis of basic cost and client information. With respect to the latter for example, it may be reported that sixty-four persons received child care services in pursuit of an employment goal, at an annual cost of $68,000; this will require reorganization of and additions to the data originally collected. Because reporting requirements frequently change, and new programs and services are continuously added and deleted, it is often recommended that both client and organizational systems be constructed of "modules," flexible information subsystems that can be combined and recombined as new or multiple reporting requirements dictate.[6]

PERFORMANCE INFORMATION SYSTEMS:
THE "HALF" DIMENSION

We have seen in previous chapters that much of the most valuable information in the social welfare enterprise requires a synthesis of that generated by client systems and organizational information systems. For example, previously discussed was the information required in the assessment of agency and program productivity. Categories of activities that comprise a unit of service provided or received are defined. In the same manner as that used to generate cost control information, the engineered and discretionary costs incurred in the provision of each unit of service are determined and allocated among various organizational units or activities; these cost estimates are then combined with service units to generate unit service costs. Finally, this information is used to compare productivity with that of other agencies or against past performance in the same agency.

Planning information is that which has been obtained in the past to be used in assessing the future, and thereby requires some system capacity to store substantial amounts of information over relatively long periods of time. Of obvious interest is information concerning the sizes of both the need and the expected user populations during the planning period. As has been previously discussed, this may require substantial amounts of information generated from a variety of sources: community forums, social indicators, community surveys, and rates-under-treatment data obtained from records of service users. Each of these sources may be mined independently or if there is some degree of compatibility among them—for example, if all incorporate the same sociodemographic, need, and service categories—may be used in combination to estimate the expected number of service users during the planning period. Of importance is information germane to the planning of resources and costs as well. Projected caseloads, estimates of the costs associated with implementing new quality standards, personnel and facilities costs, and the costs of purchased services and supplies are essential information ingredients in planning for costs.

Finally, information required in the assessment of organizational or program effectiveness ultimately must include measures that pertain to service outcome, together with information about costs. Since many service users are likely to possess multiple problems and needs and may use many different services, attempts to assess effectiveness will likely require the ability to trace the user's history of service utilization over some period of time. This in turn will require some degree of information system compatibility and integration among the agencies and programs comprising the total service network. At the very least it implies that the identity of the service user be consistently known, that a historical record of service utilization for each individual be compiled, and that it be possible to determine the status of the service user following each contact.

Were we to assess the information priorities in most social welfare programs and agencies, a typical ranking would be shown as follows:

Highest Priority: Basic client and cost control information
Planning and needs assessment information
Information about productivity
Lowest Priority: Information about effectiveness

The reason for high priority information is apparent: to ensure the continued flow of funds to the organization. That basic performance information lags so far behind, however, is the result of a complex set of political, organizational, and technical factors that impinge upon the basic elements of information system design.

elements of information
system design

The overall design of any information system proceeds with an information systems analysis, which may in a large organization require many man-hours of effort, or in a small program may consist of but a series of informal discussions between the program manager and the local computer sales representative. Systems analysis as applied to any problem involves the separation of the phenomenon under investigation into its constituent parts and the establishment of relationships among each of these parts; the result is a conceptual systems model.

Because realism must often be balanced against the need for conceptual simplicity, an extremely important decision when performing any systems analysis concerns the establishment of a system boundary, which delineates those elements and relationships that are to be included in the system. Since it is probably true that any given element will be related to any other element, the establishment of a system boundary is a matter of some discretion. Two criteria, however, are normally applied: the boundary may be drawn around those elements and relationships that are strongly related to a common purpose or function, or where the relationships among various elements weaken markedly.[7] Perhaps more than any other, this decision will greatly influence the ultimate decision-making value of a systems analysis.

Once the elements, relationships, and boundary have been identified, the conceptual system is then scrutinized to identify those alterations in its elements or relationships that would improve its performance; then desired alterations are implemented in the real system. Any given phenomenon can usually be described in terms of many different conceptual systems. An organization, for example, can be alternatively described in structural terms as a set of formal authority relationships; as a system of actors and the interpersonal relationships that exist among them; as a system for acquiring, controlling, and using resources; or as a system of information needs and flows. The perspective adopted depends solely upon the purpose for which the systems analysis is intended.

Information systems analysis is intended to improve the generation and distribution of information within an organizational setting and embraces the following activities: the identification of the various components of information required or desired by organizational participants; the identification of the specific data elements required to generate that information; and the creation of a data processing technology to facilitate the interrelationships among various data and between information and decision makers.[8] Information systems analysis may be initiated for a variety of reasons. It may be implemented to solve a problem as would be the case, for example, were the current financial information system unable to maintain the necessary accounting distinction between resources received from different funding sources. It may respond to new developments in data processing technologies, such as has occurred with the recent advent of relatively inexpensive and powerful "minicomputer" systems. Information systems analysis may be initiated to improve the performance of the existing system, often a patchwork of technology, data, and information that has evolved over the years and that is generally inadequate to support existing needs. But probably the most important stimulus in the social welfare enterprise is the imposition of new reporting requirements upon the organization—the result of a new guideline, a new law, a new accounting practice, a new budget format, a new service, a new program.

Indeed, the information and reporting requirements that accompanied Title XX have proven to be a major force behind the current emphasis on large-scale, comprehensive information systems in social service programs and agencies. Accompanying the enactment of Title XX were the federal Social Services Reporting Requirements, which initially required states to report information on the number of persons receiving Title XX services, by category of eligibility; the types of services provided to each; the problems addressed by these services and the goals to be achieved by each; and the type of agency providing the service. Also required initially was a "basic data file" for each recipient, which was intended to generate a comprehensive historical record of the various services provided by each agency to each recipient. Ultimately, however, the latter requirement was abandoned when federal administrators realized that "states varied so widely in their organization, service delivery mechanisms, and political makeups, that developing a single model to satisfy their diverse requirements was not a feasible approach."[9]

Regardless of its impetus, an information systems analysis will ultimately focus on the relationships among four major elements common to any information system: (1) a set of analytical models, (2) the system data base, (3) the methods for processing data, and (4) the general structure of the information system.

ANALYTICAL MODELS

Any model, as we have seen, is a conceptual representation of any phenomenon under investigation. In information systems design, the analytical model provides the conceptual linkage between raw data and useful information, which in turn permits one to define the system's data processing requirements; the model tells us *what to measure.* It is important to note that raw data represent but disorganized facts; information results from the accumulation and organization of facts—generally expressed as numerical measures—that are useful for problem solving and decision making. The difference between data and information has been compared to a newspaper with no headlines, no page numbers, and no spaces between the words—"an avalanche of data but a paucity of information."[10]

To better see the importance of the analytical model in creating information out of raw data, consider a "budget time line," a model that depicts budgetary expenditures over time in comparison to predicted or budgeted expenditures and is a common output of virtually any financial information system. Such a model is shown in Figure 8.2. But how does it guide the generation of information from raw data?

Suppose a community mental health center has received $60,000 in funding from a state department of mental health to operate an alcohol treatment program for a period of one year. For sake of simplicity, assume

FIGURE 8.2:

a budget time line

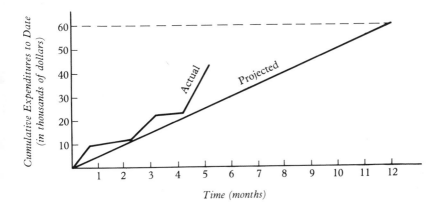

that the state is the only source of program funds and that the amount is considered sufficient by both state and local officials to meet community alcohol treatment needs during the coming year. The time line for this program will incorporate three basic elements of information: time, projected expenditures, and actual expenditures to date, each of which will be generated from a set of discrete facts about the program. But first, we need to make a basic decision: what are the appropriate increments of time during which to collect and aggregate cost data? Should we keep track of costs on a minute-by-minute basis, hourly, weekly, monthly? Unless this is already specified in the state's reporting requirements, the decision will result from a compromise between the need to control expenditures, the value of high versus low frequency cost information in facilitating that control, and the higher costs associated with more frequent cost updates. Let's say that a monthly time increment is sufficient. Thus, the first criterion for organizing the data into useful information has been specified: both budgetary and expenditure data are to be collected and aggregated on a monthly basis. This means that we must somehow keep track, not only of specific expenditures, but also the month during which they were incurred.

Following our discussion in chapter 6, expenditure data may be generated either with reference to services provided or to services received; significantly, the choice will affect the specific cost data required. If the choice is units of service received, one would need a count of the number of service users during any given month; hence we must keep track of persons served. To use this approach, we would have to establish by prior analysis both the appropriate unit of service and its cost. Suppose this has been analyzed and computed on an ADP basis at $100 per day (someone would have to decide how partial days are to be counted). Knowing the count of ADPs per month, it is a simple matter to compute the total monthly variable costs. Assuming that a method of allocating fixed costs to the program has been established, useful information has been generated by combining cost per unit service data with the number of users in a given month.

Were expenditures to be based upon services provided, one would have to keep track of the materials, supplies, and human resources expended on behalf of the program during a given month; it would not, however, be necessary to keep track of persons served to fulfill the requirements of the time line. Were alcohol treatment the only program operated by the community mental health center or were it to exist as a completely separate entity with its own facility and personnel, simply keeping track of total monthly costs would be sufficient. More than likely, however, alcohol treatment is intertwined with a host of other programs, with which it shares facilities, supplies, and personnel, but *not* the same source of funds. In this event, it is necessary to create a relationship between activity and expenditure data and the appropriate source of funds. Materials and supplies are directly billed against the program account, as is a share of overhead by mutual agreement with the state department. Personnel time of each individual provider is also billed against the program account (four hours of worker A, two of worker B, and so on) which, when combined with payroll system data pertaining to each worker's salary, generates a program personnel cost. These billings may in fact occur daily, weekly, or monthly, depending upon the other programs with which alcohol treatment shares its personnel, supplies, and facilities. But our concern is monthly, and monthly expenditure information is generated by combining time and salary data for each individual worker on the program during the month, and adding these to generate total personnel costs. When added to a predetermined monthly overhead charge and supply and material expenditure data, one has the total alcohol treatment expenditures per month. Given the comparative complexity of this as opposed to the first procedure, it should be apparent why so much time and effort has been expended upon defining standard service output and cost measures.

One final operation must be performed to satisfy the requirements of the budget time line model; a historical record of expenditures must be maintained at least throughout the funding period. A time line represents "total expenditures to date" and hence is a cumulative total of all prior months. Finally, knowing both total expenditures and projected expenditures to date allows comparison. If, for example, actual cumulative expenditures after six months of operation total $50,000 (as against a projected expenditure of only $30,000) this is information the administrator ought to have, either as the basis for a supplementary budget request, or for cutting program costs.

The budget time line is an extremely simple model, requiring relatively little in the way of data generation, retrieval, maintenance, organization, and computation; moreover, it is a model that has apparent value to program decision makers. Such simple and useful models are, unfortunately, the exception rather than the rule in the social welfare enterprise. Illustrating this point is the process model described in Figure 8.1 and the basic data described in Table 8.1. What specific models are available to guide the conversion of these data into useful information? It should not be surprising that a major barrier to the development of management information systems in the social welfare enterprise is not a shortage of data nor of data processing technology but rather a paucity of analytical models through which to create useful information.[11]

DATA PROCESSING CAPABILITIES

If the analytical model provides the conceptual basis for translating raw data into useful information, it is the data processing system that actually performs the operations and disseminates the results. Data processing may be viewed in two ways—the nature of the data and the operations required, or the specific modes by which those operations are to be carried out. With respect to the latter, data processing may be performed manually; in conjunction with a mechanical aid like a calculator, a cash register, or a microfilm system; electromechanically with the use of punched cards; or through the use of an electronic computer.[12] The particular mode selected will depend upon such factors as the volume of data elements required in the generation of information, the complexity and number of discrete operations required, the existence of data processing time constraints, and the computational complexity required. While most organizations use a combination of all four methods, our focus here will be upon computerized data processing systems.

Although many distinct data processing operations and components may be identified,[13] for our purposes it is sufficient to note that any information system will possess three primary components: (1) a means of entering data into the system; (2) a means of storing, organizing, manipulating, and retrieving these data; and (3) some means of disseminating the resulting information. There are two important sets of interfaces among these components; the "man-machine" interface, which will be discussed shortly, and those occurring within the data processing system, primarily between the computer's hardware components and its software. And while computer hardware may include a variety of input-output devices such as keypunch machines, card readers, teleprinters, and TV set-like cathode ray tube terminals, the two most important are its central processing unit (CPU) and its equipment used for data storage.

The function of the CPU is to process data, and it can do this in two basic ways. First, it can perform series of arithmetic operations on a set of numbers; in a way identical to a handheld calculator, it can add, subtract, multiply, and divide. Second, it can perform various nonarithmetic or "decision-making" operations on both numerical and nonnumerical data; for example, upon instruction from the user it can arrange a numerical sequence in ascending or decending order, or it can take a random list of names and arrange them alphabetically. The major parameter by which a CPU is normally evaluated (and a prime determinant of its cost) is its throughput—how much data can be input, processed, and output in a given amount of time.

The second major element of hardware is the computer's equipment for storing data, and this may be accomplished in a variety of ways: by maintaining boxes of punched computer cards or punched paper tapes, or by storing data on magnetic disks or magnetic tapes. The principal parameters by which each of these methods is evaluated (and the major factors affecting their cost) are first the amount of readily available or on-line storage capacity; and second is a parameter called access time, the time it takes for the CPU to receive processing instructions and to locate within the storage device the data to be processed.[14] For readily accessible, on-line storage devices like magnetic tape this number is typically measured in time increments of one-millionth of a second, although this will vary with the particular hardware used and, equally important, with the software used to control the system.

Without some means of exercising control over the computer's arithmetic and nonarithmetic operations, one merely has an inert assemblage of metal, plastic, and transistors—no whirring discs, no pleasant and reassuring hum, no blinking lights, no clatter of the teleprinter. The function of computer software is to provide that control, to issue the instructions that will ultimately create meaningful information out of raw data. This is when we enter the world of that manipulator of strange symbols and utterer of alien words—that of the computer programmer. Although it can be an intimidating world for most of us because it is dominated by a detailed and exacting logic, it is very likely here that the ultimate success (or failure) of the information system will be determined. It is essential for both programmers and users to understand the needs of and constraints faced by one another, and among the most important issues in this regard concerns the structure and logic of the information system's data base.

The data base of any computerized information system is conceptually organized into three progressively more complex categories of data, known as fields, records, and files, and it is within this basic structure that we can understand how data are processed into information. The most elementary category of data, the *field,* represents a single, isolated variable or characteristic. For example, if we were interested in establishing a user data base, we would probably establish a number of fields labeled "name," "address," "age," and so on. Were the data base designed only to deal with fields, none of these data would be interconnected. That is, we would not know that "John Doe, age 27, lives at 1224 Danville Street"; we would only know that some user was named John Doe, some user was 27 years old, and some user lived at 1224 Danville Street. About the only thing we could gain by processing these isolated independent data fields would be basic revisions of lists (names of users and addresses in alphabetical order) and elementary statistical operations on fields containing numerical data, such as average age, median age, and the frequency distribution of the ages of all service users. Interesting, perhaps, but not all that useful.

The road to really useful information begins by creating a series of logical relationships among data and hence data fields, and this is accomplished by establishing a common code which links fields together; for example, we might attach the number "1" to all those characteristics pertaining to a person who is named John Doe. As shown in Figure 8.3, this is exactly what is done when information is entered on the same computer card. Fields that can be logically related in this way are called *records.*

As Figure 8.3 shows, two separate data records have been created as part of a client information system, possibly to support different record-keeping functions performed by two different organizational departments. One, in support of the intake procedure, compiles a record that includes the user's name and age. The second, in support of case management activities, includes the user's name and the service received. (Clearly, more data would be required for each application; they have been limited here for clarification.) Each of these separate records can, in turn, be compiled into separate *files,* one for name and age and one for name and service; as shown, each can be organized and compiled in different ways (by name, by age, or by service) as the needs of the system user dictate.

As we have seen, system needs relate to the decision-making and reporting functions to be supported and these functions, in turn, are supported by various information subsystems. Subsystems can often be created by merely reorganizing the same files and records into different views of the data base (imagine looking into a box from each of its six sides), but the ability of the system to do this easily, rapidly, and without

FIGURE 8.3:

the structure and logic of the data base

Age versus Service:

Age 27, Counseling (John Doe)	
Age 32, Child care (Mary Jones)	
Age 32, Child care (Carlos Smith)	
Age 32, Counseling (Carlos Smith)	

LOGICALLY INTERRELATED FILES

Organized by Name:	*Organized by Age:*	*Organized by Service*	*Organized by Name:*

FILES

Organized by Name:	*Organized by Age:*	*Organized by Service*	*Organized by Name:*
John Doe Age 27	Age 27 John Doe	Counseling John Doe Carlos Smith	John Doe Counseling
Mary Jones Age 32	Age 32 Mary Jones Carlos Smith	Child Care Mary Jones Carlos Smith	Mary Jones Child care
Carlos Smith Age 32			Carlos Smith Child care Counseling

RECORDS

John Doe, age 27	Mary Jones, child care
Mary Jones, age 32	John Doe, Counseling
Carlos Smith, age 32	Carlos Smith, counseling
	Carlos Smith, child care

FIELDS

Name	Age	Name	Service Provided
"John Doe"	27	"Mary Jones"	"child care"
"Carlos Smith"	32	"Carlos Smith"	"counseling"
"Mary Jones"	32	"John Doe"	"counseling"
		"Carlos Smith"	"child care"

error, must generally be incorporated into the design of the *original* data base. Because information needs frequently change with the system simply evolving to meet them, however, desirable flexibility in the data base may have been sacrificed. That is, it is common practice for most organizations to maintain a large number of redundant data files to be used in support of each separate application—record keeping, reporting, cost control, and so on.

Consider the implications, however, if two separate files are constructed so that they can be logically interrelated; in Figure 8.3 this is accomplished with the code "name" common to both files. The result is new, quite useful planning and evaluation information derived from data originally used to support basic record-keeping activities—the relationship between the age of the service user and the services received. Or consider the generation of cost control information in the same way. Many organizations use time cards on which employees record the amount of time spent per day or per week on various programs. This method of collecting data creates a record pertaining to the employee's name, a program, and an amount of time worked, and also creates a logical relationship between each item. When work records for all employees are related to records within a separate payroll file (containing records of employees' names and their salaries) it becomes a relatively simple matter to keep a running tab on program costs; e.g., Clarice Hernandez worked a total of sixteen hours on program A; Clarice Hernandez' wage is $5.50 per hour; $88 is billed against program A. Files that can be thus related are said to be part of an *intergrated data base.*

Two advantages of creating a master data base within which the files for all applications can be interrelated should by now be apparent. First, it eliminates the need to collect and store the same data more than once, thereby reducing both data collection and storage costs. Second, and perhaps more important, it permits the organization to develop an information system capable of transcending basic record-keeping and reporting applications, even if little or no new data are gathered; new information is generated by simply recombining old data to establish new relationships. The creation of logically interrelated *files* allows one to establish relationships among the *data* contained in different files—the relationships between case planning records and the sociodemographic characteristics of users, which are useful in needs assessments and in forecasting utilization; the relationships between records of service use and cost control information which is the foundation of measuring service productivity; and the relationships among demographics, case records, cost control information, and service outcome that form the core of evaluation information. Moreover, were it possible to integrate the data files of different organizations it would be possible to generate a more comprehensive view of the service network than currently exists, perhaps improving integration. These, however, are issues of information system structure.

THE STRUCTURE OF THE INFORMATION SYSTEM

The final element of information systems design concerns the manner in which data and information flow through the organization, which is governed by the *structure* of the information system. System structure is ultimately concerned with the two primary elements of the man-machine interface: the relationships between data-gathering elements and data processing components, and those existing between data processing and eventual information users. Since control over the flow of information is a prime function of an organization's structure, it should not be surprising to learn that two general structural models dominate thinking about contemporary information systems design: the hierarchical and the systems model.

The *hierarchical* model mirrors the hierarchical model of organization, and *assumes* that the desirable and necessary flows of information will naturally parallel the vertical patterns of authority, responsibility, and control characteristic of that organizational model.[15] Typically, requests for information are assumed to flow downward, while information—generally in increasingly refined, distilled, and aggregated form—flows upward in the hierarchy. Also like its organizational counterpart, as Figure 8.4 shows, the hierarchical information system may either be centralized or decentralized, the only difference being that a centralized system is controlled by a central data processing department, while in the decentralized system data processing is controlled by, and staff and related equipment are generally physically located within, the departments or other jurisdictions it supports.

FIGURE 8.4:

the hierarchical model of information system structure

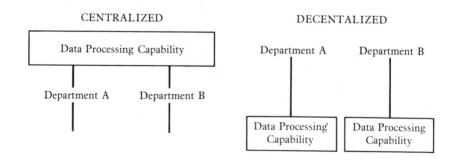

The principal problem with information systems designs that are premised upon the hierarchical model is the implicit assumption that the only important information flows occur vertically within departmental lines of authority. The effect is that the *horizontal* flows of information that must occur in any organization—those between planning and finance, for example—are not a part of the *formal* information system. In theory, this might be partially rectified through the adoption of a centralized data processing department which, in addition to being the relatively less expensive alternative, could divert the information flowing up one channel and down another as the need arises. There are a number of practical problems, as the following will illustrate, that minimize the attractiveness of this solution.

Some eighteen states currently administer and deliver Title XX services at the county level (recall that the choice of the appropriate administrative jurisdiction is a state-by-state decision). In response to the inherent inefficiencies of redundant, decentralized data processing capabilities, a number of these states have attempted to create centralized, statewide processing capabilities to support county social service activities—an endeavor which, reports one knowledgeable source, "has set back Social Service Information Systems development considerably" in those states.[16] Most of these counties already had installed their own systems, geared to their own organizational patterns and modes of service delivery; moreover, most counties had relied upon common, multi-purpose information systems shared by and supporting other county functions, police and financial record keeping for example. One cannot pull one data and software package out of an existing system and drop it neatly into another without generally suffering serious problems of data and software incompatibility. The conclusion: a rapid shift from a decentralized to a centralized system, regardless of its possible merit, will probably do more damage than good. Build a decentralized system with the *capability* for later central collection and aggregation of information for state reporting and decision making.[17]

In decentralized decision-making environments where local discretion and autonomy are the rule, a change to centralized data processing is likely to meet with resistance, for the control of information is a source of control over the organizations dependent upon that information. For example, in the case of a group of neighborhood service agencies that, together with a number of local funding agencies, voluntarily agreed to formulate and participate in a centralized data processing system, it was observed that:

> Both the neighborhood agencies and the funding organizations became dependent upon the technical experts to summarize and interpret data. As a result, these experts became involved in policy decisions that were normally internal to the other organizations.[18]

Not all organizations would be as willing as these in relinquishing decision-making authority to the "technical experts" or the external authorities that employ them.

Another difficulty with centralized data processing is that it is often both organizationally and physically isolated from operating units, which must both provide the data and use the information; the near universal result of this separation is underutilization of the system.[19] Utilization is generally improved if both the system and the individuals responsible for its operation are physically located in and under the control of the department, program, or jurisdiction they are intended to support. With respect to information system staff it has been concluded that:

> System staff should not be isolated. They should: be available for questions; expect resistance from system users, especially front line staff; and plan measures for dealing with such problems. They should anticipate design changes, and above all be realistic about computer capabilities with program staff.[20]

Significantly, continuing developments in computer technology may hold a solution to the apparent conflict between the inherent efficiencies of a centralized system and the potentially greater effectiveness of the decentralized approach. The minicomputer, which is smaller, cheaper, and less powerful, and possesses less storage capacity than most centralized units, but which is also "smart"—capable of performing basic data processing operations—is one such development. When linked to a centralized computer, the minicomputer can serve as an extension of the central unit's input and output capabilities, thereby allowing data to be processed according to the needs of the decentralized department, but stored, processed, and disseminated according to the needs of the centralized facility as well.

A second major model of information system structure is the *systems* design in which the technologies guiding information generation and transmission are designed to support the ever-changing information needs of the whole organizational system rather than those of discrete hierarchical or otherwise predetermined channels. Like the hierarchical model, however, the systems approach may incorporate either centralized or decentralized data processing capability; these are the integrated and distributed systems respectively and are shown in Figure 8.5.[21] In the *distributed* system each user possesses its own data processing capability, and information flows directly between various users as needs dictate. In the *integrated* system, the same pattern of flows may be created, but—as is true in the centralized hierarchical model—all information is assumed to flow through a single data processing unit, which maintains a common data

FIGURE 8.5:
distributed and integrated information systems

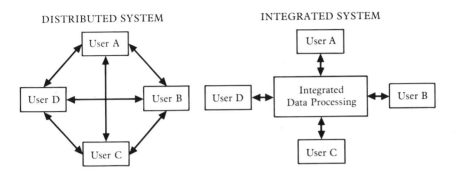

DISTRIBUTED SYSTEM   INTEGRATED SYSTEM

base for the entire network. Bear in mind that the development of intelligent minicomputers, able to communicate with other computer systems, blurs the once clear distinction between integrated and distributed systems. That is, given current technology and that projected for the foreseeable future, it is best to note that "distributed systems possess some integration and integrated systems possess some distribution."[22]

Unfettered by the view that information needs will necessarily follow those of hierarchical lines of authority, the systems model focuses upon information needs as a means of solving *organizational* (not compartmentalized) problems. Two such problems in the social welfare enterprise usually appear most amenable to solution by the integrated systems approach. The first would use the approach as a device for integrating fundamentally different types of data and information in the same system. In an application of this approach, which has been previously discussed, client information and organizational information would be integrated in a common data base to create information about organizational productivity and effectiveness, such as the cost per unit service or the cost effectiveness of various strategies for achieving valued outcomes.

The second problem area is even more intractable and the solution even more optimistic; the integrated system would be used as a means of integrating the various client information systems of all social welfare programs operating in the same geographical jurisdiction. Consider the implications of such a system for streamlining the client intake process. As it currently operates in most jurisdictions, an individual seeking assistance from a number of different agencies and programs must often go through a full-blown intake interview for each at substantial cost and time to provider and client alike. Since much of the information required by one program duplicates that already obtained and verified by other programs,

271

an integrated system could be used to extract information previously collected and stored in a common data base, requiring only that it be supplemented as the unique reporting and decision-making needs of different programs require. Furthermore, with a networkwide, common data base, decision makers would have at the press of a button a client's complete history of service utilization, a valuable source of information for any program or network-oriented evaluation study.

An information system capable of integrating historical user information—often generated by a number of different organizations—is known as a *tracking system*. Whereas basic record-keeping and reporting requirements usually demand that only aggregate user data be collected and summarized in "snapshot" form—for example the number of contacts per week or the total number of ADPs for a year—tracking systems are *dynamic*. Their focus is not a fixed set of statistics during a fixed interval of time, but rather their focus is the individual service user.

Tracking systems—in which a unique identifying code such as a social security number must be incorporated into the data base structure and maintained over a period of time, perhaps as long as a lifetime—have become a major symbolic and substantive issue in the social welfare enterprise. The Orwellian image of cradle-to-grave paternalism, coupled with the actual problems imposed by the need to maintain confidentiality lest the information be used against the individual (often meaning that information from one providing agency must be withheld from another), are very real retardants to the development of comprehensive tracking capabilities. Penetrating the emotionalism, however, it is not difficult to see the desirability, indeed the necessity, for such a capability if better program and service integration is to be achieved.

Among the most difficult and yet important phases in the design of a tracking system is the initial systems analysis of information flows in which all possible entry and exit points, as well as all possible patterns of intra- and interagency referral, must be clearly defined and incorporated into the design of the information system.[23] In defining the appropriate system boundary and the interactions within it, one needn't address the entire social welfare enterprise. Indeed, the greatest need for tracking systems probably occurs within rather narrowly defined systems of programs, systems in which casual observers would believe that substantial integration already exists. In many cases, however, it does not.

Consider the case of child welfare, in which state and local jurisdictions, supported by federal grant-in-aid funding, operate a variety of service programs in support of troubled children. Problems may range from broken homes, runaways, truancy, and other status offenses (behavior that would not be illegal were the individual not a minor) to more serious, nonstatus, criminal activities. Great attempt is made within the child welfare system to tailor services to particular needs, with services ranging from temporary foster home care, to group home care, to juvenile detention centers; the former programs may be operated by not-for-profit agencies supported by public funds, while the latter will be wholly operated by public agencies. Depending upon the specific service provided, utilization may be voluntary, initiated either by the parents or the child, or mandatory, generally through a referral made by the juvenile court system. For a number of obvious reasons, the placement of a youth in a juvenile detention center is generally regarded as a solution of last resort, and both the courts and the various child welfare agencies will adopt less harsh alternatives when possible. If these fail to resolve the problems, successively more highly structured and more closely supervised alternatives will be adopted; that is, the outcome (or lack of a desirable outcome) provides the rationale for referral and placement in another program.

Almost unbelievably, especially to those unfamiliar with the operation of social welfare programs, the information capabilities are such that many users get "lost" in a system whose parts are *purposefully* designed to be interdependent. It is not unlike the cardiac patient getting lost in the hospital somewhere between his hospital bed and the operating room. At any point in time, it is often difficult to determine the status of the individual user: that is, the nature of the program in which the child is enrolled and the specific services being provided; how long the services have been provided and their anticipated duration; the desired outcome; and prior services and sources of referral. In some cases, the information can be obtained through a laborious and time-consuming search; in most cases, however, the data are so inaccurately documented and poorly organized that no amount of effort will extract the necessary information; this is often true even if a single organization is responsible for administering the system of interest.

Tracking systems can supply the information for evaluating a large number of social welfare programs, whether the outcomes occur at the level of the individual or within the service network. With easily accessible data pertaining to individual histories of utilization-intervention-outcome it becomes possible to evaluate the effects and possibly the interactive effects of various combinations of services; it would be possible, for example to determine if program A is best performed in conjunction with or followed by program B, program C, or a program as yet undeveloped. Moreover, since it requires consistent service definitions and uniform reporting procedures and formats, the development of a tracking capability would lay much of the groundwork necessary for the achievement of more effective integration of services and programs. In short, the vast potential of integrated information systems has not been lost on systems experts and decision makers, and as one observer puts it:

Any system designer worth their salt will almost immediately see the
advantages of having a large data . . . system consolidating Title XX,
Cash Assistance, Medicaid, Food Stamps, Community Mental Health
and other human service program information.

The same observer and many others conclude, however, "*The temptation to
design such a system should be resisted.*"²⁴

The reasons for this widespread conclusion are well documented.
First, integration presents obvious problems of confidentiality, particularly
with respect to users of mental health and child protective services. And
even if adequate computer security systems can be developed, there still
remains the question of who should and who should not have access to
the information. Even if they are participants in the system, should police,
for example, have access to mental health information?

Second, while agreeing in principle to the desirability (or inevitability) of an integrated system, its actual implementation will likely prove
costly and disruptive of agency and program practices, many times involving issues of "turf." These disruptions are brought about for the most part
by the most fundamental requirement of any integrated information system, *standardization*—standardization of goals, of data, of data categories,
of information, of methods and procedures and standardization of *language.* The result is a loss of flexibility, particularly in the interorganizational relationships among system participants.²⁵ Not only does
standardization limit flexibility, and perhaps repudiate the pluralist rationale that justifies the existence of many different programs doing many of
the same things only slightly differently, but it presents operational difficulties as well. Reporting requirements, dictating what data will be collected and how they are to be transformed into information, will likely
differ from one funding agency to the next. Regardless of the ability of
system participants to work out common reporting procedures, the unique
reporting requirements of funding organizations that are *not* part of the
system must still be satisfied. The net effect is that the integrated system
may generate only a fraction of the total information needs of each agency.

Third and finally, an integrated system will allow participating organizations to make inferences about other agencies and programs—how
many clients processed, how much money spent, who's carrying their
share of the load and who's not—which, especially if funding bodies are
included in the system, may prove unsettling to program staff. "Even
where performance measures are instituted *purely for purposes of information,*" it has been noted, "they are probably *interpreted* as definitions of
important aspects of that job or activity and hence have important implications for the motivation of behavior."²⁶ Reminiscent of "criterion behavior" discussed with respect to evaluation was the finding that program

participants in one integrated information system experiment altered their behavior to ensure that they received "credit" for those activities being monitored by the system, possibly foregoing activities that were unmonitored but perhaps equally or more important.[27]

As a result of these problems, most knowledgeable persons advocate the establishment of a distributed system, but one that possesses the capability for later integration. But this "integrate later" approach presents difficulties as well. First, in most systems designed for specific applications or for use in distinct organizational settings, the development of computer hardware and software has been evolutionary, changing both with computer system developments and with identification of new information needs. The result is that over a period of time the structure as well as the content of the data base will have become inextricably entangled with the computer software, and data originally gathered and stored for particular applications cannot be easily separated from the software controls that convert it into information. Hence, either these data must be extracted from the web of software controls and stored separately for another application, or new software that creates a more independent data base must be written. Each alternative is time-consuming, expensive, and potentially disruptive of existing applications. Each also requires a substantial degree of programming expertise.

The second difficulty with the integrate later approach arises because consistent definitions of problems, needs, services provided or received, costs, and service outcomes are often lacking—even within the same organization. Moreover, many of these definitions will probably have changed over time, making it virtually impossible to use historical data to create trends and other analytical relationships that may be time dependent. Quite frequently, definitional difficulties arise because many of the applications for which adequate information capabilities do exist—reporting, cost control, and often case planning records—are performed by different agencies, different levels of government, or different departments within the same organization.[28]

An excellent example of this phenomenon concerns the attempt to develop unit cost of service estimates by synthesizing existing cost records and the service reports required of state governments under Title XX. Simply put the two together—divide services by costs from the two files already required and maintained—and *voilà,* cost per unit service. However, Title XX reporting requirements are concerned with services *received,* not those provided, defining a unit service as a "service received by the recipient one or more times" during the reporting period.[29] Thus, whether a recipient received one or a hundred counseling sessions, a single day or continuous child care support during the reporting period, each is to be reported as "one recipient"[30]—information too gross to be of much value in estimating the cost of a unit of service. This problem is not uncommon; reports are required for the purpose of maintaining accountability as it is perceived by the funding source, not necessarily for purposes of improving the efficiency and effectiveness of the program or the provider.

system implementation

The design, development and implementation of any computerized information system is a source of often profound organizational change and, regardless of its ultimate design, successful implementation demands that natural resistance to change be anticipated and overcome. One can expect such resistance even if the principles and purposes underlying the new system are supported by all participants. As is true of virtually any new organizational development—be it a program, a formal evaluation, a mode of service delivery, or an information system—the existence of a key individual or "prime mover" in the role of system planner, able to guide its implementation to a successful conclusion, is a crucial element of change.[31] With respect to the topic at hand, a key question in this regard is whether the "ideal" systems planner has a program or an information systems background. What knowledge, attitudes, skills, and biases will predominate? Thomas Whisler has noted a strong parallel between this important role and the county agricultural agent who must establish a bridge between farmers and agricultural researchers. (Note a similar parallel here to the role of the person responsible for conducting an evaluability assessment, or any activity requiring a melding of technical and operational expertise.)

> In an organization the counterpart of the county agent is a person working with both the planning elite and the operating personnel. He has divided responsibility and needs to be highly regarded by both camps, reasonably competent in the language and behaviors of both, and sufficiently motivated and strong to work under ambiguous and difficult conditions (such as dual reporting responsibilities). Obviously, the skill, experience, and personality requirements for such a person are high.[32]

As to the ideal background for this individual, opinion is divided. But in the social welfare milieu, at least one authority suggests that sensitivity to the particular organization's unique external and internal political dynamics is so crucial to successful implementation that, all else equal, "pick the program person."[33]

A second attribute of successful system implementation is the establishment of a steering committee comprised of members of all user groups —management, delivery personnel, research personnel, planners, statisticians, accountants—as well as system staff, in the initial stages of system design. A system will be valuable only if its output is both accepted and used by organizational participants. It is here that designers often confront a dilemma. Front line workers are usually charged with the responsibility for generating much of the raw data that support administrative and reporting functions, data which may seldom be transformed into useful information for their purposes (such as an easily accessible display of a client's history of services). Moreover, the gathering of data in a form suitable for system input is often disruptive to the user-provider transaction; hence needed data may be recorded in narrative form for later transcription and entry into the system. Unless seen as having value to front line service workers (or unless their maintenance becomes a criterion by which their performance is evaluated) records will often be inaccurate, out of date, and weeks and months behind on entries. Data collection and entry are not cost-free, and the earliest possible involvement in the design process by all persons expected to support (as well as to use) the system will help identify these costs, enabling a determination of whether they are offset by the value of the resulting information.

We have seen that the structure of the data base—not only what data are collected but how they are organized for storage—will largely depend upon how those data are to be organized and presented as useful information. One cannot simply extract data from an existing data base and organize them at will; what data are to be extracted and how they are to be organized—for example, would it be useful to have a list of the names of all clients served by a single not-for-profit provider, or would a list of case numbers suffice—must be known *prior* to final system design. Frequently, this requires pretesting forms, reports, and operational procedures before the system is automated. Thus, with respect to the user involvement promoted by a steering committee, one practitioner has concluded:

> The process of involving management and users . . . is time consuming and delays production of products or outcomes, but it *increases* the long-range probability of success.[34]

In sum, ever-growing demands for improved decision-making in the social welfare enterprise will make the continued development of management information systems a certainty. Each new system or a refinement of an existing system will generate organizational change. And while the nature of that change and the organizational resistance to it will vary from program to program and from agency to agency, of one additional thing

278 information systems

we can be certain: the system will require changes that make the behaviors of programs, agencies, and their participants more compatible with its logic of processing information.

notes

1. See Jeffrey Pfeffer and Gerald R. Salancik, *the External Control of Organizations* (New York: Harper & Row, Pub., 1978), p. 74.

2. Ibid., pp. 76-77.

3. John G. Burch, Jr. and Felix R. Strater, Jr., *Information Systems: Theory and Practice* (Santa Barbara, Calif.: Hamilton Publishing Company, 1974), p. 71.

4. Ibid., p. 28.

5. Thomas J. Kiresuk and Sander H. Lund, "Program Evaluation and the Management of Organization," in *Managing Human Services,* eds. Wayne F. Anderson, Bernard J. Frieden, and Michael J. Murphy (Washington, D.C.: International City Management Association, 1977), p. 288 (emphasis deleted).

6. Gary E. Bowers and Margaret R. Bowers, "Cultivating Client Information Systems," *Human Series Monograph Series* (Washington, D.C.: U.S. Department of Health, Education and Welfare, Project Share, 1977), p. 44.

7. Chadwick J. Haberstroh, "Organizational Design and Systems Analysis," in *Handbook of Organizations,* ed. James G. March (Chicago: Rand McNally & Co., 1965), p. 1175.

8. Burch and Strater, *Information Systems: Theory and Practice,* pp. 13-14.

9. Bowers and Bowers, "Cultivating Client Information Systems," p. 58.

10. Burch and Strater, *Information Systems: Theory and Practice,* p. 23.

11. Bowers and Bowers, "Cultivating Client Information Systems," p. 58.

12. Burch and Strater, *Information Systems: Theory and Practice,* pp. 27-31.

13. Ibid.

14. Ibid., p. 421.

15. Ibid., pp. 76-79.

16. Bowers and Bowers, "Cultivating Client Information Systems," p. 59.

17. Ibid., p. 60.

18. Robert E. Quinn, "The Impacts of Computerized Information Systems on the Integration and Coordination of Human Services," *Public Administration Review,* 36, no. 2 (March/April 1976), 173.

19. Bowers and Bowers, "Cultivating Client Information Systems," p. 40.

20. Ibid., p. 40-41.

21. Burch and Strater, *Information Systems: Theory and Practice,* pp. 79-92.

22. James E. Sorensen and Richard Elpers, "Developing Information Systems for Human Service Organizations," in *Evaluation of Human Service Programs,* eds. C. Clifford Attkisson, William Hargreaves, and Mardi J. Horowitz (New York: Academic Press, 1978), p. 165.

23. David W. Young, "Social Service Tracking Systems: A Public-Private Experience," *Evaluation,* 1, no. 2 (1975), 98.

24. Bowers and Bowers, "Cultivating Client Information Systems," p. 61.

25. Quinn, "The Impacts of Computerized Information Systems," pp. 168-69.

26. Pfeffer and Salancik, *The External Control of Organization,* p. 76.

27. Quinn, "The Impacts of Computerized Information Systems," p. 169.

28. Gary E. Bowers and Margaret R. Bowers, "The Elusive Unit of Service," *Human Services Monograph Series* (Washington, D.C.: U.S. Department of Health, Education and Welfare, Project Share, 1976), p. 9.

29. Cited in Ibid.

30. Ibid.

31. Bowers and Bowers, "Cultivating Client Information Systems," p. 38.

32. Thomas R. Whisler, *Information Technology and Organizational Change* (Belmont, Calif.: Wadsworth, 1970).

33. Bowers and Bowers, "Cultivating Client Information Systems," p. 39.

34. Ibid., p. 47.

In this chapter we will explore in conclusion three potential sources of social program and organizational change: major legislative reform of social policy and program, continually declining resources for social purposes, and the continuing reliance upon administrative and organizational techniques to provide solutions to problems people cannot resolve themselves.

It is concluded that the greatest challenge to the human value of the enterprise is posed by the administrative norms that must attend the adoption of large-scale formal organizations as problem-solving instruments. Paradoxically, it is the continued development of means to better implement these norms in the interests of promoting organizational needs that may further retard responsiveness to the needs of individuals who are dependent upon the enterprise.

conclusion:
sources and directions
of program change

9

In the preceding chapters we have studied the social program and have found it to be a two-faceted entity. First, it is an instrument of social policy, a mechanism for implementing often vague policy mandates regarding who is to get what; it does this by matching services to needs. Second, the program is an organizational entity, an open system embedded in an often chaotic web of interlocking but conflicting interests. These interests exert control over the program by exerting control over its essential resources, often in ways, however, that disturb the integrity of the processes by which services are matched to needs. We have investigated some of the mechanisms by which the program's multiple environments levy control over the program; some, like administrative guidelines and judicial rulings are relatively direct and straightforward, but others, like the techniques of needs assessments, management control, formal evaluations, and computerized information systems, are more subtle, influencing program operations by occupying in a selective way the administrator's limited attention.

Implicit in this view is the assumption that external forces provide the major impetus for program direction and change. In this concluding chapter we will continue this external focus. We will review the program's dual existence as a strategic element of policy and an open system with a focus upon three potential sources and directions of program change: large-scale legislative reform, steadily declining governmental resources, and continued developments in organizational and administrative technique.

policy reform
through legislative reform

Political scientists have long been preoccupied with the nature of policy change in American government. Most conclude that incremental change —tinkering with existing policy and program instead of instituting major policy reform—is both the inevitable and the desirable output of a pluralist political system. The inevitability of incremental change in pluralist society stems primarily from the limited alternatives available to participants in the web of interlocking interests that surrounds prevailing policy. Major shifts in policy can only occur if opposing interests can achieve a compromise regarding the nature of change or if new coalitions can be formed with sufficient votes to instigate change. In the social policy arena both strategies are problematical.

Compromise, it has been noted, is problematical because of the scope and intensity of the issues involved in major welfare reform, making it difficult to define the necessary common ground of agreement. "Even the most irrational features of the welfare system will benefit someone and so every reform will arouse opposition."[1] Lacking the possibility of compromise, proponents of major reform could band together to outvote the conservative opposition, but this strategy only works if the scope of reform is confined to a narrow set of issues, because "as the scope of reform grows larger, more and more interests will be adversely affected—and all the votes will move to the other side."[2] In short, "any suggestion of 'total welfare reform' will expose every aspect of the existing system to new debate, guaranteeing political stalemate."[3]

This tendency has been further reinforced in recent years by the continuing pluralization and fragmentation of authority within the Congress itself, which is largely the result of the demise of seniority as the basis of congressional power. Sources of congressional authority and leadership among the myriad committees and subcommittees, which must cooperate if policy reform is to occur, are far more diffuse and uncertain than was the case when a few elder statesmen wielded near total control over the legislative process. Even when stalemate can be overcome, we have seen that the resulting policy too often provides only the vaguest of action directives to those organizations and individuals responsible for its implementation, and creates a vacuum of legistimate authority into which litigation and the power of the courts is introduced. In this regard it does not seem hyperbolic to conclude that a fundamental reversal of roles has occurred between the legislative and judicial branches of government: the courts make policy while the legislature is engaged in the resolution of disputes.

If the dynamics of interest group politics help guarantee the inevitability of incremental policy change, there are many who contend that it is the desirable mode of change as well. Effective democracy requires an electorate informed on available policy options and the likely implications of each and both are more readily achievable when change is gradual. Major comprehensive policy reform is often equated with a centralized totalitarian state, while incrementalism is consistent with, to use Charles Lindblom's phrase, "the intelligence of democracy."[4]

Consistent with the doctrine of incrementalism is Donald Schon's observation that social systems are characterized by "dynamic conservatism," tending to adopt the least disruptive set of adjustments when change is deemed necessary to ensure their survival.[5] Paradoxically, this tendency is reinforced by the very model of change that would seek to overcome this conservatism—the "rational-comprehensive" ideal.[6] Within this model of change, societal goals are identified and a variety of experimental programs undertaken to determine the most satisfactory strategies for their achievement; the "best" strategy is then selected for implementation. In many policy areas—but in social policy in particular—the rational-comprehensive ideal may actually promote conservative policy change because of the extremely long period of time that generally accompanies the process of rational policy making: the identification of the problem, the formulation of the policy question to be researched, the conduct of the research, the dissemination of results, and their interpretation. Meanwhile the question—the policy issue—may change in definition or recede in importance with the passage of time. This phenomenon is well illustrated by the last major effort to achieve comprehensive welfare reform—the Family Assistance Plan.

Richard Nixon's abortive Family Assistance Plan—in which a negative income tax strategy was to be used as a means of providing a guaranteed minimum income to all Americans—was first announced to the American public in 1969. A major question that provided the center of debate, as one might expect, was the potential impact of this reform on individual work incentives. And a year earlier, in anticipation of this question, HEW staff initiated a series of large-scale experiments, conducted in five states, to determine the answer (these were the income maintenance experiments previously discussed in chapter 7). Only now, over a *decade* later, are the results of those experiments being brought to public awareness. Had the results been available when the issue was of political importance, they would not have boded well for the proposed reform. Not only have they indicated that negative work incentives are greater than originally anticipated, but equally important and completely unanticipated has been the finding that the proposed reform actually contributes—for a variety of hypothesized reasons over which there is little agreement—to divorce and family breakup.[7]

Meanwhile, political attitudes and political awareness have dramatically changed in the ten-year interlude. Welfare is not the national "crisis" it was in the late sixties and early seventies, having been replaced in the national consciousness by the "inflationary crisis," the "energy crisis," and the "crisis of morality." After having grown from 2.2 million in 1955, the welfare rolls had stabilized at between 11 and 12 million by the mid-seventies. And today, notes the Brookings Institution's key welfare authority and legislative adviser Gilbert Steiner, not only is the general public less concerned about welfare issues but current recipients are "quiescent, not organized, not complaining."[8] Adds another influential authority, Sar

Levitan, "It ain't such a bad system. Quit arguing over it."[9] As a result, today's reforms, as embodied in the Better Jobs and Income Program for example, are likely to be incremental and, based upon American welfare history, completely predictable: elimination of work disincentives inherent in the current system, more uniform (albeit in some cases fewer) benefits, and strengthened work requirements.[10] The latter reform assumes, of course, that the welfare system has since developed the capacity to distinguish between those who can and cannot work, a capacity that was lacking during the 1960s era of "reform."

The principal problem with adopting a legislative view of reform is that it tends to focus upon the obvious, upon those reforms that result (or more likely don't result) from well-publicized policy issues and widespread policy debate. Not infrequently, however, significant reforms will result from apparently minor shifts in social legislation, as evidenced by the amendments that created the Supplemental Security Income program. Because it nationalized and made more generous and equitable three of the four categorical public assistance programs that had theretofore been operated at the discretion of the individual states, SSI *today* is considered by many observers to have been the most significant reform in cash assistance legislation since the original Social Security Act was enacted in 1935. (Some also consider it to be an excellent example of comprehensive policy reform as well).[11] However, at the time of its adoption in 1972, in the aftermath of a defeated Family Assistance Plan, there was no clearcut Senate majority for any particular strategy of systematic welfare reform. Lacking a consensus, yet under substantial pressure from members of the House of Representatives (which had passed the Family Assistance Plan two years earlier, the Senate retreated to an assortment of modifications in the existing legislation that the newspapers—and by implication the public and many congressmen as well—"treated as technical amendments to the Social Security Act."[12]

Lacking the necessary knowledge of cause and effect, what turns out to have major policy consequences may not be seen as significant reform at the time of public scrutiny and legislative action. Conversely, (and national health insurance may eventually provide such an example), what is considered to be major, comprehensive policy reform at the time of its adoption may actually generate consequences that represent only incremental changes on the past. In sum, the significance of change rests in the importance of its consequences, and significant consequences may result from *either* major conceptual reform of existing policy or apparently minor technical "tinkering." Too often, in the arena of social policy and program, however, even seasoned experts lack the ability to predict with any accuracy the actual consequences of policy and legislative reform.

program change
and declining resources

If organizations and programs are dependent upon a continued flow of resources, what happens when those resources decline? Only a decade ago this question was of major importance only in isolated instances (OEO, for example), and even in the face of decline there were reasonable assurances that new programs (in the case of OEO, General Revenue Sharing) would emerge to cover the gaps in services and to create employment opportunities for service professionals in the aftermath of periodic program demise. Program decline was the exception rather than the rule. Today, however, many observers contend that resource scarcity will be a permanent and pervasive fact of American life for the foreseeable future. Tax revolts and citizen demands that governments pare down their activities and expenditures to the bare essentials are among the first tangible signs that the American age of abundance, continued growth, and surplus—the surplus that has enabled a capitalist state to nurture and maintain the social welfare enterprise—is over. As this reality has become more apparent, so has the need to develop alternative views of organizational and administrative behavior that see decline not as anomaly but as a normal condition of organizational life. And while the phenomenon of decline is only beginning to receive systematic attention, [13] it is possible to identify some of the changes it may bring about.

What are the implications of declining resources for current administrative and organizational practice? It will depend, as Charles Levine has noted, upon the specific causes of organizational and program decline. While declining resources is the general cause, Levine has identified four specific causes that will precipitate decline in public programs.[14] Two of these—political vulnerability and organizational atrophy—are internal factors, both of which pertain to the program's ability to adapt to, and if necessary resist, pressures to cut program resources. But it is the external cause of decline—what Levine calls problem depletion and environmental entropy—that are of interest here.

Problem depletion is a natural result of the cyclical problem-solving process, in which a problem is first identified and defined, a program is established, resources are mobilized and committed, and then eventually contracted once the problem has been solved, alleviated, simply disappears, or ceases to be an issue worthy of public support.[15] Levine has identified three common sources of problem depletion. It may occur because of demographic shifts in the population, such as is the case in school districts now experiencing sharp declines in the number of school-age children. It may occur as the result of an abrupt policy termination, as in

285

the case of programs that are the object of "sunset legislation"—programs that are designed to automatically self-destruct after a predetermined time interval unless deliberate legislative reauthorization allows them to continue. Third, and potentially most important, problem depletion may occur as the result of problem redefinition. In the field of mental health, for example, deinstitutionalization—a treatment strategy made possible by advances in pharmaceutical technology and made apparently more desirable as the cost to construct and operate mental health facilities continues to escalate—in effect both requires and results from a popular and a professional redefinition of the mental health "problem." Similar shifts in the definitional dynamic that exists among conditions, problems and service needs are already evident in corrections (deinstitutionalization), health care (self-care), education ("back to the basics"), and in the personal social services as well (in-home care for the elderly); such changes will continue to occur as costs become an increasingly important determinant of how conditions are translated into problems and needs.

Recall that many of the personal social services can be *defined* either as social utilities or as case interventions, depending upon the nature of the problem they are designed to address; utilities are geared to individual problems, while interventions are designed to alleviate societal problems. At least one observer has suggested that resource depletion in the public sector, and popular attitudes supporting a more limited role for government, will force public decision makers to adopt a more apparently instrumental personal social service posture than has been the case in recent years. It is possible that this will force a *definitional* orientation *away* from the personal social utilities on the part of the public sector, leading to the somewhat disturbing prediction that:

> service utilities for poor people in the 1980's will be supported as social interventions—that is, as important services, worthy of public support *because* they render assistance and advantage to the well-being of the social order.[16]

Not only does this possibility have implications for the specific characteristics of the services provided, the populations to which they are provided, and even a general reassertion of welfare's residual conception, but it raises the likelihood of repeating the errors of two decades past that gave rise to the era of accountability —of "selling" services as problem-solving instruments in the absence of significant evidence that those services actually contribute to the well-being of the social order.

A second major external cause of program decline, environmental entropy, refers to a community's financial inability to support public programs, regardless of desirability or level of need. The result of general economic decay—caused by such factors as natural resource depletion in mining towns, technological shifts which have led to the decline of many New England textile towns, and the widespread migration of businesses and residents from the central cities to the suburbs—environmental entropy also possesses its political dimensions as well. As the proliferation of state and local restrictions on taxation and governmental expenditure increasingly indicates,

> taxpayer resistance can produce diminished revenues which force service reductions even though the demand and the *need* for services remains high.[17]

What strategies can and are being pursued in the face of imminent resource and program decline? Levine has identified two; administrators and program supporters may adopt (or be forced to adopt) actions designed to *resist* decline or they may undertake strategies designed to *smooth* the transition from existing to lower levels of resources. Examples of familiar tactics that might be adopted by local program decision makers under each of the two external causes of decline are presented in Table 9.1.

TABLE 9.1:
common tactics for coping with decline

		Administrative Posture	
		Resistance	Accommodation
Cause of Decline	Problem Depletion	1. Diversify programs, clients, and constituents	1. Make peace with competing agencies
		2. Improve legislative liaison	2. Cut low prestige programs
		3. Educate the public about the program's mission	3. Cut programs to politically weak clientele
		4. Mobilize dependent clients	4. Sell and trade expertise with other programs
		5. Threaten to cut vital or popular aspects of a program	5. Cut back outreach and I&R activities if possible
		6. Actually cut a program a small amount to demonstrate client dependence	
	Environmental Entropy	1. Find a richer revenue base (e.g., municipal reorganization or annexation)	1. Improve targeting on problems
		2. Seek support from new sources of funds	2. Plan with preservative objectives (e.g., interventions rather than utilities)
		3. Lure new public and private sector investment	3. Yield concessions to taxpayers
		4. Adopt users' fees if possible	

Source: Adapted from Charles H. Levine, "Organizational Decline and Cutback Management," Public Administration Review, 38, no. 4 (July/August 1978), 321. Reprinted from Public Administration Review © 1978 by The American Society for Public Administration, 1225 Connecticut Avenue, N.W., Washington, D.C. All rights reserved.

While some of the tactics that might be adopted in the face of decline are unpleasant to consider, many believe that they would not be necessary were social welfare programs and organizations operated more efficiently by improving the technology through which services are produced and delivered. The increasing refinement of this technology is our last, and in many ways the most disturbing, source of program and administrative change.

technical sources
of change

This book began with a conscious and conspicuous reference to NASA, the technocratic standard of organizational and administrative excellence by which complex, modern organizations are often judged. In stark contrast in mission, technology, environment, and apparent accomplishment, was juxtaposed the social welfare enterprise, the organized response to problems of individual and societal well-being. While radically different, both NASA and the enterprise are founded on the pervasive belief that the large-scale modern organization represents the most efficient and effective instrument for the achievement of valued ends—perhaps the *only* instrument for achieving those ends. Although they are instruments, organizational technologies are not value neutral, but instead promote—indeed require—the adoption by participants and clientele alike of behavioral norms that are essential to the maintenance of the organization's instrumental role. Much of the preceding discussion has been concerned with techniques that are consistent with these norms, but not without the often disquieting implication that the repeated confrontation between individual and organizational needs may easily be resolved in favor of the latter. It is appropriate in conclusion to further explicate this conflict.

In assessing what they have called the "organizational imperative," David K. Hart and William G. Scott have identified three administrative norms that *must* follow the general proposition that the achievement of valued ends can only occur through the modern organization: rationality, stewardship, and pragmatism.[18] While rationality is normally seen as a process of adopting the best means to achieve a given end, Hart and Scott argue (convincingly, I believe) for a more narrow definition, with rationality ultimately translating into the simple norm of efficient resource utilization. One may counter with the proposition that goal achievement— effectiveness—is an equally important dimension of rationality, which may in fact be appropriate where notions of effectiveness can be premised upon readily identifiable and widely agreed upon standards and measures. We have seen, however, that such is seldom the case in social programs, and lacking this important reference it is not difficult to conclude that rationality—at least as it is understood by those who reward administrative performance and who are at least in part responsible for ensuring continued organizational survival—*is* the achievement of efficiency. The norm of stewardship, that the "administrator must manage the more important affairs of the organization in the interests of 'others,'"[19] is identical to the administrative concern with accountability and requires no further elaboration here. The third behavioral norm, pragmatism, quite simply holds that the administrator will take such actions—be they proactive or reactive—that will enable the program or the organization to "survive in good health in changing environments."[20]

Significantly, both the fundamental proposition and norms that comprise the organizational imperative know not the bounds of sector, function, or espoused organizational purpose; "good administration" is good administration, be it in General Motors, a hospital, a child welfare program, or a university. And if, as is the widespread popular belief regarding the social welfare enterprise, an organizational sector is *not* well administered, it stands to reason that advice and counsel will be forthcoming from those sectors that ostensibly are. Indeed this is happening, with administrative tinkering (and the policy changes it will bring about) increasingly the domain of administrative "experts," not only from the social service professions and ranks of the public bureaucracy, but increasingly from private industry as well. After all, the dominant view in America today holds that, while possibly not revered, at least industry is better run than government.

As Guy Benveniste has noted, however, policy and program experts must maintain an apparently "apolitical" stance if they are to be effective; moral exhortations in place of sound expert advice can only serve to diminish the possibility that the advice will actually influence change.[21] Exhortations instead are couched, as the following statement by IT&T president Robert Geneen indicates, in the most politically acceptable rhetoric of social responsibility.

> We, in industry, owe it to our society to use our resources to cure a social ill. . . . We, in industry, have the capital, the manpower, the skills, the technology . . . to get the job done.[22]

Nonetheless, as we are cautioned by Benveniste, even while such public-spirited rhetoric may serve to downgrade the *apparent* political influence the administrative expert has in the making of policy, the role is the exact opposite of its apolitical definition, because "it provides access to social power without political election."[23] But how might expert advice, even of the most purely technical variety, deviate from the apolitical?

Probably the most striking examples—all taken in the interests of improved efficiency—concern industrial views of how service delivery should be improved. But as management expert Theodore Levitt has noted the use of industrial techniques to achieve greater efficiency requires a fundamental revision in the way we normally think about services.

> The concept of "service" evokes, from the opaque recesses of the mind, time-worn images of personal ministration and attendance. It refers generally to deeds one individual performs personally for another. It carries historical connotations of charity, gallantry, and selflessness, or of obedience, subordination, and subjugation . . .
>
> In the higher status occupations, such as in the church and in the army, one customarily behaves ritualistically, not rationally. In the lower status service occupations, one simply obeys. In neither is independent thinking presumed to be a requisite of holding a job. The most that can therefore be expected from service improvements is that, like Avis, a person will try harder. He will just exert more animal effort to do better what he is already doing.[24]

In short, he concludes, "service thinks humanistically and that explains its failures."[25] While Levitt's propositions and conclusions are directed at services provided primarily by private sector organizations, McDonald's for example, the organizational imperative suggests that there has been a blurring of distinction between public and private organizations—an increasing number of human services are being provided by private, *profit-making* organizations with public subsidy—and his advice is not much different from what other experts on "good" administration might recommend for public programs as well.

In particular, through the time-honored industrial technique of substituting tools for motivation, administrative experts would reduce the detrimental impacts of individual discretion, "the enemy of order, standardization and quality."[26] In effect, by adopting the techniques of industrial organization they would, with the most honorable of motives, "productize" the delivery of social and human services. While this may not represent a particularly desirable stream of developments, remember that this is the very strategy that permitted modern industrial organization to achieve its comparatively high degrees of efficiency over earlier collective efforts. And remember as well that both motivation and discretion are very real problems in the social welfare enterprise. But what "tools" are available for implementing this strategy? An obvious example is the computer, which I believe to be the single most important source of future change within the social welfare enterprise, and whose "potential" has been described by one service administrator as follows:

> My fond hope is that one day we shall never have to deal with people —the machines will do that.[27]

And while one may derive some temporary security and perverse satisfaction by noting that the above remark is attributed to a bank executive, both quickly vanish when one realizes that it could just as easily have come from a social service employee, for many of whom Bell Telephone's persistent claim that, "The system is the solution," may not be far off the mark. The "apolitical" character of the administrative expert's most cherished norm—efficiency—is thus not apolitical at all, requiring (if we are to believe the experts) dehumanization, standardization, and the subsequent administrative centralization implied by the latter. Like the norms of accountability and pragmatism, the net effects of doggedly pursuing efficiency are those of rigidifying organizational behavior, minimizing the likelihood of potentially beneficial innovation and stultifying personal creativity.

Many of the perspectives, models, ideas, and techniques that have been explored in the preceding chapters have dealt with both the apparent barriers and opportunities for "good administration," an understanding of which—with no apologies—I believe is required if social programs are to be effective in matching services to needs. Moreover, we can expect the continued proliferation of organizational and administrative tinkering in the enterprise; modern society is too highly interdependent to believe otherwise. But I am left—like no doubt many of you—with a profound sense of foreboding over the values those of modern organization and good administration may displace, and indeed many writers have lamented the resultant demise of pluralism, democracy, and individual freedom.[28] And lacking adequate policy guidance, we have seen that adherence to the precepts of good administration in its place, may but serve to enhance the organization's survival at the expense of those individuals who must rely upon it for some measure of their well-being. "The great problem," as Pressman and Wildavsky aptly put it, "is to make the difficulties of implementation part of the initial formulation of policy."[29]

What are possible solutions to these problems? Many alternatives have been offered, most concerning policy and structural changes — decentralization for example — that would alter the prevailing balance of power in the social welfare enterprise. But as Heinz Eulau has remarked of these reforms:

the problems involved in the provision of human services are not soluble simply by recourse to facile policy panaceas, faith in benign administrative palliatives, or dependence upon political mobilization of inadequately served groups of clients.[30]

If there is indeed a remedy to these problems, Eulau finds it in the service professional who, by extending his normal *consultative role* with clients and colleagues to embrace organizational, administrative, and political concerns, would invoke his professional authority to "complement, supplement, and implement other governmental processes like democratic participation, bureaucratic organization, pluralist bargaining, or oligarchic decision making."[31] In effect, through consultative processes would be infused "professional expertise as well as client perspectives into the policy process and the delivery of services,"[32] making professional consultation the principal "linkage mechanism between democracy and bureaucracy."[33]

My hope is, that through any insights gained in studying social program administration, both service and administrative professionals will be better prepared to undertake this complex yet vital task.

notes

1. Frederick Doolittle, Frank Levy, and Michael Wiseman, "The Mirage of Welfare Reform," *The Public Interest,* no. 47 (Spring 1977), 77.

2. Ibid.

3. Ibid.

4. Charles E. Lindblom, *The Intelligence of Democracy* (New York: Free Press, 1965).

5. Donald A. Schon, *Beyond the Stable State* (New York: W. W. Norton & Co., Inc.), Ch. 2.

6. Charles E. Lindblom, *The Policy-Making Process* (Englewood Cliffs, N.J.: Prentice-Hall, 1968), Ch. 3.

7. See Stanley Masters and Irwin Garfinkel, *Estimating the Labor Supply Effects of Income-Maintenance Alternatives* (New York: Academic Press, 1978).

8. Carol R. Richards, "Welfare Crisis Is Over, According to Experts," *Salem (Oregon) Statesman,* July 4, 1977.

9. Ibid.

10. Irwin Garfinkel, "What's Wrong with Welfare," *Social Work,* 23, no. 3 (May 1978), 189–90.

11. Robert B. Albritton, "Measuring Public Policy: Impacts of the Supplemental Security Income Program." A paper presented at the 1977 Annual Meeting of the Midwest Political Science Association, Chicago, Illinois, April 21-23, 1977.

12. Lance Leibman, "The Definition of Disability in Social Security and Supplemental Security Income," *Harvard Law Review,* 89, no. 5 (March 1976), 856.

13. See Charles H. Levine, ed., "Symposium on Organizational Decline and Cutback Management," *Public Administration Review,* 38, no. 4 (July/August 1978), 315–57.

14. Charles H. Levine, "Organizational Decline and Cutback Management," *Public Administration Review,* 38, no. 4 (July/August 1978), 318–19.

15. Ibid., 318.

16. Melvin Mogulof, "Future Funding of Social Services," *Social Work,* 19, no. 5 (September 1974), 612, emphasis added.

17. Levine, "Organizational Decline and Cutback Management," 319.

18. David K. Hart and William G. Scott, "The Organizational Imperative," *Administration and Society,* 7, no. 3 (November 1975), 259–85.

19. Ibid., 262.

20. Ibid., 263.

21. Guy Benveniste, *The Politics of Expertise* (Berkeley, Calif.: Glendessary Press, 1972), p. 65.

22. Cited in Murray Gruber, "Total Administration," *Social Work,* 19, no. 5 (September 1974), 631.

23. Benveniste, *The Politics of Expertise,* p. 65.

24. Theodore Levitt, "Production-Line Approach to Service," *Harvard Business Review,* 50, no. 5 (September–October 1972), 43.

25. Ibid.

26. Ibid., 44, 46.

27. "Readers Report," *Business Week,* May 28, 1979, p. 7.

28. See generally Jacques Ellul, *The Technological Society* (New York: Vintage, 1964).

29. Jeffrey L. Pressman and Aaron B. Wildavsky, *Implementation* (Berkeley and Los Angeles: University of California Press, 1973), p. 143.

30. Heinz Eulau, "Skill Revolution and the Consultative Commonwealth," *American Political Science Review,* 67, no. 1 (March 1973), 174.

31. Ibid., 189.

32. Ibid.

33. Ibid., 191.

bibliography
of cases

Long used successfully in legal and business education, the case method provides students with the opportunity to apply theoretical and abstract concepts to real problems in realistic settings. Only recently, however, has the availability of a sufficient number of high quality cases permitted an extension of this valuable teaching and learning opportunity to students of public and social welfare administration.

Below are selected abstracts of pertinent cases in social program administration, identified with the chapter in which their use is most appropriate.* While identifying only a few of the many possibilities currently available, those listed have been screened according to the following criteria: short to moderate length, requiring nominally two to three hours of outside preparation and one to two hours of class time each; good balance between substantive and administrative issues; and overall consistency with general level and thrust of *Social Program Administration.* Although one and in some instances two cases have been identified as appropriate for use in conjunction with each chapter, this is not necessarily to suggest that all (or any) cases need to be adopted—for example, those listed for chapter 9 may easily stand alone as capstone exercises in courses using this text. Instead, potential users are encouraged to examine and to adopt the cases to their own educational objectives and constraints.

*From *Intercollegiate Bibliography: Cases in Public Policy and Management,* Spring 1979. Compiled by members of the Public Policy and Management Program, Intercollegiate Case Clearing House. Reproduced by permission of the President and Fellows of Harvard College. Sample copies of these cases, costing $1, with a 50% discount for educational institutions, and teaching notes—which cost $1, are not discounted, and require that the order be placed on your university letterhead—are available from: Intercollegiate Case Clearing House, Soldiers Field, Boston, Massachusetts 02163.

chapter one

Transportation for the Elderly: Happy   9-379-723
Faces on a MARTA Bus

R. T. Golembiewski, C. W. Proehl, Jr., University of Georgia (College of Bus. Admin.)

Setting: Atlanta, Georgia, rapid transit authority, 1970–78 (field)

Examines the Metropolitan Atlanta Rapid Transit Authority's (MARTA) transportation program for elderly citizens. This program reflects a basic characteristic of all public programs: doing something, no matter how well, typically highlights only how much more could be done. Specifically, focuses on how one public program was initiated and implemented. Also reflects on those processes that led to meeting some, but not all, of the transportation needs of the elderly.

Case: 14p.

chapter two

Title IV-D Program   **9-378-504**
in New York State: A Case Study
in Program Management

J. F. Plant, W. A. Wallace, D. Axelrod, Rensselaer Polytechnic Institute and State University of New York at Albany

Teaching Note: 5-378-505

Setting: New York, county social services department, 1977 (field) Title IV-D is a federal-state-local intergovernmental system for locating absent parents of families receiving Aid to Families with Dependent Children payments and collecting court-ordered child support payments from them. Describes the experience of a local county attempting to implement the program. An issue in particular is the direction the program should take: Most return of money for program dollar spent, or most parents located, even if they cannot afford to make payments. Also explores the intergovernmental nature of the program and the need for cooperation among several government agencies. Studies must prepare an organizational and program plan for a IV-D unit that will be able to collect $3 for every $1 spent.

Case: 24p.
Teaching Note: 7p.

chapter three

District of Columbia   **9-378-512**
Summer Youth Program

E. Cherian, W. A. Wallace, D. Axelrod, Rensselaer Polytechnic Institute and State University of New York at Albany

Teaching Note: 5-378-513

Setting: Washington, D.C., city government, 1968 (field)

A summer youth program is being conducted in the District of Columbia in an atmosphere of tense racial relations. Although the program is in its third year, this year's planning was done hurriedly in the aftermath of racial street riots. The program depends on federal funds and must be evaluated. A private consultant is called in. The consultant chooses an interview method as a way to assess attitudes about the program. "Street-wise" youths are hired to interview the primarily "street-wise" program participants and youthful nonparticipants. Interview results show general lack of awareness of the program's objectives and a significant amount of hostility toward it, even among participants. Students must review all data given and develop a plan for the next summer youth program. Emphasizes planning as the first and most important function of management. Also examines ways to evaluate an ongoing program when little hard data are available.

Case: 25p.
Teaching Note: 9p.

Reorganization   9-378-574
of Florida's Human
Services Agency (A)

L. E. Lynn, Jr., Harvard University (JFK School of Govt.)

Setting: Florida, 1969–75 (field)

The first in a four-part series, Reorganization of Florida's Human Services Agency (A-D) (9-378-574 through 9-378-577), examining the issue of human services reorganization from three distinct perspectives: the state legislature; an operating division affected by the reorganization; and the governor's office. The series as a whole serves as a vehicle for examining the origins of the different perspectives and for analyzing the ways in which interactions among different actors in a political setting can influence policy outcomes. Part A of this series recounts the history of the Florida Human Services Agency; describes the problems legislators faced in creating a truly responsive human services agency; and concludes with the reorganization bill of 1975, a radical and controversial piece of legislation designed to insure integration through the regionalization of service delivery and the abolition of program-oriented divisions. Students may be asked to assess the strategy of the Florida legislature and to determine what steps should be taken in order to make the delivery of human services more efficient and more responsive to the needs of its beneficiaries.

Case: 46p.

chapter four

Nutrition for the Elderly   9-378-522

E. A. Lehan, W. A. Wallace, D. Axelrod, Rensselaer Polytechnic Institute and State University of New York at Albany

Teaching Note: 5-378–523

Setting: Unspecified, local government, 1970–76 (field)

Describes, in narrative form, the history of a hot lunch program established to provide good nutrition for the elderly population of a small city. Shows how political factors and pressure from special interest groups were allowed to override careful study of the situation and to push through a simple solution to a complex public problem. Tables give pertinent demographic data and statistics on the operation of the hot lunch program. Students are asked to make the neglected careful study of the problem. Can be used to teach students to diagnose a complex public problem, analyze alternative solutions, and present their results in a structured format.

Case: 16p.
Teaching Note: 9p.

chapter five

Richardson Center for the Blind   9-573-004

B. P. Shapiro, Harvard University (Grad. School of Bus. Admin.)

Teaching Note: 5-573–074

Setting: Minnesota, rehabilitation of blind, $1 million revenue, 1972 (student)

Concerns the broad policies of a rehabilitation center for the blind. Emphasis is on the determination of product policy (products and services offered) and on communications strategy (the recruiting of trainees). Provides good historical and organizational material. Prepared by Miss Roberta N. Clarke, graduate student, under the supervision of Assistant Professor Benson P. Shapiro.

Case: 21p.
Teaching Note: 6p.

**Organizational Planning
for Service Delivery   9-479-649
in a Community
Mental Health Center**

M. R. Suib, J. R. Walsh, University of Mississippi (School of Bus. Admin.)

Teaching Note: 5-479-650

Setting: Unspecified, community mental health center, 7-county area, 1976–77 (field)

Contains a review of the early development of and current federal requirements for comprehensive community mental health centers. Details of a specific center are included, showing three staff reorganizations. Students are encouraged to analyze organizational structure for strengths and weaknesses in service delivery, and to redesign the organization from both a medical and a social service orientation.

Case: 8p.
Teaching Note: 1p.

chapter six

Middlevale Health Center   9-178-667

C. T. Horngren, Stanford University (Grad. School of Bus.)

Teaching Note: 5-178-668

Setting: Unspecified (field)

An elementary description of program budgeting and its application to a small health organization. Requires the actual preparation of a simple program budget for four health programs conducted by a community health organization.

Case: 5p.
Teaching Note: 1p.

Office of Economic Opportunity (B)   9-112-006

R. F. Vancil, U.S. Civil Service Commission

Teaching Notes: 5-112-075; 5-176-211, R. E. Herzlinger

Setting: Washington, D.C., government, 1966 (field)

After two years of rapid growth, this new agency is considering a reorganization of the budget function, moving it from the office of finance to the research, plans, programs and evaluation division. The purported advantage is better integration of planning, programming, and budgeting, but a consultant's report (also included in the case) favors the status quo.

Case: 16p.
Teaching Notes: 5p.

chapter seven

Monitoring and Evaluating   9-378-520
a State Day Care Licensing Program

K. Lounsbury, J. Lounsbury, D. Hall, W. A. Wallace, D. Axelrod, Rensselaer Polytechnic Institute and State University of New York at Albany

Teaching Note: 5-378-521

Setting: Illinois, state government agency, 1974 (field)

Examines the failure of a state day care licensing agency to provide the regulation of those facilities that is mandated by state law. Includes discussions of the requirements and intentions of the law; the structure, staffing, workload patterns, and costs of the agency; the concerns of day care facility operators and agency staff members; and the findings of a review of the situation by a state legislative commission. Students are asked to analyze the day care licensing program and to propose ways of making it effective and efficient. An issue is the reconciling of the ideal of public protection through governmental regulation with the reality of the financial resources and personnel available to do the job. Students will see that careful program analysis is vital to the structuring of a program that will both meet its objectives and make the best use of its resources.

Case: 35p.
Teaching Note: 15p.

chapter eight

Computers, People, and the Delivery   9-378-536
of Services: The Implementation of a Management Information
System

R. E. Quinn, W. A. Wallace, D. Axelrod, Rensselaer Polytechnic Institute and State University of New York at Albany.

Teaching Note: 5-378-537

Setting: New York, university and private agencies, 1966 (gen. exp.)

Examines an attempt to institute a central computerized management information system for the use of several community social services agencies. Through narratives and dialogue among those involved, students learn that while the system offers attractive benefits in increased efficiency and reduced costs, it is seen as threatening to the autonomy and established work patterns of the agencies. Fears of the system cause the agencies to become increasingly uncooperative, until the visibility of the entire system is in jeopardy. Students are asked to diagnose the situation and propose ways to resolve the problems associated with developing and implementing a management information system, and to learn some of the steps that can be taken to manage that process successfully.

Case: 33p.
Teaching Note: 10p.

chapter nine

Agency for Child Development   9-378-905

J. R. Russell, E. Smith, Boston University (Pub. Mgt. Pgm.)

Teaching Note: 5-378-906

Setting: New York, New York, city agency, 1976 (field)

A young "interim executive director" must decide how to reduce the cost of running the Agency for Child Development from $150 million to $116 million per year. Most of the reduction must come in the city's 410-center day care program. Students must decide what criteria to use in developing a plan to achieve the savings, develop the plan, and recommend an approach to its implementation.

Case: 41p.
Teaching Note: 5p.

Department of Youth Services 9-378-940

C. S. Diver, Boston University (Pub. Mgt. Pgm.)

Teaching Note: 5-378-941

Setting: Massachusetts, state agency (field)

A dramatic transformation of a youth corrections agency from institutional to community-service emphasis has left the department in fiscal and administrative chaos. A career employee, appointed as chief administrative officer by the new commissioner, must resolve immediate problems and begin to build new systems for budgeting, expenditure control, hiring, and contracting suited to the department's new program orientation and structure. May be used to explore the personal role of a fiscal officer in affecting "program" and "policy" decisions, or to contrast the administrative requirements of managing a direct-service vs. a purchase-of-service program.

Case: 30p.
Teaching Note: 3p.

index